Contents

Note on contributors

Michael Beveridge is Lecturer in Psychology in the Department of Education at the University of Manchester. He was formerly Tutor in Philosophy at the University, and Research Fellow at the Hester Adrian Research Centre for the Study of Learning Processes in the Mentally Handicapped. His current research includes the study of children's graphical representation using microcomputers, and the involvement of parents in children's linguistic and cognitive development. He is the author (with Peter Lloyd) of *Information and meaning in children's communication* (Academic Press, 1981).

Chris Brierley is Research Associate in the Department of Education at the University of Manchester.

Allayne Bridges is a lecturer in the Department of Psychology at the University of Birmingham. As well as the development of case-like categories and syntactic comprehension, her research interests include children's perspective-taking skills and mother-child discourse.

Richard P. Brinker is the Intervention and Evaluation Coordinator for the Educational Testing Service of the Institute for the Study of Exceptional Children in Princeton, New Jersey.

N.H. Freeman is Reader in Psychology at the University of Bristol. His research interests are children's spatial skills, language and drawing. He was Director of the Social Science Research Council project 'Language and representation in normal children and subnormal' (1976–1979); and is the author of *Strategies of representation in young children* (Academic Press, 1980) as well as numerous articles.

Elena Lieven is a Lecturer in Developmental Psychology at the University of Manchester. The main focus of her research is early language acquisition, and she is currently working on second-language acquisition in immigrant children. She has also published on feminism.

Paul Light is a lecturer in psychology at the University of Southampton. His research interests are in social aspects of cognitive development in children, in children's drawings, and in remedial approaches

Children thinking through language

edited by Michael Beveridge

Edward Arnold

© Edward Arnold 1982

First published 1982 by
Edward Arnold (Publishers) Ltd
41 Bedford Square, London WC1B 3DQ

British Library Cataloguing in Publication Data

Children thinking through language.
1. Cognition in children   2. Children—Language
I. Beveridge, Michael
155.4'13   BF723.C5

ISBN 0-7131-6352-6

Printed in Great Britain by Richard Clay (The Chaucer Press) Ltd, Bungay, Suffolk.

for nonspeaking children. He is the author of *The development of social sensitivity* (Cambridge University Press, 1979).

Peter Lloyd is a lecturer in psychology at the University of Manchester. His research interests are communication skills in children, development of word meaning, children's friendships, and metacognition. His publications include (with Michael Beveridge) *Information and meaning in child communication* (Academic Press, 1981); and 'Language and communication: the influence of Piaget', In S. Modgil (ed.), Jean Piaget: A British tribute (Harvester, forthcoming).

David Porter is a research student at the University of Southampton. He has held posts as Senior Residential Child Care Officer at a school for autistic children, and research assistant on a Social Science Research Council funded project.

Bob Remington is a lecturer in psychology at the University of Southampton. His teaching and research is concerned with the psychology of learning and its applications, particularly in the areas of behaviour therapy and behaviour modification. He is the author, with T.H. Foxen and J. Hogg, of 'Auditory reinforcement in profoundly retarded multiply-handicapped children' (*American Journal of Mental Deficiency* 82(1977)).

James Russell is a lecturer in Psychology at the University of Liverpool. His research interests include cognitive development and philosophical psychology, and their relations within genetic epistemology. He is the author of *The acquisition of knowledge* (Macmillan, 1978) as well as papers in the leading developmental and theoretical journals.

C.G. Sinha is Research Fellow at the Hester Adrian Research Centre for the Study of Learning Processes in the Mentally Handicapped, University of Manchester. He was the Principal Investigator on the Social Science Research Council project 'Language and representation in normal children and subnormal' (1976–1979). His research interests are language and mental representation in normal and severely mentally handicapped children.

J.A. Stedmon is Lecturer in Psychology at the University of Manchester. Her research interest is children's problems with referential language.

Cathy Urwin is a lecturer in developmental psychology at the University of Warwick, but is at present based at the University of Cambridge as a Margaret Lowenfeld Research Fellow. She has carried out research into parent-child communication and language development in blind children; and her current interests include the interface between psychoanalytic theory and the empirical study of mother-infant communication, and the development of social relationships between infants.

Valerie Walkerdine is Research Fellow at the University of London Institute of Education. Her research interests include cognitive development and school practices, particular mathematics; mathematics and gender; gender and schooling; and particularly attempts to develop theories of the subject and subjectivity. Her publications include (with C. Sinha), 'The internal triangle: language, reasoning and the social context', in I. Markova (ed.), *The social context of language* (Wiley, 1978); (with D. Adlam *et al.*), 'Psychology, ideology and the human subject' (*Ideology and Consciousness* 1(1977)); (with G. Corran) *The practice of reason: investigations of the teaching and learning of mathematics in the early years of schooling*, vol. 1, *Reading the signs of mathematics* (University of London Institute of Education); and vol. 2 (with R. Eynard) *Girls and mathematics*.

Preface

Dan I. Slobin
(*Department of Psychology, University of California, Berkeley*)

The book you are about to read will fill your head with echoes of conversation – the talk between children and parents, between children and teachers, between children and experimenters, and among children themselves. The authors are at pains to not only analyse this talk, but to *situate* it – to place it in contexts of expectations, emotions, values, and understandings both shared and unshared. Chapter after chapter presents leitmotifs for the 1980s. The child must be looked at as an individual. 'Language', 'cognition', and 'society' are not separate entities in interaction, but aspects of a common system constructed by individuals in processes of discourse and exchange. And these very processes are the constitutive bases of the individual.

If you are influenced by these chapters, you will find it difficult to study groups of children without attending to individual differences; difficult to design experiments without worrying about what the experimental setting means to the child; difficult to study separate systems of grammar or concepts without attending to the matrix of 'sociodialogic' factors in which language and cognition are embedded.

In addition to these broad and well-written ideological manifestoes and methodological caveats, you will find a wealth of new discoveries and theoretical insights. The authors take you to the homes of blind and retarded children, to the laps of mothers and fathers, to classrooms and laboratories. One has a clear sense of researchers at work – and children trying to make sense of their work. And, in the background, there are careful reviews of the literature, theoretically-oriented reevaluations and extensions of earlier work, promises of more to come.

If you read on, you will embark on a stimulating, often controversial journey. The editor has selected a group of writers who present a consistent theme, echoing and reflecting from chapter to chapter. It is not clear yet how we shall succeed in integrating the many factors that these writers call upon us to consider in interaction with one another. And in

ix

a full theory of 'children thinking through language' we shall want to pay attention to additional factors as well. To mention but two of my own interests, I would worry about situating the development of thought and discourse within the social structures and communicative systems of particular cultural groups, as mediated through the grammatical and semantic means of particular languages. There is clearly more to be done in integrating linguistic and social structure with patterns of mental and communicative development. Readers from other fields of endeavour will have their own points to add. But we must thank Michael Beveridge and his friends for involving us in a socio-dialogic dialogue.

Dan I. Slobin
Manchester
September 1981

Introduction

The central theme addressed by the authors of this volume concerns the ways in which our understanding of children's language interacts with the study of their cognitive processes. Obviously there are many approaches to such a complex problem and the chapters which follow reflect this diversity. It may be helpful therefore to approach the book with some guiding questions in mind and the purpose of this short introduction is to indicate a framework which might prove useful to the reader in getting an overall sense of the chapters which follow.

In the first chapter Elena Lieven illustrates how children's real-world knowledge can interact with their linguistic performance. Her argument suggests that a full understanding of a particular child's language development demands that we can locate his/her utterances in their social and psychological context. For example, systematic word order appears first for utterances with animate agents and Lieven suggests that the category 'animate agent' may at this stage be more psychologically real than the more general grammatical category of 'subject'. In what I find to be an extremely interesting analysis of how we should conceptualize children's language, Lieven discusses the way children talk about possession of different classes of things, e.g. people or objects, and the way children use syntax to mark 'highly transitive events'. Lieven is specifically concerned whether this type of evidence can be incorporated into a model of language development; and she concludes by hinting at a possible model involving an amalgamation of psycholinguistics and information processing.

Allayne Bridges raises a number of similar points in her chapter on children's comprehension of language; a process which she views as the integration of information from a wide variety of sources. Bridges discusses differences between children's response strategies in comprehension tasks and also considers the general principles which lead to response biases and preferences. For example, the child's knowledge of the likely behaviour of objects under the prevailing conditions is identified as an important factor in predicting success or failure in comprehension tasks. Bridges suggests how response biases and preferences can be theoretically valuable; and although she does not spell out a

1

general model of comprehension, she indicates many of the issues which will need resolving before such a model could be provided. Perhaps most interesting is her idea that comprehension and production may *not* have some common 'underlying unity'.

When talking about comprehension tasks, Bridges notes that introductory talk might have a strong influence on the features of the context that children see as significant. And this question is taken as a central problematic by Freeman, Sinha and Stedmon in their chapter on the relation between word meaning and discourse. They particularly emphasize the problem of establishing joint reference with children, illustrating the importance of knowing that children are answering the same question as the adults think they are when they perform in comprehension tasks or tasks which are tests of cognitive abilities.

This chapter takes a discourse analysis approach to the process of topic-setting in cognitive tasks, and reports a series of intriguing studies which plot the interaction between the linguistic and nonlinguistic contexts in topic-setting. The studies show that manipulation of this interaction can induce the same type of 'errors' in adults as those that are demonstrated by young children. And Freeman *et al.* argue that children have been described as miscomprehending when they could equally well be said to be making rational sense of discourse by using nonlinguistic information. In these cases children's answers may be wrong but could still be reasonable.

Russell takes a similar view to Freeman *et al.* on the importance of understanding why children are giving 'wrong' answers, and he also emphasizes the importance of understanding how children construe the question. Russell develops an extremely interesting argument which uses the philosophical notion of 'propositional attitudes' to suggest that Piaget's 'conflict of perspectives' hypothesis about the loss of egocentrism makes no sense without considering how children view their own statements and actions. Russell argues for an explanation of the move into operational thinking in terms of the development of intersubjectivity. Russell suggests, as do Urwin and Walkerdine in later chapters, that social interchange is important, even necessary, for cognitive development because sharing joint perspectives with others is an important aid to thinking.

Certainly Russell's evidence shows that young children have a disposition to allow non-joint perspectives; they are very tolerant or 'liberal' on this point. And as they grow older they demand more agreement both in the answers given and in beliefs about these answers. However, shared propositional attitudes do not always guarantee that it is 'truth' which is being agreed about. This would only be the case for propositional attitudes which do not permit alternatives. Children believing their answers to be true means that they have propositional attitudes of the form 'my view of X is such that it would cause my view to change if I allowed that others could have a different view and be correct'. Russell's chapter highlights the relevance for the study of cognitive development of the way in which children come to the position of accepting 'truth' as a possible propositional attitude. And more especially why they do so in some domains and contexts before others.

Elena Lieven stressed the importance of linguistic 'formats' to language acquisition. Cathy Urwin, in her chapter, looks at the development of this formatting process in blind children and argues that it shows how they come to know the signs of the world. She also makes a case that the usual view of how sighted children come to know these signs places too great an emphasis on what they can see and neglects social and linguistic exchange routines.

Urwin shows how language can allow the blind child to see that joint perspectives are possible. She argues that the development of discourse modes plays a crucial role in coming to understand the activities of other people and the way they act independently on the environment. Urwin suggests for example that naming games give the blind child a clue to the idea that objects can be accessible to both participants in the games. And she also suggests that language is the basis for learning the contrast between sharing and possession. In common with the other contributors Urwin links cognition to discourse context, and her argument requires that psychologists take a fresh look at the role of language in the development of human subjectivity.

Valerie Walkerdine adopts a similar approach in her chapter on the way children come to terms with 'cognitive' problems in school. She extends the arguments of Freeman *et al.* to the explicit view that objects cannot be understood externally to any discourse; and that the key to understanding children is being able to identify the position they have taken up within a discourse. Walkerdine proposes that children are better at reasoning in familiar contexts primarily because they are able to reflect on the language more easily than when the context is unfamiliar. This can be done by relying on what she calls the 'metaphoric content' of the task. And the suggestion is that so-called 'abstract thinking' develops through gradual shedding of this dependence, a process which she suggests is facilitated by successful teachers.

Walkerdine questions and then rejects the view that reasoning is in the child's mind and context is outside it. She believes that knowledge of discourse formats which are rooted in everyday activities allows the child access to a world in which 'thinking' is driven externally. As this position is part of an attempt to give an alternative to dualistic accounts of thinking, it would be difficult to fully accept Walkerdine's reanalysis of the problems she discusses without also accepting the theory that people's 'psychology' is primarily, if not entirely, identifiable in their social practices. However even if the reader finds this position either untenable or unclear, Walkerdine taps a rich vein for future inquiry.

The chapter by Beveridge and Brierley describes a participant observation study which uses some concepts from George Kelly's Personal Construct Theory to provide a model of the way 3-year-old children describe their world. The study is dependent for its validity on having achieved two aims: First, establishing joint perspectives between children and researchers during the months of the study and secondly, having appropriately interpreted the way the children's utterances can indicate the operation of different constructs. A substantial sample of the children's utterances are presented in the chapter, and the reader should at least be able to judge whether the second criterion has been satisfied. However, the 'achievement of joint perspectives' is difficult to demonstrate but is more likely to be possible when – as in this case – the adults conducting the study are part of the real-world context experienced by the children, and not just strange people in a strange experimental context.

Peter Lloyd's chapter raises a number of questions about the relationship between communication skills and performance on cognitive tasks. The dislocation between action and language observed by Lloyd should be considered in relation to Russell's emphasis on children's beliefs about their own statements. It is likely that the more certain children are about their statements, the more they will try to keep their actions and those of others consistent with what they have said. Lloyd also notes the important cognitive function for children of talking to themselves, and shows, given an appropriate context, that such self-directed language can be interpreted as being communicative in intent. His question of how much of children's language in social contexts is also 'thinking aloud' is relevant to all the chapters in this book.

The last two chapters take different analytical approaches to the language of less able children. Light and Remington describe carefully-thought-out training studies using techniques based on Premack's work with chimpanzees. They conclude that training procedures can provide a *set* which influences how further learning can occur. Thus, even with severely retarded children, it may be important to incorporate information about the context in which linguistic forms are acquired if we are to understand how one stage of linguistic development leads into the next.

Brinker presents both evidence and theory in support of this view. He reminds us that children often rely for successful communication on adults interpreting ideosyncratic language appropriately, which means they must rely on knowledge of the context, the language and the child. Brinker indicates how this process may not always be to the advantage of the retarded child. Light and Remington, in the more structured context, also show the difficulty of knowing precisely what mentally handicapped children are attending to when they generalize the use of linguistic labels. And, as Brinker's initial example shows, adults need to know the features of objects which are salient for children. Brinker goes on to argue, in a similar vein to Freeman *et al.*, that approaches to cognitive development which rely on Rosch's prototypes or Nelson's functional core concepts may need to be qualified by an appreciation of the social meaning of the context for the child.

In this short introduction I have tried to draw together some of the themes which run through this book. From their different perspectives the authors consider how we make sense of children via their language. The importance of the discourse context is particularly stressed, as is the role of communication in cognitive development. The overall picture presented seems to be a conceptually rich area of inquiry, and I hope the reader finds the chapters which follow as interesting as I have.

1
Context, process and progress in young children's speech[1]

E.V.M. Lieven

Introduction

Too often, we take the person apart for the purposes of our studies and then face the almost impossible task of reintegrating our findings in different areas back into some unified theory. Thus we divide our study of how children learn to talk into areas such as 'communicative skills', 'language structure', 'semantics', 'cognition', 'social influences' and are left with the question of how, if at all, the theories and descriptions generated by these different areas of study should be related to each other. In what follows I shall explore evidence for some of the possible relationships which may exist between these various areas in terms of the child's developing abilities to 'talk like an adult'.

If we try to think of a child talking in a real-world situation we must be interested both in the factors which lead the child to be able to produce a particular utterance at a particular moment and in the ways in which the child's different talking skills change over time, since the latter presumably bears on the former. Research always involves generalizing from descriptions of the 'data' made at one or other level of abstraction. It is in these various processes of abstraction, description and generalization that one particular conceptual object – 'the psychological child' – often seems to get lost. Whenever a child says something all of the following factors will be involved: contextual priming, memory, current strategies for producing utterances, and the conventions and attitudes which govern talk in the world in which the child lives. Some of the processes that underlie the production of speech in the child may be purely specific to language, others may involve much more general learning abilities. In either event there is no dispute about the fact that the child uses what s/he hears as one basis for her/his own speech – the disputes are all about the way in which this is done and the precise relationship between the speech environment in

[1] I wish to thank the following people for their very helpful comments and suggestions on this paper: Elaine Baker, Phil Barnard, Mike Beveridge, Anatol Lieven, Chris Sinha, Dan Slobin, Catherine Snow, Cathy Urwin, Valerie Walkerdine. They are, of course, in no way to be held responsible for the final product.

which the child lives, the processing mechanisms and procedures by which her/his utterances are generated and those utterances themselves.

In what follows I shall be suggesting (in the first section) that progress in skills for talking may be interwoven with the child's social world and the speech addressed to her/him in more complex ways than would be reflected in correlational studies on mothers' speech to children and children's skills at language relative to each other. In the second section of the paper, I consider the question of structure in young children's speech. Seemingly superficial similarities in structure between different children's utterances may disguise fundamental differences in their use. The differences may prove crucial if we are to describe the actual process of language development rather than imposing formal rules on the child which reflect theoretical presuppositions more than actual behaviour. I discuss the issue of continuities and discontinuities in children's procedures for producing utterances in terms of (a) the points at which they can and do make internal reorganizations of these procedures and (b) the support that they get for doing this from their environment. Finally (in the third section), I take up this last point in terms of the routines and frameworks within which the child may be able to gain sufficient automatization of procedures such that reorganization can take place. The paper, therefore, examines studies of adult speech to children and studies of children's early rules for generating utterances with a view to suggesting some possible contextual and interactional aids to the child in her or his acquisition of language structure.

Speech to children

We know that, in starting to talk, children are abstracting information from the speech that they hear. However the question of whether different kinds of speech environment make any difference to either the speed with which children learn to talk, the processes involved in their doing so or to the final outcome, however defined, is the subject of considerable dispute. On the one hand, it may simply be a matter of differences in rates of learning, with the actual processes involved in constructing language being the same in all cases. On the other, it may be that children subjected to very different inputs may have to rely on different processing devices to construct their language, and that there may be important and systematic differences in procedures for generating utterances, at least in the period before the child's language approaches that of the adult. In either case an adequate characterization of the speech that children are actually hearing is an important prerequisite to any claims about the relation between adult speech to children and children's own language development.

One important question here is how children learn to talk in environments where they are either spoken to very little and/or mainly hear speech that is not directed to them (e.g. from radio or television). There is no direct evidence on this, but Tizard and Rees (1974, 1975) report that a group of children brought up in institutional environments are 'behind' on conventional measures of language ability at 2 years by comparison with a group of matched working-class controls. Of course this may be due to many things other than the specific nature of the speech to the institutionally-reared children, but it is interesting that they were not behind on other developmental and cognitive measures and also that they had 'caught up' with the control groups by the age of four. The suggestion is then of a specific effect on rate (at least) of language learning. The fact that the effect 'washes out' by the age of 4 in terms of conventional measures of language ability would make this a finding of no interest to those who make a distinction between 'language competence' and 'language performance' and are only interested in the acquisition of the former. However, the question arises as to whether slow learning may also, in some cases, be different learning (in either process or outcome) and this is clearly of interest to those whose concern is the actual psychological processes involved in learning to talk.

There is plenty of evidence that speech to children differs from adult-adult speech (Snow 1977, Newport *et al*. 1977). Researchers agree that it is characterized by shorter utterances and repetitiveness, that it is more closely tied to the immediate situation and that it is often slower, with more highly-accentuated pitch and stress. Since many of these features also characterize the speech of adults to foreign-language learners and of very young children to language-learning children (Shatz and Gelman 1977, Dunn and Kendrick in press) they are thought to be concomitants of the attempt to communicate with a non-competent speaker. However, that in itself does not invalidate them as potential aids to the language learner.

A couple of examples will serve to highlight the importance of knowing what speech the child is actually hearing before we move on to a discussion of the possible effects on children's language learning of differences in adults' speech to children. Ochs (1980) explains the absence of the ergative marker in the speech of young Samoan children by reference, not to the cognitive complexity of this linguistic form, but to the fact that it is not used in private domestic speech and, in particular, in women's speech. It is a characteristic of men's public and formal speech – that speech most closely studied by linguists writing a formal grammar of Samoan. A point with similar implications is made by Smoczyńska (in press) when she argues that the overgeneralizations and regularizations that Polish children perform on some gender endings may be derived, in part, from the diminutives which are frequent in the speech of Polish adults to children and which show greater simplification and consistency for gender endings than do the adult forms. Such examples suggest that a category of language *per se* is too simplistic when considering how children learn to talk. Language forms will vary according to the practices of which they are a part and this makes a crucial difference to the study of language development.

Thus, I would argue, it is clear that the type of speech encountered by children is an important variable in their learning of language. However, the interpretation of individual studies on this issue can be far from straightforward. Particular methodological problems occur because one has to attempt to control for the effects of the child on the mother and to find some basis for identifying the different groups of children to be compared.

In the case of the study by Cross (1977, 1978) the child variable was rate of acquisition as measured by a receptive language test and measures of MLU (mean length of utterance) and upper bound length. The children were matched in pairs on the basis of these measures and the younger child in each pair was considered 'accelerated' by comparison with the elder ('normal') child (Cross 1978, 202). The main finding was that semantic extensions and, more particularly, synergistic sequences (utterances and utterance sequences which were both semantically related to the child utterance and self-repetitions on the part of the mother) in the mothers' speech, were positively correlated with 'language advance'. With the exception of mean preverb length (also positively correlated with language advance), syntactic aspects of the mothers' speech did not differentiate the two groups. A difficulty with this study is that measures of the children's speech are so minimal. As we shall see in the second section of this paper, two children may have the same MLU and even average upper bound length and yet vary substantially in important aspects of their speech.

In contrast to the Cross study, Newport *et al.* (1977) take comprehensive measures of the child speech (from the point of view of a strictly linguistic analysis) but not of the mothers' speech. They look only at frequencies of the variables rather than at any measure of contingency to child utterance with the exception of 'expansion' and this does not include semantic extensions. Their data base is two two-hour 'interviews' held six months apart with 15 mother-child pairs. The children ranged in age from 12 to 27 months and in MLU from 1.00 to 3.46. A central focus of the paper is an examination of correlations between growth rates in various aspects of the children's speech over the six months and various aspects of the mothers' speech to them. Newport *et al.* controlled for differences in initial language level of the children by partialling out the variance due to both age and language measures at the first interview, and for the effects of the child on the mother by partialling out the variance due to both the above factors in the mothers' speech at interview 1 — measures of mothers' speech were not made at interview 2. Using these double partial correlations, they found no correlations between measures of 'propositional complexity' (number of verbs per utterance and noun-phrases per utterance) and the various measures of the mothers' speech that they employed. They did, however, find correlations between some other aspects of the children's speech and their mothers' speech to them – specifically, between the number of auxiliaries per verb phrase in the children's speech and the number of yes/no questions in the mothers' speech, and also between the number of inflections per noun phrase in the children's speech and the number of deictic utterances in the mothers' speech. The authors conclude from these results that adult speech to children may have effects on the acquisition of parts of the language system that are specific to a particular language (e.g. the auxiliary system in English) but are unimportant when it comes to 'universal aspects of language structure and content' (Newport *et al*. 1977, 133).

The finding of relatively few correlations between specific syntactic features of adults' speech to children and relative language 'advance' in children supports the idea put forward by Newport *et al*. and by many others that the child plays an active role in her/his own development of increasing complexity in language. One way of thinking about this is in terms of an 'assimilation-accomodation' model. The child is presumably only able to analyse the speech that s/he is hearing in terms of the current processing procedures available. S/he thereby restricts the scale of the problem. Within a broad range, therefore, purely syntactic variations in the speech that is heard may make no difference. We can however elaborate upon this conclusion somewhat by considering two points that arise from Newport *et al*.'s study.

First we must conclude that there may be some instances where we *can* make a theoretical prediction about the relationship between the development of a particular structure in the child's language (e.g. the auxiliary system) and the frequency of particular types of utterances in the input in which this structure receives high prominence from a processing point of view (e.g. auxiliary fronting in yes/no questions). This of course depends on having a clear theory of the characteristics of language processing in the child. In Newport *et al*.'s case the finding of this correlation may have been the result of post-hoc analysis, but it does in any case provide a model for future theoretical predictions.

Secondly, the issue of what to measure in both the adult's and the child's speech is critical to the kinds of conclusions that can be drawn. Propositional complexity (as measured by numbers of noun-phrases and verbs per utterance) may not be a theoretically coherent entity in the speech of children of this age range (see the second section of this chapter). More importantly, it may simply not be relevant to look at features like MLU, sentence types, deixis and syntactic expansions, when attempting to look for effects of adults' speech to children on the growth of something like propositional complexity. It may be that it is styles of discourse between adult and child which are critically involved here, and this would not be reflected in any way by the sorts of measures used by Newport *et al*. The study by Cross cited above is suggestive on this point, and we turn now to other work which, while it in no way proves a connection between discourse features and children's structural and propositional language development, does indicate the kinds of analyses that might have to be undertaken if this question were to be seriously investigated.

While Cross's study suggests only an effect of the dynamics of discourse on rate of acquisition, Nelson, in her 1973 study, argues that differences in the ways that the mothers in her study talked to their children may, in part, account for differences in early speech 'style' between the children. There are two sorts of difficulties with these studies. One has already been mentioned – the nature of the measures of child speech used (see Lieven 1980a for a discussion of this in relation to Nelson's study). The other is that a more advanced child may actually be influencing her/his own mother in a systematic way. A linguistically interesting child may 'generate' a linguistically interested mother by eliciting more contingently related speech.[2] While I think that such effects are highly likely, and indeed have presented some evidence for them (Lieven 1978a), I also think one can make a good argument for the potential importance to children of both a high degree of responsiveness to their utterances and a high degree of contingently-related speech. This is not to say that children cannot learn to talk under conditions that do not meet these criteria, but it raises the question of whether they may have more difficulty in doing so and/or may have to learn somewhat differently. What is at issue is the processes and procedures with and by which a child learns to talk and the potentially different interplay in these between cognitive, linguistic and social factors for different children.

Nelson makes this argument in terms of 'accepting' and 'non-accepting' mothers while I (1978b) place the discussion more in terms of what speech is used for in the child's environment. For example, in my own study of three children there were strong consistencies between sessions both in how generally responsive the mothers were to anything that the child said and in how much they expanded their utterances. The least responsive and least expanding mother was also relatively speaking much more likely to respond to her child with monosyllabic responses such as *yes*, *no*, *mm*, *oh*. These patterns showed up in the earliest sessions with the children – well before they were producing any 'interesting' multiple-word utterances. In this paper, I demonstrate how the more responsive of the mothers manages to weave a conversation around the rather minimal imitations and repetitions of her child while the other mother is either non-responsive or very directive in trying to elicit a specific word (the 'correct' one) from her child.

---

[2] Newport *et al*. (1977) might have disambiguated this issue for the group that they studied had they investigated these kinds of discourse variables.

We can make two points here: first, that it may not be the individual expansions which are important as such but more what they reflect about the more general context of talk and the support that the child gets for attempting to take part in it; secondly, that one important consequence of these differences in maternal speech styles may lie in the extent to which a child is thrown back on her or his own resources when s/he wants to say something. Thus a child who is not participating in the repetition, extension, build-up sequences and imitation which characterizes the conversations of many of the child-adult pairs studied may have to rely much more heavily on rote-learned routines and her/his already overlearned rules than will the more 'conversationally supported' or 'scaffolded' (Bruner 1975) child. These points illustrate how the child's progress in talking may reflect, and be reflected in, her/his social world. We shall see the kinds of differences between children's speech that this might lead to at the end of the section on combination and structure below.

Combination and structure

When writers such as Cromer (1981) and Shatz (1981) argue that work on the development of communication has not aided our understanding of how language is acquired, they are referring to the problem − as they see it − of how language *structure* is acquired. There is no question but that the sentences people speak can be analysed in terms of certain formal, and often semantic-free, rules. Examples are grammatical gender, where nouns are divided arbitrarily into a number of gender declensions which have little or no semantic basis (Karmiloff-Smith 1978); rules for various kinds of embedding and subordination; agreement rules in different languages; rules for word order, such as auxiliary inversion in English for *wh*-questions.

A central question in the study of language development is when and how children begin to manifest the more semantic-free rules of the language they are starting to speak, and the degree of continuity or discontinuity in their speech that this new behaviour represents. On the one hand children are involved from an early stage in putting together combinations of words and morphemes that are orderly abstractions of what they are hearing, and it is the child who is making these abstractions i.e. they are not given in any obvious way in the speech that children hear. On the other hand there is considerable evidence that children's early utterances can be described by rules which are semantically based, i.e. that children use meaning as a way into structure (Slobin 1973). A recent paper by Slobin (1981) provides an example of this. He demonstrates that children start by using the syntactic devices available in their language for marking transitivity by applying them only to highly transitive events, independently of whether the language uses the same devices (e.g. an accusative inflection) to mark other semantic roles (or related but less transitive events). He argues that there may be some types of events in the child's world which have sufficient cognitive saliency and coherence ('prototypicality') that they underpin the child's discovery of the linguistically 'canonical' way of referring to such events.[3] The issues that arise here are how specifically language-based the skills that children use to make these 'rules' are, and the manner by which such semantically-based rules 'bleach' into formal, syntactic rules. A precondition to answering these formidable questions is an accurate description of the actual procedures by which children can be inferred to be generating utterances, and it is to a discussion of this in relation to the specific issue of early word combinations in English that we now turn.

When a child produces more than one word under one sentential contour, what is it that s/he has combined? Has s/he just produced the words relevant to the situation in a random order? Alternatively has the child made use of a constant positional occurrence of a particular word or of inferred word classes? Work on this area of child language development has largely concentrated on the issue of how to make correct inferences about word classes and on developing rules for their combination. It is worth pointing out that theories on the origin of word classes in children's early combinations have ranged through the whole nativist-environmental spectrum. Thus while McNeill (1966) suggested that the categories of 'pivot' and 'open' might be innate, Braine (1963) used a basically associationist argument to account for the same inferred word classes. Over the years we have had a number of different formulations of this problem – some arguing for a direct translation from some nonlinguistic underlying cognitive (Schlesinger 1971) and/or social (Greenfield and Smith 1976) bases for the child's utterances, others for their basis in semantic relations (Bloom *et al*. 1975, Leonard 1976). A difficulty with the former type of theory is that it faces severe problems in explaining how the child ever moves from such a nonlinguistic basis for combination to the more complex and abstract ways of producing utterances which seem to characterize the speech of only slightly older children. A problem with the latter type is that it is quite unclear how children form or identify such abstract categories as 'agent' or 'action' in terms of groups of words that can then be combined in an orderly fashion.

The central issue in relation to categories is that of their scope. One way in which these problems have been tackled by both Bowerman (1973) and Braine (1976) is to suggest that, where children's early word combinations do appear to be following some generative procedure,

---

[3] The extent to which such cognitive saliency and coherence are constructed and presented within the kinds of routines and frames discussed in the third section of this chapter is an open question. See Sinha (in press) for a theory of the relationship between social constructed canonical frames and cognitive representations.

such rules or precedures may operate on much less abstract groupings of words than the kinds of word classes previously suggested. For example, when a child starts to mark a grammatical case (for instance in the nominative or accusative) using either systematic word order or morphology, s/he may only do it for a subclass of items in that case, e.g. for animate agents in the nominative. If so, then it makes more sense, psychologically speaking, to think in terms of the category 'animate agent' than in terms of 'subject of the sentence'. Thus it is argued the child's categories are indeed an abstraction but not at as abstract a level as the syntactic roles of subject and object. Braine suggests that the categories of children's early combinations may even be of much lower scope than this. Thus, according to Braine's analyses, children may slowly build up their 'parts of speech' categories from productive combinations based on just a few, or sometimes one, lexical item. An example would be a set of utterances in a child's corpus which could be described as fitting the formula: *hot/cold* + X where X is a group of words semantically restricted in some way. This formula could be productive given the following types of evidence. First, evidence that the child produces combinations, based on the formula, which s/he is most unlikely ever to have heard. Secondly, that there are no instances in which *hot* or *cold* come at the end rather than the beginning of the child's utterance.[4] The important point is that the productivity or otherwise of this formula does not rest on the assumption that the child has a category such as 'property of an object' or 'attribute'. Braine makes a convincing argument for the slow build-up of word classes in at least some children, from just one or two words through to something much more like a semantically-based category. The advantage of this approach is that we can follow individual children as they build up their word classes and as both these classes and the rules for combining them become more complex. Thus we are in a much better position to ask questions about how particular 'positional patterns' (Braine 1976, 9) get established and to investigate the sorts of skills involved as these categories and formulae gain in complexity and scope.

One consequence of Braine's method of analysis was to demonstrate that, although the children that he studied were talking about the same sorts of things e.g. 'action', 'possession', they were doing so using idiosyncratic formulae for combination. Furthermore, these operated often over different and very restricted semantic ranges. To give an example of this from my study (Lieven 1980b): all of the three children in this study (Beth, Jane and Kate) 'talked about possession' but the ways in which they did so differed considerably. Thus Beth had three possessive words: *my, your* and *our*. The words with which these

---

[4] In fact the definition of 'productivity' is considerably more problematic that I have indicated here. See Braine 1976 and MacWhinney 1980 for a discussion of the relation between corpus size and the identification of productivity.

appeared in her utterances were most likely to be personal names as in: *my Mummy*, or *our Daddy, Mummy* or without clear reference as in: *there my, more my, Mummy*, or *look your, your, my Mummy*. There was also contextual evidence that she may have been 'talking about possession' when she used the names of people who were not present, as she did very often: *there Julian there, Mummy* (when Julian, her brother, was not present and she was pointing to something in a book – the inference is that she was claiming that the object in the book 'belonged' to Julian). By contrast, Jane appeared to have a productive formula for explicitly referring to her possession of objects: *my/mine + X* where X referred to a large number of objects that either really were Jane's or which she was laying claim to. Kate, the third child, also used a similar, lexically based, pattern but she also used the *'s* morpheme for expressing possession in what appeared to be a generative manner i.e. in utterances that she was unlikely to have heard before. Thus to describe these three children as having rules with which to produce utterances about possession might possibly be accurate at one level of theoretical description but would tell us little about the origin of such rules, the content of the utterances generated by them, or about the rules themselves. It seems from these data that the children are talking about possession in different ways. In addition they may be talking about different kinds of possession. Kate, an only child, uses the possessive morpheme to talk about other people's possessions, e.g. *Laina's tape recorder* (in the context of being forbidden to touch it); to express a transient relation, e.g. *Gerald's turn* (when she wants Gerald to take a turn) as well as when she wishes to assert her claim on something, e.g. *Kate's toast*. Beth on the other hand, seems much more concerned to simply indicate possession without specifying what is possessed. Possession by members of the family seems of primary concern to her and this may well be related to her position as the younger of two children. It does not seem that the difference between Kate and Beth lies merely in Beth's lack of names for objects, since her spontaneous vocabulary range is nearly as wide as Kate's – she just does not use it (Lieven 1980a). One potentially very important factor, then, in understanding these differences in possessive utterances is the possible differences in the practices of possession within the families. Different relations to private property and ownership may be reflected in the ways in which children talk about possession and, perhaps, in the ways in which they structure their utterances to do it. One would have to follow the development of these children's 'possessive' utterances in great detail to see whether these initial differences affected either how they developed the syntax of posession and/or whether there remained differences in later usage.

This kind of difference between Kate and Beth occurs not only in their 'possessive' utterances but can be detected in nearly all the utterances they produce. Thus while Kate would seem to have a large number of systematic formulae, some based on lexical items, others based on more abstract categories, Beth's utterances are mainly combinations of a very few words and phrases e.g. *there, more, look, Mummy, Julian, somemore.* Similar differences have been noted by other authors. Thus Bowerman (1976) noted that there were at least three types of early multiple-word formulae: those which depend for their meaning on the presence of a specific lexical item, e.g. *more + X;* those whose relational meaning is independent (more or less) of the meanings of the words used to fill the categories, e.g. agent + action; and those in which the relational categories are not entirely independent of a specific lexical item, e.g. *X + it.* She makes the point – as does Braine – that all three of these patterns may be present in the speech of one child. Yet there is also evidence from my own longitudinal data and those of others (Leonard 1976, Ramer 1976) that children may differ considerably in the extent to which their speech depends on lexically-based patterns and the duration of this dependence. If we are to understand the processes involved in learning to talk we have to ask how such differences arise and how they are involved in the child's continuing development of more complex speech.

In Lieven 1980a I argue that the differences in the children's multiple-word utterances can be linked to differences in their use of single-word utterances. Thus Beth's very early speech is heavily dependent on a few words with which she builds her longer utterances. In contrast Kate *uses* a far wider range of words particularly names of objects and their attributes than do either of the other two children. Again the difference between Kate and Beth lies not so much in the spontaneous vocabulary range that they manifest (i.e. the number of types) but in the ways they choose to use this range (i.e. the number of tokens) – Beth using a very small number of words very frequently while Kate talks about a large number of objects and events. These two children appear to have very different procedures for talking. Thus even when she is only using single words, Kate is already explicitly commenting on the existence of objects and their attributes while Beth is seemingly more immediately concerned to use language as a direct vehicle to getting the attention of those around her. In Bates's (1979) terms, Beth is more dependent on formulaic speech while Kate is already demonstrating evidence of a separation between words and the objects and situations they refer to (i.e. a greater degree of analysis of vehicle-referent relations (Bates 1979, 328)).

One important conclusion that is clearly indicated by the data discussed above is how careful we have to be about abstractions from children' utterances when we are trying to talk about the rules that may underlie (or can be used to describe) the generation of such utterances. Neither MLU nor some kinds of semantic analyses would necessarily have distinguished the three children discussed above, and yet anyone studying the development of language skills would find it necessary to separate them for analytical purposes.

A second suggestion is of the potential influence of the social-interactional environment on the ease with which children start to show evidence of less 'context-dependent' language structure and the methods by which they do so. This may be a relatively direct influence, as in Schieffelin's 1979 example of the Kaluli of Papua New Guinea who believe that children have to be taught to talk. In this society there are explicit frames for teaching children to speak and other kinds of child speech may be discouraged, e.g. monologues, word and sound play. Here then, children's speech is explicitly evaluated against the adult view of what correct language is. In other societies such evaluation is often less clear, but a sense of what talking is for and the correct forms for doing it will no doubt be present in any interaction though they may differ from one group of people to the next. This, in turn, will affect the routines and frameworks within which adults talk to children and thus, what children say and how they say it (Bryce-Heath pers. comm.).

In Lieven 1978b I suggest that differences in the styles of interaction and attitudes to what language is for in the mother-child dyads may be affecting how the children 'bootstrap' themselves up into more complex ways of talking. Kate's mother is highly responsive to Kate's utterances, hardly ever misses an opportunity to expand on them, and is accepting of what Kate says. By contrast, Beth's mother appears to have a more utilitarian attitude to language and uses it for getting everyday things done and to encourage Beth to use correct referential speech. She expands Beth's utterances at a very low rate and, unlike Kate's mother, does not really engage in play talk or in talk about the world. Beth is a child who, at much the same age as Kate and with very similar lengths of utterances, says very little in terms of lexical specificity. As we have already seen, her speech seems very closely tied in to a small number of words used for attentional ends. Kate is already using her speech to engage in complex negotiations with her mother, to joke, to contradict, and to comment explicitly on the world. These skills gave her, at least with her mother and myself, a distinct edge on self-assertiveness over both Beth and Jane. Whether such skills would have been either welcomed or recognized in Beth's family is open to question. The message that Beth is getting is that language is not for engaging in a game – thus there is an emphasis on correct speech and on the mother defining the topic of conversation. Given that Beth's mother is also unwilling or unable to elaborate on Beth's utterances in such a way as to keep the conversation going, Beth is left much more to her own devices in her attempts to produce utterances. This is clearly true in the short term and it may well also be true as a description of the methods by which she starts to produce more complex utterances. It seems doubtful to me that Beth will end up with a radically different version of adult 'grammar' from Kate – at least under current ways of thinking about grammar and psychological processing. A more open question is whether Beth has to rely on different procedures for constructing a grammar, and what the similarities and differences between her rules for generating utterances and those of Kate are at later dates.

Whatever specifically linguistic skills children bring to the process of language learning, it can surely be described as a continuous process by which the child, trying to bend words to her/his own needs, is forced to move away from a one-to-one relation between context and utterance, between cognitions and the words to express them, and between function and form. I would argue that children go through these processes time and time again in their development of language in a much greater variety of ways and at a much wider range of ages than has perhaps been fully realized, and that the speech environment in which they grow up is one important influence on when and how different aspects of language become more formal and less contextually and semantically based. The problem is to relate such structural discontinuities to the functional continuities that children's speech manifests on the one hand and to processing mechanisms available to the child on the other.

Defining functional continuity also raises problems, however, since there is always the danger that the proposed continuity is more metaphorical than real. Thus it is probably correct to point to the turntaking games of the preverbal period as structural precursors for turntaking in conversation (Bruner 1975). But this is only a partial background for the procedures involved in deixis, anaphoric reference, presupposition and implication as they are realized in the structures of utterances.

On the one hand then, we have to go beyond imposing some kind of metaphorical continuity on the developing language skills of children if we are ever to unravel the ways in which interaction and conversation, cognition and processing capacities, combine in the individual child to produce changes in their ways of talking. On the other, the search for genuine continuities in children's development also involves a challenge to some ways of conceiving of structure in early child speech – as I have been arguing in the first half of this section. If we are not accurately describing precisely what *is* abstract in this speech, then we may be analysing our own linguistic or psycholinguistic preconceptions rather than any actual child's ability to speak in increasingly complex ways.

In the final section of this paper, I present a few examples of children's ability to reorganize their language system into more abstract ways of using language, in the context of suggesting that one powerful interactive aid to the child in doing this may be that of familiar, and partially routinized, events and conversations.

Routines and metaprocedural 'leaps'

So how does a child come to 'bootstrap' her or himself into treating some particular feature of language or its usage in formal rather than purely meaning-related terms? At a minimum this must involve the registration of patterns in the input as a function of the child's already available patterns and words. How this registration occurs is an extremely complex issue, but to my mind it is highly likely to involve some 'wired-in' capacity for the analysis and production of fast temporal sequences in both the acoustic and articulatory domains. Some of Slobin's (1973) operating principles may reflect such processing mechanisms, e.g. 'pay attention to the ends of words' (191). This could be recast in terms of some kind of priority for recency which, when combined with the child's current representation, would lead to the identification of new elements in the speech stream (Barnard and Lieven, in preparation). Work on speech segmentation in children has not proceeded very far but Peters (1980) provides some interesting examples of missegmentations, and the possible sources for them in the input, from which it might be in principle possible to isolate some of the processing mechanisms involved. However such an analysis would also have to include certain higher-order cognitive processes – perhaps similar to some other of Slobin's operating principles, e.g. 'the use of grammatical markers should make semantic sense' (i.e. one-to-one mapping form to function) (1973, 206). It is as yet quite unclear how specific to language such higher-order processes might be – though, whatever their origin, their operation in the domain of language may well be reflected later in development in other cognitive domains, e.g. the interplay of procedures that children demonstrate in various cognitive tasks such as conservation (Walkerdine and Sinha 1978).

Karmiloff-Smith (1981) argues, when discussing the 'metaprocedural' behaviour of somewhat older children that 'once each separate, isolated procedure has become automatized, then children step up to a metaprocedural level . . .'. I want to conclude this chapter by considering some possible aids to 'automatization' for the child and some examples of the 'step-up to the metaprocedural level' which antedate the examples given by Karmiloff-Smith by several years in the child's development. I shall be arguing that the sources of 'automatization' (i.e. routinization of procedures) very often lie with the child's interactive and social world – and that if they do not, a child may be at somewhat of a disadvantage. I shall also be reiterating the point made in the preceding section, namely that superficially similar behaviour on the part of children may disguise differences in the extent to which children have made such abstractions.

There is evidence for the involvement of various kinds of routines in at least some children's language development. Usually when this is discussed in the literature it refers either to the very early frameworks of joint action and exchange that Bruner (1975) describes and/or to the rote-learning of phrases in the context of games such as peekaboo or patacake. However it seems clear that more or less routinized and familiar frameworks are a pervasive feature of most children's lives – and it may be in just these frameworks that initatives towards contextual detachment (or the 'step-up to the metaprocedural level') can occur. Snow (in press) has a beautiful example of just such a detachment on the pragmatic and discourse level. N, the subject of her study, produced the following utterance in the context of wanting to go outside to play after dinner – something he often wanted to do which was always refused at that time of day: *Go out in the garden. Play with the red car. That's a good idea*. The intonation pattern of *That's a good idea* 'mimicked precisely that normally produced by N's mother who used this expression regularly in attempts to convince him to carry out nondesired behaviours.' Here N has analysed certain aspects of the pragmatic use of the phrase *That's a good idea* and generated it for his own similar pragmatic purposes. This implies that the phrase has been registered across a number of different contexts and that the child has, at some point, been able to analyse out the commonalities in these various situations. An important point about Snow's paper is that she convincingly demonstrates one child's ability to store whole utterances spoken to him and to remember and reproduce linguistic material over lengths of time which stretch to months – presumably such abilities are a prerequisite for the internal reorganization of procedures for producing utterances.

Bruner has, of course, long argued the importance of routines such as book-reading for the learning of words (Bruner 1975, Ninio and Bruner 1978) and many parents also explicitly teach words to children and play elicitation games with them. McShane (1980) argues that the routinization of 'naming games' may continue for some time before the child 'realizes' that everything has a name. Such a realization is an example of a procedural reorganization. Both Bowerman (1976) and Clark (1980) support this notion when they argue that children's semantic development must be seen as involving some of the same processes of generativity that are traditionally thought of in relation to the development of structure in children's speech. However, I think that children may differ quite radically in the point at which they make such an inference and that some, perhaps like Beth, may be producing large numbers of multiple-word utterances without having reached the stage of contextual distance achieved by other children before they move to multiple-word combinations. Such differences would presumably be reflected in the ways in which children generate their multiple-word utterances – as I have argued for Beth and Kate – and in some cases this may also reflect the attitudes to language use in their immediate social world which I have already discussed. This would also explain the contradictory findings in the literature on the subject of whether children do or do not show a vocabulary 'boom' at some point after they first start learning words (cf. McShane 1980 for a discussion).

The search for routines and frames which may aid the child in her/his analysis of speech is a complex one, since what constitutes a routine or frame for the child will presumably vary as a function of her/his current representations. Thus a child who has a 'canonical' form established (Sinha in press) on whatever level will be in a position to identify non-canonicality – and perhaps to generate it. At the early stages in the development of representations it may be necessary for a routine to follow a very tight format for it to be identified as a routine by the child. Ninio and Bruner's (1978) book-reading formats may be an example of this. Later, however, what constitutes a routine or frame for the child may have more flexibility.

A possible example of the latter type of frame can be found in the transcripts of Eve's speech from the Harvard study undertaken by Brown and his colleagues (Brown 1973). Eve's early use of time adverbials occurred, at least in the context of the four hours per week that recordings took place, in a highly specific context – that of Eve requesting that she be allowed to drink milk from her baby sister's bottle. This request was often allowed but always involved discussions of turn-taking: *First baby X can have a drink, then Eve; After baby X, then Eve can have a turn; No, its baby X's turn now then Eve can have a turn;* etc. Eve imitated parts of such utterances and spontaneously produced time adverbials and related words (*after, first, then, turn*) in shorter utterances related to the same, obviously highly emotionally important and very frequent routine.[5] It was a considerable time before these time adverbials were to be seen in contexts other than these. One example indicates some of the effort involved for Eve when she did start to try and use time adverbials in other contexts, though it must be said of this example that she was also trying to refer to events that had already taken place – a considerable endeavour in itself:

Eve at 25 months

Father	Eve, what did you do this morning? Tell Pop. What did you do this morning while I was gone?
Eve	[I] play in the sand-box.
Father	What did you make in the sand-box?
Eve	A birthday cake with Becky and with Cathy.
Father	Who was the cake for?
Eve	For for . . . a horse hada hab a drink of water.
Father	The horse hada have a drink of water?
Eve	Yeah.

[5] The role of emotion and desire in the development of language and the construction of routines and frames is an important issue which I have not dealt with at all. See Urwin (this volume) for a discussion.

Father	What's that got to do with the birthday cake?
Eve	Because we haba make it.
Father	We made a drink of water? Where? In the bucket? Where?
Eve	In . . . a bucket.
Father	In the bucket too?
Eve	*After* drink of water had go in go go go in it.
Father	*After* the drink of water, *then* the birthday cake?
Eve	Yeah. *After* drink of water go in it, *then* the birthday cake. *After* the drink of water had a *turn*.
Father	Ah, the drink of water had a *turn first* in the bucket. Uh huh. *Then* the birthday cake. That's pretty good. What else did you do?

Parts of the routine are underlined. Note how Eve's father struggles to make sense of what Eve is saying and accepts her way of describing the events. Note too how, in Eve's final utterance, the notion of *after* and having a *turn* are combined — as they are in the original routine — but in a slightly odd way, perhaps, from the point of view of adult speech.

Conclusions

The overriding conclusion of this paper is that by separating the study of child language into areas such as 'cognitive underpinnings', 'input', 'generation of formal linguistic rules', we distort the object of study. The answers to questions posed within one of these paradigms of research depends on factors which are studied in the other paradigms. Further, it must be recognized that children may differ considerably in the ways in which they construct their speech and what they use it for — superficial similarities disguise the fact that aspects of language and language use may become decontextualized for different children at different points in their development. Finally the process of such decontextualization is, I suggest, not a 'once and for all' leap into formal grammar, but occurs over and over again as children learn to talk.

References

Barnard, P. and Lieven, E.V.M. (in preparation): Cognitive structures and linguistic experience: an information processing approach to language acquisition.

Bates, E. 1979: *The emergence of symbols*. New York: Academic Press.

Bloom, L.M., Lightbown, P. and Hood, L. 1975: Structure and variation in child language. *Monographs of the Society for Research into Child Development* **40**, Serial 160.

Bowerman, M. 1973: *Early syntactic development*, Cambridge: CUP.

—— 1976: Semantic factors in the acquisition of rules for word use and sentence construction. In D.M. Morehead and A.E. Morehead (eds.), *Normal and deficient child language*. Baltimore: University Park Press.

Braine, M. 1963: The ontogeny of English phrase structure: the first phrase *Language* **39**, 1–13.

—— 1976: Children's first word combinations. *Monographs of the Society for Research into Child Development* **41 (1)**, Serial 164.

Brown, R. 1973: *A first language: the early stages*. Cambridge, Mass.: Harvard University Press.

Bruner, J.S. 1975: From communication to language. *Cognition* **3**, 255–87.

Clark, E. 1980: Convention and innovation in acquiring the lexicon. *Papers and Reports on Child Language Development* **19**, 1–20.

Cromer, R. 1981: Reconceptualizing language acquisition and cognitive development. In: R. Schiefelbusch and D. Bricker (eds.), *Early language intervention*. Baltimore: University Park Press.

Cross, T. 1977: Mothers' speech adjustments: the contribution of selected child-listener variables. In C. Snow and C. Ferguson (eds.), *Talking to children: language input and acquisition*. Cambridge: CUP.

—— 1978: Mothers' speech and its association with rate of linguistic development in young children. In N. Waterson and C. Snow (eds.), *The development of communication*. Chichester: Wiley.

Dunn, J. and Kendrick, C. (in press): The speech of two and three year olds to infant siblings: 'baby talk' and the context of communication. *J. Ch. Lang.* **9**.

Greenfield, P.M. and Smith, J.H. 1976: *The structure of communication in early language development*. New York: Academic Press.

Karmiloff-Smith, A. 1978: The interplay between syntax, semantics and phonology in language acquisition processes. In R. Campbell and P. Smith (eds.), *Recent advances in the psychology of language* **1**. New York: Plenum.

—— 1981: Language as a formal problem space for children. In W. Deutsch (ed.), *The child's construction of language*. New York and London: Academic Press.

Leonard, L.B. 1976: *Meaning in child language*. New York: Grune and Stratton.

Lieven, E.V.M. 1978a: Conversations between mothers and young children: individual differences and their possible implication for the study of language learning. In N. Waterson and C. Snow (eds.), *The development of communication*. Chichester: Wiley.

—— 1978b: Turn-taking and pragmatics: two issues in child language acquisition. In R. Campbell and P. Smith (eds.), *The psychology of language* **1**. New York: Plenum.

—— 1980a: Different routes to multiple-word combinations. *Papers*

and *Reports on Child Language Development* **19**, 34–44.
—— 1980b: Language development in young children: children's speech and speech to children. Doctoral dissertation, University of Cambridge.
McNeill, D. 1966: Developmental psycholinguistics. In F. Smith and G.A. Miller (eds.), *The genesis of language*. Cambridge, Mass.: MIT Press.
McShane, J. 1980: *Learning to talk*. Cambridge: CUP.
MacWhinney, B. 1980: Levels of syntactic acquisition. In S. Kuczaj (ed.), *Language development: syntax and semantics*. Hillside, NJ: Erlbaum.
Nelson, K. 1973: Structure and strategy in learning to talk. *Monographs of the Society for Research in Child Development* **38**, Serial 149.
Newport, E., Gleitman, H., and Gleitman, L. 1977: Mother, I'd rather do it myself: some effects and non-effects of maternal speech style. In C. Snow and C.E. Ferguson (eds.), *Talking to children: language input and acquisition*. Cambridge: CUP.
Ninio, A. and Bruner, J. 1978: The achievements and antecedents of labelling. *J. Ch. Lang.* **5**, 1–15.
Ochs, E. 1980: Social environment and acquisition of ergative case marking in Samoan. Unpublished paper presented at Child Language Research Forum, Stanford, March.
Peters, A. 1980: The units of language acquisition, *Working Papers in Linguistics* **12 (1)**. Dept. of Linguistics, University of Hawaii at Manoa.
Ramer, A. 1976: Syntactic styles in emerging language. *J. Ch. Lang.* **3**, 49–62.
Schieffelin, B. 1979: How Kaluli children learn what to say, what to do and how to feel: an ethnographic study of the development of communicative competence. Doctoral dissertation, Columbia University.
Schlesinger, I.M. 1971: Production of utterances and language acquisition. In D. Slobin (ed.), *The ontogenesis of grammar*. New York: Academic Press.
Shatz, M. 1981: On mechanisms of language acquisition: can features of the communicative environment account for development? in: L. Gleitman and E. Wanner (eds.), *Language Acquisition: State of the Art*, Cambridge, Mass: Harvard University Press.
Shatz, M. and Gelman, R. 1977: Beyond syntax: the influence of conversational constraints on speech modifications. in: C.E. Snow and C.A. Ferguson (eds.) *Talking to Children: Language Input and Interaction*, Cambridge: CUP.
Sinha, C. (in press): Representational development and the structure of action. In G. Butterworth and P. Light (eds.), *The individual and the social in cognitive development*. London: Harvester.

Slobin, D.I. 1973: Cognitive prerequisites for the development of grammar. In C.A. Ferguson and D.I. Slobin (eds.), *Studies of child language Development*. New York: Holt, Rinehart and Winston.

—— 1981: The origins of the grammatic encoding of events. In W. Deutsch (ed.), *The child's construction of language*. New York and London: Academic Press.

Smoczyńska, M. (in press): The acquisition of Polish. In D.I. Slobin (ed.), *The crosslinguistic study of language acquisition*. Hillsdale, NJ: Erlbaum.

Snow, C. 1977: Mother's speech research: from input to interaction. In C. Snow and C. Ferguson (eds.), *Talking to children: language input and acquisition*. Cambridge: CUP.

—— (in press): Saying it again: the role of expanded and deferred imitations in language acquisition. In K.E. Nelson (ed.), *Children's language* **4**. New York: Gardner Press.

Tizard, B. and Rees, J. 1974: A comparison of the effects of adoption, restoration to the natural mother, and continued institutionalization on the cognitive development of 4-year-old children. *Ch. Dev.* **45**, 92–9.

—— 1975: The effect of early institutional rearing on the behaviour problems and affectional relationships of 4-year-old children. *J. Ch. Psychol. and Psychiat.* **16**, 61–73.

Walkerdine, V. and Sinha, C. 1978: The internal triangle: language, reasoning and the social context. In I. Markova (ed.), *The social context of language*. Chichester: Wiley.

2
Comprehension in context

To anyone who has not recently had much contact with the study of children's syntactic comprehension, the field must have appeared a rather quiet and subdued one over the last decade. Indeed there may be psychologists and linguists within the area of child language research who could be forgiven for thinking that nothing at all has changed since the 1960s.

To a certain extent these onlookers would be justified. For, strangely, not much attention has been directed towards investigating the ontogenesis of syntactic comprehension in preschool children — not as much, that is, as one might expect given the closeness of the concerns of this particular area with the development of either the semantic or the pragmatic aspects of language, and yet both of these latter aspects have flourished during the same period. Perhaps the lure of the novel (or at least the less familiar) is responsible. Possibly some would-be researchers have felt that in the light of post-transformational grammar all the questions had been answered, or that questions about children's syntactic awareness were of limited significance to anyone interested in communication and language use in a broader sense. Whatever the reasons for the relative neglect of the ontogenesis of syntactic comprehension in the past, the indications are that it will be reinstated as an area of study because, as I hope to indicate in this chapter, it has a special contribution to make to our understanding of the basic mental processes underlying language interpretation. Indeed, once we begin to inquire about the cognitive and linguistic bases on which children attempt to make sense of what has been said to them, a range of questions emerge. There are questions concerning the interface between a child's 'real-world' knowledge and linguistic (and metalinguistic) awareness that are of especial relevance to young children's attempts to make sense of what has been said to them. There are questions which touch on the level of sophistication of the child's construal of the social and physical circumstances. There are questions about the development of cognitive and case-like concepts such as those of actor and agent, and questions about the relationships between the processes underlying comprehension and production. As can be seen, the type of issues still to be resolved are far from being limited or uninteresting. Some may look rather familiar (e.g. the comprehension/production reference) but the need for a re-examination of even these arguments in the light of recent research findings is urgent (cf. Chapman 1978, Bridges 1980).

The last 10 years have seen some quite fundamental changes in the way in which language comprehension has been conceptualized. The growing realization that an utterance's meaning is not something which resides in a sentence like a speck of gold in a lump of rock (or like a maggot in an apple) has had the effect of shifting the emphasis of experimental studies away from concentrating exclusively on the sentence as the unit of analysis and towards a broadening of the scope of inquiry to include the child's construal of the nonverbal and inter-personal events that accompany a speaker's utterances as well as the utterances themselves. Even isolated instruction-sentences, according to this view, are interpreted in terms of a listener's perception of the pre-vailing social and physical setting. References to children 'extracting meaning' from sentences are going. In their place is a characterization of language comprehension as a constructive mental activity based on the interaction and integration of information from a variety of sources, both linguistic and nonlinguistic. Examination of the nature of these information sources by tracing age-related changes in the reliance on various types of cues and careful error analyses is beginning to reveal the extent to which cognitive processes are involved in early sentence interpretation.

In this chapter, some of the more recent evidence regarding preschool children's syntactic comprehension will be presented and reviewed. No special attempt will be made to paper over the cracks that exist in the available data. Instead I intend to exercise an author's right to act as devil's advocate and highlight the gaps in the story. The discussion will centre largely around children's apparent understanding (or mis-understanding) of active and passive sentences. This may seem to be concentrating on a grammatical contrast that has already received a dis-proportionate amount of attention. But it is precisely the established, almost traditional position in syntactic comprehension research and the extensive coverage which this construction-pair has received that makes it a good starting point for a reassessment of the assumptions and argu-ments (implicit or explicit) which were advanced in the 1960s and early 1970s.

The chapter falls into three main sections. The first reviews the litera-ture and examines the adequacy of methods of analysis used in the past. The second section seeks to describe and discuss the evidence con-cerning some of the observed response regularities made by preschool children. The final section examines some of the issues raised in the earlier sections and speculates on the implications of these data for any model of children's developing interpretive powers.

What grouped data can tell us

One of the first tests of children's comprehension was described by Fraser, Bellugi and Brown in 1963. The experiment and the replications which followed (Lovell and Dixon, 1967, Nurss and Day 1971, Fernald 1972) were concerned to demonstrate preschool children's differential ability in three tasks: imitation, comprehension and production (ICP). Each of the tasks consisted of a set of 40 sentences (two pairs of 10 grammatical contrasts). Included amongst the test sentence-pairs were:

(i) Subject/object in the active voice e.g. the train bumps the car/the car bumps the train

(ii) Subject/object in the passive voice e.g. the train is bumped by the car/the car is bumped by the train.

In the comprehension task, the children were presented with pairs of pictures depicting contrasting sentences and asked to identify the picture that matched first one and then the other sentence from each pair. The general conclusion of these studies was that comprehension (as operationalized by this task) was at least as advanced as production. Active sentences, however, were found to be more frequently matched correctly with their pictures than passive sentences. Evidence from other comprehension tests in which children were asked to 'act out' events have also found this difference in performance between young children's responses to active and passive sentences. Again and again, preschool children have been found to perform less well on passive sentences than on active sentences (Bever 1970, de Villiers and de Villiers 1973, Maratsos 1974, Strohner and Nelson 1974, Bridges 1980). The percentage of correct responses to passive sentences only begins to reach the same performance level as for active sentences when the children reach 5.0 years of age. Between the ages of 2.0 and 3.6, for example, the average percentage of correct responses to passive sentences is usually found not to exceed 50 per cent whereas the corresponding performance figure for active sentences ranges between 70 and 90 per cent.

Given this discrepancy between active and passive performance data, many researchers have been tempted to treat the findings as evidence for the existence of a word-order rule in which the first-mentioned participant is always assigned the role of agent in the described action. Obviously, any child applying this rule systematically to every active and passive instruction presented during a comprehension test would act out the meaning of every active sentence correctly but would systematically reverse the intended role relationships of any passive sentence, since the first-mentioned participant in a passive sentence refers to the object of the action, not the actor. Bever (1970), for example, attributed the poor performance of the 4-year-olds in his experiment to the overgeneralization of a rule of this form.

There are several reasons, though, why we should be cautious about accepting this conclusion or adopting this type of reasoning. One source of disquiet is the way in which researchers in the past, such as Bever (1970) and Strohner and Nelson (1974), have tended to base their arguments on the evidence of generalized age trends in comprehension test performance (i.e. how 3-year-olds as a group respond on average to a set of passive sentences). To assume a direct correspondence between group and individual patterns of behaviour, however, can be quite misleading. An analysis which requires data about the performance of a group of children to be averaged may, if we are not careful, conceal important information about the coexistence of two or more response strategies. This point was demonstrated clearly by Sinclair and Bronckart (1972) in one of the earliest studies to be analysed at an individual rather than a group level. French speaking children (aged 2.10 − 6.11 years) were asked to use toys to act out the meaning of 3-word strings (e.g. boy-push-girl, boy-girl-push, push-boy-girl). By comparing the response-profiles of individual children across related test items, Sinclair and Bronckart found that the children were very consistent in the way in which they interpreted the 3-word strings, but that not all children of the same age interpreted the word-strings in the same way. There was evidence of at least 6 distinctly different response patterns at one stage: some children, for example, treated the noun nearest the verb as the patient; other children treated the first mentioned noun as the agent; yet others treated the last-mentioned noun as the patient, regardless of the position of the verb. This important information about the existence of different response patterns would have been lost if the data had been expressed in the more common form, i.e. in terms of the percentage of correct responses for the age group as a whole. Generalized performance figures therefore present enormous problems of interpretation because, although they give a gross indication of how well 3- or 4-year-olds can be expected to perform, data of this sort cannot provide information regarding qualitative differences in the response patterns of individual children. Neither can they be expected to give any indication about how the characteristics of those response patterns might change as the children grow older. If information about the nature of two or more coexisting response patterns is to be preserved and it is considered important to reflect cognitive and linguistic abilities at an individual level, then the data analysis chosen needs (wherever possible) to be in terms of the response patterns or profiles of individual children across contrasting test items, and should not be based on the relatively uninformative measure of the average number of adult-like responses per age group.

Which individual patterns of response do we know about? What do they tell us of the cognitive and linguistic knowledge of children of different ages? What types of concepts and assumptions underlie children's interpretations of acting-out instructions? Unfortunately, the amount of data available at present regarding individual children's sensitivity to such variables as the order of mention of referents in active and passive sentences is meagre, but what evidence there is very intriguing. In the next section, the evidence for four general response regularities will be discussed. Each of these response patterns has been observed to be characteristic of the preschool population.

Four elementary response patterns: the bases of preschoolers' interpretation

1 Primitive approaches

The majority of preschool children respond to a request to 'show how the boy pushes the girl' by selecting the named objects and making one of them act on the other in some way. Occasionally, though, one encounters 2 to 3-year-old children who consistently fail to make one toy act on the other. Even after repeated representation (and demonstration too sometimes) these children persist in responding in an 'intransitive' way in which neither toy can be said to be unambiguously portrayed as the actor and the other as the object of the action.

The most detailed analysis of these early responses comes from Sinclair and Bronckart (1972), but they have also been recorded by other researchers (e.g. de Villiers and de Villiers 1973, Bridges 1980). Two general categories of response were identified by Sinclair and Bronckart:

(a) Intransitive responses, with one or both of the named participants performing an intransitive action. So, for example, when asked to act out the event described by the sentence 'the dog chases the cat', these children may pick up just one toy and move it about the table top or may take both toys and act out an event in which neither toy is the clear recipient of the action: the toys may be made to race side by side for example. Certain verbs may attract a similar type of difficulty in which both objects are agents. Requests to show how 'the car hits the lorry' or 'the girl kisses the boy' may result in reciprocal actions being portrayed (i.e. the vehicles are made to collide head on or the boy and girl dolls are brought together to indicate kissing).

(b) 'Child as agent' responses, where the child acts on one or both of the named participants himself. That is to say, one or both of the toys becomes the patient of the child's own action. Asked to act out the sentence 'the boy pushes the girl', a child responding in this way knocks one or both toys down himself. According to de Villiers and de Villiers (1973), children who respond in this way show no particular preference for making either the first or last named participant the patient of their actions: either may be used.

It is not clear why young children respond in either of these ways. One reason could be that these children are incapable of simultaneously treating a toy as the patient of their own actions and the object of a portrayed event. Interestingly, studies of children's spontaneous play have found that some children are 3 years old before they make one toy act on another in a make-believe scene (Lowe 1975). Failure to make one toy act on another may not therefore be anything peculiar to a comprehension task: it may reflect a more fundamental cognitive conceptual shortcoming. Another possibility is that children of this age fail to acknowledge the transitive nature of verbs such as 'to push', 'to chase' or 'to kiss'. That is, their semantic awareness of these verbs may not have yet developed to include the notion of activities such as pushing, chasing or kissing, as unidirectional, target-oriented actions.

The main feature of both these categories of response is that the children make no attempt to make one object act on the other. They either act directly on one or both of the objects themselves or make the objects perform an intransitive or reciprocal activity in which the roles of two objects are identical. Although at first sight these responses may appear to be of limited interest, they could in fact represent the first, most rudimentary stage in children's understanding of role relationships and case-like categories. For, judging from their responses, children who respond in either of these ways do not acknowledge that implicit within the request to act out a sentence such as 'the car pushes the lorry' is the requirement that one of the named objects has to act as actor (i.e. pusher) in the described action and that the other should be treated as the recipient or target of that action. They understand something of the demand on them to perform an action on the toys. But, in failing to acknowledge the transitive nature of the event, these children completely avoid the question of the relation between the two participants and the problem of which named object is meant to be actor. No other response pattern fails in quite this way. This lack of directed action is what distinguishes these responses from the later patterns. In this sense, we may be justified in classifying 'child as agent' and 'intransitive' responses as primitive syntactic comprehension response patterns. This characterization is supported by the fact that 'child as agent' responses and intransitive responses are typically reported amongst younger children. Bridges (1980), for example, found that the 'child as agent' response pattern was exhibited by 7 of the 15 2.6-year-olds in her sample, but that no child over 3 years of age responded in this way. In contrast, children of 3 and over almost always respond to the request to act out 'the X pushes the Y' either by making the X push the Y or by reversing the intended meaning of the sentence and making the Y push the X. At the very least, therefore, one must conclude that these children appreciate that they are being asked to make one of the named objects act directly on the other. What cannot so easily be stated is the basis on which these children come to use one referent as actor and the other as object of the action. At least three possible bases for response consistency have been suggested in the literature: event probability or plausibility (including, as a special case, agent animacy), spatial arrangement, and order of mention (word order). Each of these will be discussed in turn.

2 Event probability

Not all events relating two objects have an equal likelihood of occurence. For example a statement about a ball, a boy and kicking is more likely to convey the relation described by the sentence, 'the boy kicks the ball', than the highly improbable and bizarre relation, 'the ball kicks the boy'. In contrast to these nonreversible sentences are reversible sentences such as 'the boy kicks the horse' where the actor and the object acted-upon can be interchanged and still leave a sentence which is semantically plausible. The effect that this type of semantic constraint has on the comprehension of active and passive sentences was described many years ago by Slobin (1966).

The effect of the plausibility or probability of the event described by a sentence on young children's interpretations has since then been the subject of several investigations (e.g. Bever 1970, Strohner and Nelson 1974, Chapman and Kohn 1977), although most of them have relied on grouped data. Presented with reversible but improbable sentences such as 'the baby feeds the girl' or 'the mouse chases the bear', 2- and 3-year-old children are often found to reverse the relationship between the referents and make the girl and the bear represent the actors (the feeder and the chaser respectively) and make the baby and the mouse the objects of the actions. The suggestion here is that the children draw on their past experience concerning the usual or more likely relative status of the two named participants and act out what, from the children's point of view, is the intelligent and previously acceptable type of event. Given what the children know from stories or personal experience about feeding times, babies and girls, or the general qualities of mice and bears and their respective propensity for being chasers and victims of the chase, they anticipate the more common role relationships amongst the referents. Whether the children are aware of the 'silliness' of some of the adults' requests is not a matter which has even (to my knowledge) been investigated explicitly. I suspect such a study would call for elaborate procedures for surrogate test administration (similar to Donaldson's talking panda) to circumvent the problem of children's reluctance to disagree with an adult experimenter.

Plausibility or event probability is not restricted to semantically anomalous test sentences involving just animate referents, however. A related but slightly different state of affairs exists when children are presented with instruction sentences in which only one of the referents is animate (e.g. 'the boy hits the ball'/'the ball hits the boy').

The possibility that children might use animacy to assign participant roles has been explored by several investigators. Chapman and Miller (1975) presented 15 children aged 1.8 to 2.8 with reversible active sentences in which the animacy of the agent and the animacy of the object were systematically varied. Comprehension of the subset of sentences with animate agent and inanimate object (as indicated by the percentage of correct responses, given grouped data) was between 90–95 per cent, whilst the performance of animate-animate and inanimate-inanimate sentences overall was 66.5 per cent and 65.2 per cent respectively. Sentences with inanimate subject and animate object meanwhile achieved a mean correct score overall of only 50.1 per cent. There is no discussion, however, of the discovery of any individual patterns of response.

Evidence from other sources, such as young children's spontaneous utterances (e.g. Limber 1976) and their replacement of nonsense nouns within active and passive sentence frames (Dewart 1979), supports the idea that children commonly take the noun in preverb position to refer to an animate referent and the noun in postverb position to refer to an inanimate subject.

More recently, Lempert (1978) has extended Chapman and Miller's work to consider the influence of animacy on 3.4 to 5.3-year-old children's interpretation of passive sentences. Once again the performance figures (grouped data, *n* for each age group = 10) for the animate-animate and inanimate-inanimate passive sentences were very similar: they rose from 63 per cent to 87 per cent and 63 per cent to 80 per cent respectively with increasing age. But the results of the mixed-animacy sentences suggested that there was a tendency for children under 5 years old to interpret the *inanimate* noun as agent. This was especially striking amongst the 3-year-olds, whose group performance figures for the inanimate agent/animate object and animate agent/inanimate object subsets of sentences were given as 90 per cent and 27 per cent respectively. (Performance on a matched set of active sentences was reported to be over 95 per cent for all age-groups). Lempert has interpreted these findings as support for the idea that young children make a distinction between agentive causation and 'non-agentive' causation, on the one hand, and a distinction between actives and passives on the other, and that they assume that the purpose of passives is to mark the inanimate noun as the agent or instrument of the action and the animate noun as the object of the action. Unfortunately Lempert does not report the number of children demonstrating such a systematic inanimate-agent-in-passive-sentences response pattern in her study, although she does mention in passing that two (but only two) children systematically produced a response pattern consistent with an order-of-mention strategy.

Lempert's findings are intriguing, standing as they do in such marked contrast to previous studies' conclusions, and the significance of the result if replicated with other objects would be considerable. For if 3- and 4-year-old children are capable of making and acting on an agent v. instrument distinction within a presumed broader case-like category of actor, then their metalinguistic skills are far more advanced than the data from studies of active sentence comprehension have suggested.

One issue that continues to persist is whether the observed animacy preferences are the result of the salience of animacy *per se* (as an abstract concept) or are a function of regularities in the real world which are reflected in the children's knowledge concerning the referents mentioned in the test sentences. In other words, if a child responds to the sentence 'the car pushes the man' by making the man push the car, are we to interpret this as the natural outcome of a generalized preference for any referent which happens to be animate without special consideration of the identity and characteristics of the named participants, or as a more specific judgment on the child's part regarding the probability of one particular referent being the actor in the described event? Unfortunately grouped data again serves to obscure the picture. For whilst results continue to be averaged across test sentences, we run the risk of giving the impression that interpretation is the result of the application of generalized or abstract semantic principles, whereas perhaps the relative properties of each pair of referents are actually considered separately.

Chapman and Kohn (1977) have commented on the fact that many of the younger children they tested consistently preferred one interpretation of a sentence pair. Fourteen of the 18 2- and $2\frac{1}{2}$-year-old children responded to both 'The kitty pushes the door' and 'The door pushes the kitty' by making the toy cat act on the door, and 7 of the same 18 children interpreted 'the girl bumps the swing' and 'the swing bumps the girl' to mean the girl bumps the swing both times. It would be easy to argue that these responses are the result of children applying an animate agency rule, but Chapman and Kohn are cautious about attributing the children with a general semantic strategy in which the animate object is treated as the actor. They write, 'The statistically significant effects of the group data analysis . . . appear to stem from children's consistent interpretations of some, but not all, sentence pairs. This finding means that children often regard animate nouns as the more probable agent; but that their preference could be viewed as a special instance of a probable event strategy rather than a general animacy strategy applied equally across all sentences' (18).

What can be deduced from the nature of these errors about the relative reliance of young children on cognitive, semantic and syntactic processing of sentences? The general conclusion from these studies is that children's responses are guided by their knowledge of the likely behaviour of certain classes of objects given certain types of activity. But at what point during the comprehension of a sentence such as 'The baby feeds the girl' do semantic and cognitive considerations influence interpretation? Some researchers (e.g. Huttenlocher and Strauss 1968, Bem 1970) have characterized the successful listener's achievement in terms of a transformation of the test sentence. According to this view children would be expected to assign the preverb noun (i.e. 'the baby') the role of agent and the other noun, 'the girl', that of patient and afterwards exchange the roles on semantic grounds. With more cognitive, constructivist (e.g. Bransford and McCarrell 1974) or intentional (Clark 1978) views of comprehension, though, it becomes proper to ask whether young children of preschool age engage in any such linguistically-derived assignment of roles, or whether the basis for the children's assignment of roles is entirely nonsyntactic in origin. Does hearing the sentence 'the baby feeds the girl' do no more than direct the children's attention to the two dolls and suggest an activity which the children then act out according to their understanding of what the most likely (intelligent and generally acceptable) relationship between a girl and a baby is at feeding time?

Two rather basic questions are raised by making a distinction between knowledge-based and syntactic approaches to role assignment. The first is whether these children are merely uncertain how a sentence's structure dictates the role which a particular object should play in an event or whether they are completely ignorant of the implication for meaning of grammatical differences. The other question concerns why children should favour one particular interpretation over all others. Is it a mark of social sensitivity or one of egocentric presumption? These are questions which recur and which will be discussed later in the chapter.

3 Spatial arrangement

Some sentences offer very little in terms of semantic cues. Reversible sentences, such as 'the red car pushes the green car'/'the green car pushes the red car', encode no 'obvious' real-world relationship between the two referents. If young preschoolers perform no more than a lexical analysis on the sentences addressed to them, then how will they respond when the properties of the referents are such that the two events are equally probable? Stripped of this support, will the children have to resort to a primitive strategy reminiscent of an earlier developmental stage? Or were semantic considerations in fact a distraction? Once these are removed, will the 3-year-olds demonstrate their ability to use syntactic information to assign participant roles? Or will the children have to look outside the sentence and rely on extralinguistic sources of information to guide their interpretation of sentences?

The notion that features of the linguistic input (and pseudolinguistic cues such as word-order) constitute the primary source of information for children when they are interpreting spoken utterances has been implicit in the way investigations of syntactic comprehension have been designed and analysed. Results are grouped across test items of the same sentence-type and well-established experimental procedures are invoked to ensure that other factors (such as the physical arrangement of the toys in front of the children) are randomized. Unfortunately, there is no reason to suppose that randomizing the positions of the toys had ever actually *prevented* children from relying on extralinguistic variables, although it may well have had the effect of making any response patterns that were based on extralinguistic considerations less obvious to adult experimenters. Note that it is not the practice of randomization itself that is the problem; it is the subsequent failure to report whether or not any of the randomized variables had predictive power. So, whilst there are quite a considerable number of experiments in the literature which have investigated the importance of regularities in the form of the instruction sentences for the way children respond, the possible influence of the extralinguistic context (including the experimenter's own actions, the child's past experience of activities similar to those being used in the test, and the child's construal of the set of objects themselves) has so far received only sporadic attention and is therefore considerably less well documented.

One aspect which has been investigated (initially by Huttenlocher and her colleagues; e.g. Huttenlocher and Strauss 1968) has been the effect of the physical arrangement of the referents on the comprehension of active and passive sentences. Imagine the situation in which a young child is given a red Dinky car to hold, is shown a green car already in position on a road and is then asked to 'make it so that the green car pushes the red car'. Many 2.6 to 3.6-year-old children, when faced with this situation, consistently respond by making the red car (or whichever toy is in their hand) act on the green car (which is in place) and thereby systematically reverse the meaning of the sentence by interchanging the roles of the referents. This is a robust finding which has been reported by several researchers (Bem 1970, Dewart 1975, Bridges 1980).

What seems to have been overlooked in the past is the possibility that a similar positional rule may be operating in the traditional acting-out task setting. Is it necessary to have one toy actually in the child's hand and one already in position? Perhaps it is simply enough that one car is nearer to the hand with which the child prefers to push. This possibility was investigated by my (1980) study in which the sentence voice and the arrangement of the toys were systematically manipulated. I found that as many as 30 per cent of the 95 2.6- to 4.0-year-old children consistently responded (individual response pattern data) by making whichever referent was nearer their dominant hand the actor. Certain methodological features (e.g. the use of a toy road laid across the children's line of sight) in this experiment may have increased the salience in the children's minds of the relative position of the referents and thus make this response pattern more favoured than in previous comprehension experiments, although it is interesting to note that a similar positional bias has been reported by Chapman and Kohn (1977) amongst the individual response patterns of 2.6-year-olds.

Cromer (1976, 313) has claimed that 'a child uses an extralinguistic strategy when he does not know how to make use of the grammatical structure in the adult manner.' The positional response pattern is significant because it suggests that many 2.6 – 4.0-year-old children do not draw on syntactically-derived information even when they are trying to understand active sentences. The children who responded this way in Bridges' study were just as likely to reverse the participant roles in an active sentence as they were to act out that sentence correctly: it was the spatial arrangement of the referents that influenced their ultimate response, not the form of the sentence.

The positional response pattern thus bears many similarities to the semantically sensitive responses described earlier, in terms of its implications for a model of 2- and 3-year-old children's comprehension processes. For again, the simplest explanation is that the children's linguistic analysis extends no further than the lexical level, and we have to consider seriously the possibility that many children under the age of 4 do not detect the difference in meaning involved between two active sentences such as 'The car pushes the lorry' and 'The lorry pushes the car'. They grasp that a car and a lorry are involved and that the activity engaged in is pushing, but which vehicle actually does the pushing is something which is determined by extrasyntactic considerations. This is a puzzling finding, for it suggests that even children who might be expected to know their language well because they spontaneously produce well-formed multiword utterances (i.e. 3-year-olds) will frequently fail to attend to the grammatical form of an utterance when they are trying to understand/respond to what has been said to them. Again, this is a point which we will return to later.

4 Order-of-mention

What then of the word-order pattern? How much support is there at the individual level for the suggestion that preschool children are sensitive to word-order? Is there, as Bever claimed in 1972, evidence of the overgeneralization of a 'first-mentioned noun is actor' rule when children are aged 4.0 to 4.6 years?

Several investigators who have analysed their data in terms of individual response patterns have noted consistent order-of-mention patterns being produced by some children. A high proportion of order-of-mention response patterns is rare, though. In an acting-out task which used normal and deviant word order passive sentences, Dewart (1975) found that only 2 of the 18 3.8- to 4.9-year-olds in her study made the first-mentioned referent the actor. De Villiers and de Villiers (1974) found that only 2 of the 12 4-year-olds they tested consistently reversed the meaning of passive sentences. Another researcher to find very few cases of word-order response patterns was Lempert (1978): only 2 of the 40 3.4- to 5.3-year-old children produced response patterns of this sort, although it should be noted that Lempert's criterion for consistency was extremely stringent (covering 32 responses). Bridges' (1980) study, too, found that the order-of-mention response pattern was relatively infrequent amongst the preschool population: only 14 of the 152 2.6- to 5.0-year-old children responded in this way, and this accounted for no more than 20 per cent of the children tested at any one age group. The response pattern was most commonly found amongst two and three year old children. Only 5 per cent of the 4.0-, 4.6- and 5.0-year-old children responded in this way. The response patterns of the 4-year-old children in Bridges' study were more advanced than the simple order-of-mention response pattern: either they responded correctly to the active sentences and seemed to rely on situational cues to guide their interpretation of passive sentences (this accounted for 14 per cent of the children), or they responded in a completely adult-like manner and acted out both active and passive sentences correctly (54 per cent of the 4.0-; 4.6- and 5.0-year-olds responded in this way). Responding in either of these ways demands that attention is paid to the syntactic form of the instruction sentence. In summary, therefore, one has to conclude that although there is evidence that individual children respond in such a way as to make the first mentioned referent the actor, this response pattern is not particularly common amongst preschool children and, so far, has certainly not been found to be typical of 4-year-old children.

What does the order-of-mention pattern of responses tell us about children's interpretation processes? The answer, unfortunately, is very little, because the order of mention response pattern is very ambiguous; it could be the result of any one of several quite different mechanisms, each of which implies a different degree of linguistic sophistication.

The most commonly-quoted characterization of these errors, the explanation of the order-of-mention response pattern as the over-generalization of a 'first-mentioned noun is actor' rule, supposes that a child is capable of contemplating . linguistic concepts such as agent/subject and patient/object and mistakenly treats passive sentences as though they were active sentences. This view of children's errors has been allowed to go unquestioned for many years now, so strong is the conviction that comprehension precedes production and that both depend on the same core of linguistic knowledge. Almost without further discussion, the fact that a young child can spontaneously produce subject-verb-object sentences is taken to imply that the related syntactic rule will be automatically invoked when she or he is interpreting similar sentences. This argument may however need to be reviewed.

One problem concerns the specificity of the 'first noun is actor' description, for in another of Dewart's (1975) experiments, it was found that the order-of-mention response pattern was not peculiar to test sentences involving agency; an identical set of responses (i.e. in which it was always the first-mentioned referent that was picked up and made to perform an action on, or with respect to, the second object) was recorded for normal and deviant word-order sentences involving direct and indirect objects (e.g. 'send the cat to the dog'), instrumental sentences (e.g. 'hit the cat with the dog') and cleft sentences (e.g. 'it's the wolf that bites the duck'). Nineteen of the 30 4.0- to 4.11-year-olds tested and 3 of the 10 3.4- to 3.11-year-olds responded in this way on a significant proportion of the test sentences. Redefining the actor as 'the thing moved' Cromer (1976) has suggested 'that children use the same strategy, that the first noun is actor, to identify a number of disparate grammatical functions' (332). How can we be sure, though, that all of these 'disparate grammatical functions' are psychologically real for preschool children? Come to that, what evidence is there that preschool children have a mental representation of the concept of agent and can use it deliberately to ascribe a particular function to a particular object during a comprehension task? Do the children look to the sentence to tell them which object ought to be the actor and then search for the named object in order to make it fill that role? Or does the object merely 'end up' as the actor because of certain extrasyntactic factors? Undoubtedly if one looks at these responses from an adult's point of view, then in the indirect/direct object sentences, the moved piece comes to be interpreted as the patient; in the instrumental sentences, the moved object will be judged to represent the instrument of the action; and in the passive sentences and the cleft sentences the moved object will be seen as the agent of the action. But is this how the children themselves interpret the demands of the task? Do they knowingly assign those roles to the objects they are handling? Or is their analysis of each test sentence restricted to identifying the two referents mentioned and making one act on the other in the manner of the verb in that sentence? Regularities in the organization of the actions that make up the acting-out response could describe the observed behaviour of preschool children just as well as the overgeneralization explanation. If, for example, a child tended to pick up the referents in the order in which he heard them mentioned in the test sentence, and always reached out first with his preferred pushing hand to pick up objects, then a fully-fledged order-of-mention response pattern would be generated without any more elaborate an analysis being performed than was the case for the positional response pattern. This explanation is, at the moment, pure speculation. My intention in including it here is merely to demonstrate how very young preschool children might be able to produce order-of-mention response patterns without it necessarily implying that any syntactic analysis had taken place.

Usually, in psychological literature, the suggestion that a set of results may be the function of 'response biases' or 'response preferences' is a kiss of death. It is traditionally a dismissive comment, reserved for inexplicable or uninteresting data. But language comprehension research may be one area in which so-called 'response biases' and 'response preferences' are worth taking seriously, and they may yet be shown to be more significant and theoretically valuable than has so far been recognized. For whatever else they may be, these response regularities are clearly not the result of idiosyncratic preferences or momentary lapses of concentration: the fact that identical patterns of response are exhibited by so many 2-and 3-year-olds argues strongly against such a suggestion. The prevalence of the positional pattern of responses, for example, is too striking to be explained away as mere coincidence. So the regularities in response have to be viewed as reflecting the persistent misinterpretations which preschool children make about what they are being asked to do and the consistent way in which they attempt to meet the task demands as they see them. All the more reason therefore that we should be sure about which is the best description of the observed behaviours and which social, cognitive and linguistic skills we are attributing to children as a consequence.

Three-year-olds' comprehension and the concept of agent

The previous sections have brought up several issues which invite further discussion.

One of the questions raised concerns the reasons for 2- and 3-year-old children's apparent failure to use syntactic cues to meaning. It will be recalled that sometime around 3.9 − 4.0 years of age most children begin to respond correctly to active sentences, although they may still respond incorrectly to other types of sentence. This is the first point in development at which children may be said to be differentiating clearly between sentences of different types in their response patterns. Children's response patterns are systematic and predictable, but before this point is reached they seem to be influenced not by the syntactic structure of the instruction sentence but by semantic and extralinguistic considerations. The children respond as though they have performed no more than a lexical analysis on the sentence addressed to them and then been influenced by such factors as how the toys are arranged or what they understand the normal relationship between similar objects to be. As a consequence each sentence is treated identically, there is no differentiation in the children's way of responding to active or passive sentences, and it is as though children of this age do not detect the differences in meaning involved.

Why should 3-year-olds pay so little attention to the syntactic form of sentences when they are trying to understand and respond to what has been said to them? Two possibilities exist: the first is that these children are genuinely ignorant of the implication of syntactic structure for a sentence's meaning. So, although these children may appreciate that active and passive sentences are not identical in form they may not suspect that these formal dissimilarities are more than stylistic differences. (According to this view, children know that, by listening carefully to the instruction sentence, they will find out which particular objects the experimenter wants them to manipulate and which type of activity is to be portrayed, but they do not seem to appreciate that the experimenter's instruction sentence also tells them how those two objects are to be related. The instruction sentence thus serves a directive function for them but not a descriptive one.) The other possible explanation of the 2- and 3-year-olds' behaviour is less extreme. It states that children are aware of the power of syntax to dictate participant roles, but that such knowledge is not yet consolidated and so, in the face of complex response demands or very strong extralinguistic contrary indications, the children became unsure and overlook syntactic considerations in favour of producing an apparently more sensible or straightforward solution. The requirement for children to manipulate named objects, for example, could be argued to constitute a distraction and thereby to induce confusion and errors that might not otherwise occur. If this were true, then clearly the reliance on acting-out as a technique of investigation would yield highly misleading performance estimates. An examination of the performance of 2- and 3-year-old children in other comprehension tasks is called for. If children of this age reveal themselves to be capable of responding differentially to different sentence constructions when they are asked merely to recognize rather than to create the correct state of affairs, then there is reason to suspect that the need to organize the sequence of actions that makes up an acting-out response detracts attention from the accuracy of the event depicted.

The distinction between a sentence as a description of an event or end-state and a sentence as an instruction concerning certain actions was one that was made a decade ago by Bem (1970). She argued that children's difficulty in comprehension tasks arises from their failure to consider the nature of the desired end-state. She found that training sessions involving paired presentation of the instruction sentences and the appropriate object-arrays subsequently led to an improvement in the performance of 7 3.10- to 4.6-year-old children. Brown (1976) has also commented on the effectiveness of the combined presentation of an acted-out event (with toys) and an appropriate descriptive sentence as a means of improving 3.6- to 5.0-year-olds' performance on passive sentence comprehension task. Four-year-olds at least, it would seem, can be induced fairly easily to alter the way in which they interpret instruction sentences so as to give more adult-like responses, but the extent to which younger children's interpretations can similarly be manipulated has still to be demonstrated.

In the meantime, the issue of whether 2- and 3-year-old children can recognize syntactically-defined role relationships in circumstances other than acting-out tasks still has to be answered. What evidence is there from non-acting-out tasks to demonstrate that young children can appreciate the differences in meaning between 'the boy chases the girl', 'the girl chases the boy' and 'the girl gets chased by the boy'?

After acting-out, the next most common experimental paradigm in studies of syntactic comprehension is that of 'recognition' or 'selection' in which the child is shown two or more scenarios (either object arrays or pictures) and is asked to point to the one which matches the sentence spoken by the experimenter. This procedure was used by Fraser, Bellugi and Brown in their ICP study and has been used in many other studies since (e.g. Bem 1970, Baldie 1976), although frequently only group data is reported.

In Fraser *et al.*'s (1963) experiment, for example, the 12 3.1- to 3.7-year-old children were shown two contrasting pictures and were asked to indicate first the picture which was described by one of the contrasting sentences and then, immediately afterwards, to indicate the picture which was described by the other sentence. In view of the fact that some children at this age have been found to respond by spontaneously alternating, pointing first at one picture and then at the other, it is possible that experiments which require both items in a sentence pair to be responded to appropriately before a correct reply is recorded may be reporting slightly inflated performance figures. Even so only 16 of the 24 active sentence pairs and 7 of the 24 passive sentence pairs administered (2 to each child) were responded to correctly, representing a possible maximum of three children who could respond to both actives and passives completely correctly at this age and a possible maximum of 8 who could respond correctly just to active sentence pairs. In another experiment involving sentences such as 'the red block is on top of the blue block', Bem (1970) reported that 3.5- to 4.6-year-old subjects who were unable to respond correctly on an acting-out task were also unable to respond correctly on a selection task. As a group, these children responded correctly in only 55 per cent of the selection trials. Brown (1976) also reports only grouped data, but again the performance figures are close to 50 per cent; the mean percentage of reversible passive sentences during a 12-item selection pretest for his sample of 48 3.6- to 5.0-year-old children was 60 per cent. Baldie's (1976) data were unusual in that he reported that all the youngest children (aged 3.0 to 3.11) in his study responded correctly to the single reversible active sentence with which they were presented. In contrast only half of them responded correctly to the (solitary) reversible passive sentence. Bridges (1980) found that, up to the age of 4.0, most children repeatedly selected the same array (perseverance) or pointed first to one array and then to the other in a regular fashion (alternation) without apparently paying any attention to the form of the sentence they heard. Just over half the 3.0- to 4.0-year-old children responded in one of these two ways. Only 10 per cent of children at this age however responded correctly just to active sentences and 15 per cent responded correctly to both active and passives. Overall (i.e. expressed as grouped data), these 3.0-, 3.6- and 4.0-year-olds selected the correct array after 61 per cent of the active sentences and 61 per cent of the passive sentences. Not until the children were 4.6 years old did more than half of them give completely adult responses and thereby demonstrate that they could reliably select an array to match either active or passive sentences.

The evidence of all these selection task experiments leads one to conclude that performance on selection tasks is remarkably poor. Certainly there is little in any of these experiments' data to suggest that 3-year-olds' performance on active and passive sentences is any better in selection tasks than it is in acting-out tasks. In both types of tasks adult-like response patterns do not seem to emerge as a common way of responding until the children are 4 years old.

Another task which has occasionally been used to investigate pre-school children's sentence comprehension is that of verification, in which the children are required to say whether or not a particular sentence is an accurate description of an event. Hall (1975) recorded children's eye movements to study their 'interrogation' of a visual array during a series of verification tasks. She concluded that a 4-year-old 'finds it difficult to interrogate and represent the world in terms of relationships, but rather prefers to maintain objects as "topics" about which different comments or relationships can be connected' (383) However, the youngest children tested in Hall's study of active and passive sentences were aged 4.8 to 5.3, and were already able to give accurate judgements on both passive and active sentences; so it is not clear from this experiment how children under the age of 4 would respond. Bridges (1980) gave younger children a verification task and found that the children were over 4.0 years old before more than half of them responded in an adult-like way to both active and passive sentences. Before this age, the children tended simply to answer 'yes' to every test sentence (a response which could be explained either as a response bias or, equally well, as the result of a limited lexical analysis by the children.) Once again, though, the picture emerges of preschool children being able to respond differentially to active and passive sentences only after they are 4 years old.

Yet another experimental paradigm used to examine preschoolers' understanding of the importance of word order is their ability to correct grammatically deviant sentences. De Villiers and de Villiers (1973, 1974) used this technique and found that children tended to choose semantic means to correct reversed word-order sentences; so the earliest attempts at correction changed 'House a build' into 'Live in a house'. Word-order corrections did not become frequent until the children were about 4.6 years old.

Three alternative experimental tasks have now been discussed: selection, verification and correction. None of these has indicated strongly that the removal of the need to organize an action sequence allows young children to demonstrate full awareness of syntactic structure and its implication for defining participant roles.

What then can be concluded about the nature of the problem facing young children? Is it that they are unaware of the significance of a sentence's structure or are they merely uncertain?

For those children who demonstrate some differentiation of active and passive sentences without necessarily producing completely adult-like responses, one may argue that the problem is one of uncertainty. These children, typically about four years old, respond correctly to active sentences even in circumstances where they are faced by strong extralinguistic distraction (e.g. Bridges 1980), and thereby show that they are aware of the difference in meaning between two sentences such as 'the lorry pushes the car' and 'the car pushes the lorry'. In so far as different participant roles are being assigned on the basis of differences in sentence form, one may argue that these children have some concept of agents and patients as syntactically-defined entities. As yet the link between intended participant roles and the formal characteristics of sentence constructions other than active sentences has still to be established for these children. In their uncertainty, though, they do not over-generalize their newfound linguistic knowledge but allow themselves to be guided by their interpretation of the social and physical context within which the utterance is perceived. Their responses to active sentences, however, are enough to reveal 4-year-old children as capable of more than a lexical analysis and as capable of contemplating linguistic as well as cognitive case-related categories. The picture is less clear where 2- and 3-year-olds are concerned, though.

Virtually all the work on child language comprehension has assumed, often without even cursory discussion, that 2-, 3- and 4-year-old listeners have control of basic (though possibly incomplete) linguistic concepts. But are we justified in attributing such sophisticated metalinguistic skills to very young children? Are 3-year-old children genuinely capable of contemplating abstract *linguistic* entities such as agent, patient, possessor or instrument? Or do they rely on real-world knowledge and contextual cues to suggest participant roles?

Braine and Wells (1978) attempted to investigate children's understanding of case categories such as actor, instrument and object by training children to put tokens on pictured referents according to the participant role each played in a sentence. In the general discussion of their paper, Braine and Wells raised the problem of whether the children were responding to the sentences or to the pictures. They maintained that 'since case categories are presumed to be cognitive categories involved in the perception of events or states of affairs (e.g. Fillmore 1968), then, so long as responses are based on such categories, it is irrelevant whether they are primarily determined by the sentence or the picture' (119). I would argue, however, that it is important to know which of the two, the sentence or the nonverbal array, is the primary source of information for young children. For if young preschool children determine participant roles only by direct interrogation of the nonverbal array, then abstract linguistic concepts such as agency are arguably not known to them. It should then come as less of a surprise to discover that 3-year-olds tend not to attend to the structure of a sentence in an acting-out task. It is to be hoped that research in the next few years will clarify the distinction between cognitively-derived and syntactically-derived participant role assignment and thus provide a clearer indication of the relationship between children's real-world knowledge and their knowledge of their native tongue. Hildyard and Olson (1975) studied 6-year-olds' verification of active and passive statements following the description of pictures using either active or passive sentences. They comment: 'children of age 6 and under are apparently unaware that actives imply passives, as evidenced by their inability to answer 'Was John hit by Mary?' after hearing 'Mary hit John'. Hence children encountering a mismatch between the event and the sentence cannot simply recode the sentence. What they can do is reconsider what they know of the original display, that is they recode the event into a form compatible with the test sentence' (14). In another experiment with 5-year-olds, Olson and Nickerson (1975) presented pairs of matched or mismatched active and passive sentences either in isolation or in the presence of an appropriate picture. In all conditions the presence of a picture aided comprehension, and for the mismatched sentence pairs, performance in the picture condition was twice as good (with an approximate mean score of 70 per cent) as for isolated sentences. The lower than chance level of performance on the isolated sentences suggests that some children may have been responding on the basis of the order of mention of the referents in the test sentences, but without individual response data it is impossible to gauge how plausible this explanation might be.

Meanwhile there remains the problem of whether or not 2- and 3-year-old children are aware of sentences as a source of information about intended role relationships. At the moment there is insufficient evidence to settle the question, although preliminary results from an experiment currently being carried out at the University of Birmingham suggest that, whilst many 3-year-olds are able to indicate which of two objects is the actor after they have watched an acted-out event, they have difficulty indicating which is actor after simply hearing a sentence describing the event.

Whatever the precise status of the concept of agency etc. for these children, however, children nevertheless give the impression most of the time of having understood the gist of what has been said to them. So whilst 2-and 3-year-old children may not yet grasp fully the literal or propositional sense of 'what is said' by adult experimenters in test settings, they are already past-masters at divining 'what is meant'. Children's interpretation of the pragmatic aspects of comprehension tasks is long overdue for closer inspection and worthy of investigation. What influence, for example, does the introductory chat between the adult and child have on the features of the apparatus or procedure the

children judge to be significant? How much does the negotiation that goes on in the 'warm-up' period lead the children to interpret sentences, words or actions in one way rather than another? Children at this age are quick enough to perceive the parameters of and willing enough to cooperate in the (test) game as outlined to them, and in the broadest sense, their responses are what is called for. In the comprehension tasks described earlier in the chapter, most young preschoolers respond in vaguely appropriate ways: they say 'yes' or 'no' in a verification task, point in a selection task, offer alternative sentences in a correction task and make one toy act on another in an acting-out task, and they offer these responses in reply to the adult's clear invitation to act. A child's social or interpersonal sensitivity may however prove to extend further than these discourse- and response-type considerations. For there is still the unresolved issue of why the responses of so many children are influenced by specific factors in so uniform a way. Could it be that children pay attention to variable X or feature Y because they believe that is what the adult means them to do? Do they interpret the arrangement of the toys in an acting-out task, or the fact that there are only two pictures to choose from in a selection task, as the adult's way of helping them to play the game? Do the children think that these regularities are intended as outsize hints about what they are supposed to notice? Or are their responses the result of more general ideas (based perhaps on past conversations with adults) about what 'ought' to be – about fairness or orderliness or being 'sensible'? Such propositions are clearly at odds with the traditional Piagetian view of preschoolers' capabilities. For many the prospect of socially aware 3-year-olds may be totally unacceptable. At the moment we can only speculate about why certain features of test situations and not others come to be seen as salient. We look forward to future research in this field.

In the past semantic, syntactic and pragmatic aspects of language comprehension have tended to be treated as separate areas of investigation, each with very different questions to answer. But all of them share a basic goal: the description of the mental processes underlying a young child's attempt to work out what the other person means him to do. Essentially, this is a problem in communication, a problem in 'reading' a situation as a speaker intends, of looking for the most likely messages within the context of patterns of social interaction. Three-year-old children, it would seem, are adept at construing 'what is meant', despite (or perhaps because of) their restricted analysis of sentences. No handicap automatically accrues merely because the analysis goes no further than finding out which things are being talked about. 'Under normal circumstances, of course, this may be all that is necessary for successful communication, especially in a situation where all the referents are visible to both speaker and listener. After all, once the participants have been identified, the relationship between them, literally, "goes without saying". It is not until the young child is put in a comprehension test situation that it becomes apparent that he does not yet subscribe to the conventional (adult) way of extracting meaning from grammatically contrastive sentence pairs (or at least, that such rules are not yet consolidated and he is prepared to relinquish these considerations very easily in favour of extralinguistic ones)' (Bridges 1980, 101).

Evidence demonstrating changes in the way preschool children interpret sentences is gradually becoming available; and as more and more of it becomes known, the more urgent becomes one final question: what is the relationship between comprehension and production?

For many years the underlying unity of comprehension and production was a widely held and unquestioned assumption. A speaker-hearer's knowledge was thought to be coherent and common to all language processes. But now theorists are faced with the possibility that, in development, the production of a particular syntactic cue might not necessarily imply the use of that cue in comprehension, and that there might be many normal 3-year-old children whose own spontaneous utterances mainly consist of well-formed, multiword sentences and yet who do not appreciate the implication of the structure of even simple active sentences for intended role relationships. Could it really be that children might subsequently misconstrue an utterance which they themselves had produced in non-test circumstances earlier the same day? Apparently so.

One consequence of assuming that 2- and 3-year-old children routinely attend to syntactic detail in comprehension tasks is that it may make the performance of children known to have language problems seem to be more unusual than it really is.

It is interesting, for example, to compare observations made concerning the linguistic development of Genie (Curtiss 1977) with individual response pattern data from normal preschool children. As part of a monitoring programme to evaluate Genie's progress in learning to use grammatical information in the comprehension of language, a series of tests was compiled. One of the tests used was a selection task involving a set of 3 pictures and active and passive sentences. The pictures showed a boy pulling a girl, a girl pulling a boy, and a boy and a girl pulling a wagon. Genie's performance in terms of percentage correct responses, summed over the 12-month period October 1971 – October 1972, was very close to 50 per cent for both sentence types (42.9 per cent for the actives and 47.6 per cent for the passive sentences). Curtiss *et al.* (1974) comment: ['Genie's] performance on the active/passive test . . . has been totally inconsistent . . . This is peculiar and confusing, since Genie has used consistent and correct word order (in terms of the adult model) to indicate SVO relations...in her own productive speech' (531). But, as we are beginning to realize, the fact that her average performance to active and passive sentences was near to 50 per cent at a time when she was producing well-ordered SVO utterances in her spontaneous speech does not necessarily mark Genie out as being deviant. Genie is not alone in her inattention to syntactic structure when she is interpreting sentences. Many normal 3-year-old children also fail to attend to the grammatical form of a sentence when they are engaged in comprehension tasks. This chapter has asked many questions, more than its fair share perhaps. But if nothing else, the number of questions shows that there is still a great deal to be learned about the development of language interpretation processes. The techniques are available and, with appropriate analysis, many important questions concerning the relationship between cognitive and linguistic knowledge, the extent of linguistic knowledge and the nature of children's interpersonal skills wait to be answered.

References

Baldie, B.J. 1976: The acquisition of the passive voice. *J. Ch. Lang.* **3**, 331–48.

Bem, S. 1970: The role of comprehension in children's problem solving. *Dev. Psychol.* **2**, 351–8.

Bever, T.G. 1970: The cognitive basis for linguistic structure. In J.R. Hayes (ed.), *Cognition and the development of language*. New York: Wiley.

—— 1972: Perceptions, thought and language. In J.B. Carroll and R.O. Freedle (eds.), *Language and comprehension and the acquisition of knowledge*. London: Halsted.

Braine, M.S. and Wells, R.S. 1978: Case-like categories in children: the actor and some related categories. *Cog. Psychol.* **10**, 100–22.

Bransford, J. and McCarrell, N.A. 1974: A sketch of a cognitive approach to comprehension: some thoughts about what it means to comprehend. In W. Weimer and D. Palermo (eds.), *Cognition and the symbolic processes*. Hillsdale, NJ: Wiley.

Bridges, A. 1977: *The role of context and linguistic cues in the language comprehension of preschool children*. Doctoral thesis, University of Bristol.

—— 1980: SVO comprehension strategies reconsidered: the evidence of individual patterns of response. *J. Ch. Lang.* **7**, 89–104.

Brown, I. 1976: Role of referent concreteness in the acquisition of passive sentence comprehension through abstract modeling. *J. Exp. Ch. Psychol.* **22**, 186–99.

Chapman, R.S. 1974: Discussion summary: developmental relationship between receptive and expressive language. In R.L. Schiefelbusch and L.L. Lloyd (eds.), *Language perspectives: acquisition, retardation and intervention*. Baltimore: University Park Press.

—— 1978: Comprehension strategies in children. In J.F. Kavanagh and W. Strange (eds.), *Speech and language.in laboratory, school and clinic*. Cambridge, Mass: MIT Press.

Chapman, R.S. and Kohn, L.L. 1977: Comprehension strategies in two and three year olds: animate agents or probable events? Paper presented at Stanford Child Language Research Forum, Stanford University.

Chipman, H.H. 1979: The comprehension of passive sentences by mentally deficient children and adolescents. In G. Drachman (ed.), *Salzburger Beiträge zur Linguistik* 4, pt. 3: *Sprachpathologie*.

Clark, H.H. 1978: Inferring what is meant, In W.J.M. Levelt and G.B. Flores d'Arcais (eds.), *Studies in the perception of language*. London: Wiley.

Cromer, R.F. 1976: Developmental strategies for language. In V. Hamilton and M.D. Vernon (eds.), *The development of cognitive processes*. New York: Academic.

Curtiss, S. 1977: *Genie: a psycholinguistic study of a modern day 'wild child'*. New York: Academic.

Curtiss, S., Fromkin, V., Krashen, S., Rigler, D. and Rigler, M. 1974: The linguistic development of Genie. *Lang.* **50(3)**, 528–54.

de Villiers, J.G. and de Villiers, P.A. 1973: The development of the use of word order in comprehension. *J. Psycholing. Res.* **2**, 331–41.

—— 1974: Competence and performance in child language: are children really competent to judge? *J. Ch. Lang.* **1**, 11–23.

Dewart, M.H. 1975: *A psychological investigation of sentence comprehension by children*. Doctoral thesis, University College London.

—— 1979: Children's hypotheses about the animacy of actor and object nouns. *B. J. Psychol.* **70**, 525–30.

Fernald, C.D. 1972: Control of grammar in imitation, comprehension and production: problems of replication. *JVLVB* **11(3)**, 606–13.

Fillmore, C.J. 1968: Lexical entries for verbs. *Foundations of Language* **4**, 373–93.

Fraser, C., Bellugi, U. and Brown, R. 1963: Control of grammar in imitation, comprehension and production. *JVLVB* **2**, 121–35.

Grieve, R., Hoogenraad, R. and Murray, D. 1977: On the young child's use of lexis and syntax in understanding locative instructions. *Cognition* **5**, 235–50.

Hall, L. 1975: *Linguistic and perceptual constraints on scanning strategies: some developmental studies*. Doctoral thesis, University of Edinburgh.

Hildyard, A. and Olson, D.R. 1975: *On the mental representation and matching operations of active and passive sentences by children and adults*. Mimeo.

Hoogenraad, R., Grieve, R., Baldwin, P. and Campbell, R. 1978: Comprehension as an interactive process. In R.N. Campbell and P. Smith (eds.), *Stirling Psychology of Language Conference,* **1**: *Language development and mother-child interaction*. London: Plenum.

Huttenlocher, J. and Strauss, S. 1968: Comprehension and a statement's relation to the situation it describes. *JVLVB* **7**, 300–4.

Huttenlocher, J. and Weiner, S. 1971: Comprehension of instruction in varying contexts. *Cog. Psychol.* **2**, 369–85.

Kemper, S. and Catlin, J. 1979: On the role of semantic constraints in sentence comprehension. *Lang. and Sp.* **22(3)**, 253–67.

Lempert, H. 1978: Extrasyntactic factors affecting passive sentence comprehension by young children. *Ch. Dev.* **49**, 694–9.

Limber, J. 1976: Unravelling competence, performance and pragmatics in the speech of young children. *J. Ch. Lang.* **3**, 309–16.

Lovell, K. and Dixon, E.M. 1967: The growth and control of grammars in imitation, comprehension and production. *J. Ch. Psychol. Psychiat.* **8**, 31–9.

Lowe, M. 1975: Trends in the development of representational play in infants from one to three years – an observational study. *J. Ch. Psychol. Psychiat.* **16**, 33–47.

Maratsos, M. 1974: Children who get worse at understanding the passive: a replication of Bever. *J. Psycholing. Res.* **3**, 65–74.

Neisser, V. 1976: *Cognition and reality: principles and implications of cognitive psychology*. San Francisco: Freeman.

Nurss, J.R. and Day, D.E. 1971: Imitation, comprehension and production of grammatical structures. *JVLVB* **10**, 68–74.

Olson, D.R. and Nickerson, N. 1975: *On children's inability to draw implications from sentences*. Mimeo.

Sinclair, H. and Bronckart, J.P. 1972: SVO: a linguistic universal? A study in developmental psycholinguistics. *J. Exp. Ch. Psycho.* **14**, 329–48.

Slobin, D.I. 1966: Grammatical transformations and sentence comprehension in child and adulthood. *JVLVB* **5**, 219–27.

—— 1972: Seven questions about language development. In P.C. Dodwell (ed.), *New horizons in psychology* **2**. Harmondsworth: Penguin.

Strohner, H. and Nelson, K. 1974: The young child's development of sentence comprehension: the influence of event probability, nonverbal context, syntactic form and strategies. *Ch. Dev.* **45**, 567–76.

3

All the cars - which cars? From word meaning to discourse analysis*

N.H. Freeman, C.G. Sinha and J.A. Stedmon

1 Introduction

The hope of psycholinguistics is that if the meaning of an utterance can be specified, then it should be possible to tell whether children understand the meaning. But it is very difficult to specify the meaning of an utterance without going beyond units of analysis like sentence or sentence-part (de Beaugrande 1980) to the consideration of context-dependent meanings (Strawson 1950, Searle 1975, Grice 1968). This necessarily involves taking into account not only the speaker's intention in selecting his words, but the range of expressive powers that those words might have for a listener under those particular circumstances (Bennett 1976, 253–64). This means going beyond highly formal dictionary-dominated models to open the lumber-room of pragmatic rules which, like all lumber-rooms, has to be put in order. Recently both psychologists and philosophers have come up with some quite precise formulations. Rules for defining presupposition (e.g. Langendoen 1971, Oh and Dinneen 1979, Gazdar 1979), and Grice's (1975) work on rules for distinguishing between conventional and conversational implicatures, suggest that pragmatics might indeed be orderly if we had a sufficiently detailed and technical analysis.

Psychology is not only concerned with how pragmatic aspects of meaning can be brought into line with other aspects, but also with the question of how communicants can form a mental representation of an extended series of interchanges, a 'shared discourse', as it is often termed. We suggest, in what follows, that discourse analysis too can lead to highly formal models of cognition, to frame-analysis, the structure of scripted knowledge, and the like. We began the work reported here with an apparently clear case of children failing to grasp the meaning of simple utterances. We came to recognize that their unadult responses were quite rational from a discourse point of view.

* This work was supported by grants from the Social Science Research Council and the University of Bristol

2 From word meaning to word use

The relation between what a word means and the rules for its appropriate use has remained problematic ever since Frege (1892) initiated modern linguistic logic. Clearly there is a device by which one can present the meaning of words without classifying their rules of use: it is called a dictionary. Dictionaries have a long history; formulations of their underlying principles are more recent. Modern linguistics (de Saussure 1966) treats words as having fixed core meanings with restricted rules of variation around the core. One can find the core meaning of a word by constructing a semantic field in which the word is positioned in relation to other words which are agreed to be its relatives. For example, 'up' is *contrary* to 'down', *orthogonal* to 'left', has a *dual existence* as word and particle in 'put up with', and so on. Lyons (1977) presents a beautiful analysis which sustains one's intuition that the meaning of a word is *contrastive* in nature, and he systematizes many contrasts. Yet Miller and Miller (1979) showed, *inter alia*, that it cannot be assumed that we know the conditions under which Lyons's contrasts have psychological reality. To take a more general view: when do the relationships which are given in dictionaries register in the mind of someone hearing one or more words which supposedly exemplify the relationships?

For example, it is easy to see that the words 'beer' and 'wine' have something in common; but it is less easy to see when this relationship has psychological reality and when it does not. Jacoby, Craik and Begg (1979, 585) point out that 'the meaning of an event is determined by the set of contrasts *generated during initial processing*' (italics added). Put less formally, the work which a word does in a given context can be defined by the distinctions that it conveys in that context, and to that extent is context-dependent. 'If "beer" is initially encoded as an alcoholic beverage, it may be poorly distinguished from "wine" or "vodka", but if "beer" is encoded as a good thirst-quencher after baseball, it may be poorly distinguished from orange juice or Coca-cola. Consequently it is impossible to specify the distinctiveness of an event without specifying the alternatives in question' (Jacoby *et al.* 1979, 598). Thus, even the contrastive or intensional specification of the meaning of a word cannot be defined independently of the context or occasion of its use: 'the point is that meaning is not a static characteristic of individual words, but is rather a variable set of interpretations depending on the distinctions the word is intended to convey' (Jacoby *et al.* 1979, 597).

It follows, then, that at least part of the proper study of word meaning is the study of interlocutors' ability to agree on (a) the set of applicable distinctions it is reasonable to draw, and (b) the selection rules for discrimination within the set. Coming to such agreement is a social act with conventional rules, and this is what our account is about. The first step is to focus on the phrase 'the distinctions that the word is intended to convey'. Talk of intentionality threatens to lead us into an epistemological minefield, but even the most basic distinction-words like 'same/different' exemplify the case. Here is some recent evidence.

Early research on children's comprehension of 'same' and 'different' (Donaldson and Wales 1970) reported that children failed to distinguish between them, treating them both, apparently, as if they meant 'same'. This was taken to be evidence of incomplete semantic acquisition, and was interpreted within a theory of context-free lexical marking by Clark (1970). However, as Glucksberg, Hay and Danks (1976) showed, the assumption was unwarranted. They adapted the paradigm for use with adults. This time, references to 'same' and 'different' items were made by a stooge ostensibly engaged in the task of repairing a tape recorder. When the stooge held up a screwdriver and asked for a 'different one', adults interpreted this as a request for another screwdriver: a different token of the same type. They therefore responded identically to 'same' and 'different' requests, since there was only one available screwdriver: a perfectly reasonable interpretive strategy in the context. As with Frege's classical analysis of the morning/evening star, two *semantically distinct* referring expressions can be made to have the same *referential function* because their interpretation depends upon conventional rules of use of words in a discourse context.

The experiment serves to bring out a crucial point. To understand the way a speaker intends an utterance to be *used* in context requires agreement over a *frame of reference*. The point is not new: it was made nearly three centuries ago by John Locke (1690). In sections 7–9 of the chapter on Simple Modes, he deals with the field of reference indexed by the term 'same place'. If a company of chessmen remain on the squares of the board where they have been placed, they may be described as being in the same place, even if the board has been carried into another room 'because we compared them only to the parts of the chess board, which keep the same distance one with another'. Locke argues that place-specifications are developed by 'common use', by making 'reference to these adjacent things which are best served to their present purpose, without considering other things which, to another purpose, would better determine the place of the same thing'. In short, 'our idea of place is nothing else but such a relative position', a landmark specification within a frame of reference determined by the speaker's purpose. Nothing in the formal semantics of 'same place' will guarantee an appropriate understanding without a grasp of the speaker's purpose and intended frame of reference. William James (1892, ch. 13) generalized Locke's point: 'Reasoning is always to attain some particular conclusion. . . . conceiving [the datum] rightly means conceiving it by that one particular abstract character which leads to the one sort of conclusion which it is the reasoner's temporary interest to attain.'

The common image of developmental psychologists is precisely one in which they invite children to reason 'to attain some particular conclusion', noting whether or not the appropriate conclusion is in fact attained, thereby inferring something about the child's reasoning capacities. Only recently have psychologists questioned whether or not the child's reasoning processes were governed by the same 'particular abstract character' as that which referentially framed the conclusion from the experimenter's point of view; whether the child's 'temporary interest' really did coincide with the experimenter's. The notion of 'temporary interest' is well expressed by Chafe (1976, 28) when he points out that rules for organizing conversation in context depend upon assumptions that speakers make about 'temporary states of the addressee's mind'. Context-specific rules for understanding have been explored in perspective-taking (Hughes 1978, Light 1979), conservation (McGarrigle and Donaldson 1975, Sinha and Walkerdine 1978a, Sinha and Carabine 1980), comprehension of spatial terms (Grieve *et al.* 1977, Walkerdine and Sinha 1978), and class inclusion (McGarrigle *et al.* 1978, Finn 1979). It is however, only fair to note that such rules may not always strongly show up (Freeman, Sinha and Stedmon 1981); and we do not yet have adequate methods for measuring the effects of 'socio-dialogic sense' (Karmiloff-Smith 1979), 'social logic' (Sinha and Walkerdine 1978b) or 'human sense' (Donaldson 1978) upon comprehension of words in context.

The task is formidable. The 'same/different' problem (and the other areas briefly referred to above) shows that nothing in the formal semantics of linguistic descriptions alone will guarantee that interlocutors 'will interpret a word in the same way' without their 'temporary interests' coinciding. Appeals to shared background knowledge, common presuppositions, reciprocal development of purposes seem essential, yet they only loosely embrace the solution to the problem. It is clear that the problem is one of how we are to formulate the use by interlocutors of an extended representation of knowledge. The structure of such knowledge is incredibly difficult to guess at. At the very least, *context-specific frames of reference* must be set up during social negotiation, and must be extended and coherent enough to integrate linguistic and nonlinguistic information. They must also be sensitive to conventional rules regulating conversation, and must contain procedures for making some alternatives of interpretation more salient than others, so that the interlocuters can find a ready route for agreement over what to concentrate on.

To develop these last points further, let us return to the beverage example. Suppose someone appears poorly to distinguish beer from a blank sheet of cardboard, would that not strain any account of communicative competence? Not necessarily. Suppose A were to say: 'A beer would refresh us now, what a pity there isn't any', and B were to hand A a cardboard sheet with every expression of goodwill. B's response might be intelligible as an act resulting from framing the utterance in terms of its original purpose: acquiring a means of cooling down. In this context, a piece of cardboard used as a fan is an appropriate alternative means to the same end (airstreams have psychological reality as reinforcers for creatures as lowly as rats). The intelligibility of B's response depends upon (a) the assumption that the topic of the utterance is not beer, but means of refreshment (b) the framing of 'beer' within a contrast set constituted not by 'other drinks' but 'other means of refreshment'. So the example of Jacoby *et al.* moves from word meaning to word use, but only works to draw the contrasts they propose if the word use coincides with the word as topic. This is a notion taken from discourse analysis, and that deals not with words but with whole sets of utterances in context. So many analyses of word meaning are built upon completely unrecognized assumptions about regulations governing conversation. It is high time to unpack some.

This chapter, then, is concerned with discourse rules as ways of representing local knowledge. In particular, we shall be concerned with the notion of discourse topic, as a means of access to the appropriate referential framing of context, and consequently to the determination of the implicit contrast set for a referring expression. We shall show that children may appear not to comprehend a word because the adult speaker unwittingly fails to convey the topic of the discourse to the child, and thereby fails to secure agreement over the appropriate frame of reference. First, however, we shall examine further the concept of discourse topic.

3 From utterance meaning to utterance use: the discourse topic

As the title of this section shows, we are going to parallel the previous section on a higher plane of analysis: dealing with even more unwieldy 'units' such as whole sentences and utterances in context. The area is called 'discourse analysis'. It might as well be called 'homilectics' – the art of holding converse and delivering extended messages. That is what many psycholinguistic experiments on children are really about. But, as Chafe (1976) discussed, how do we decide 'what a sentence is really about'? According to him, the topic of a sentence is just that. There are many devices for assigning, emphasizing, shifting and maintaining topic. These range from the canonical topic-as-subject/ comment-as-predicate construction, to cleft and pseudo-cleft devices handling phonic reference and foregrounding, relativization and so on. Amid the proliferation of overlapping concepts and distinctions available in the literature, the concept of topic is the one upon which there has been maximal recognized and unrecognized convergence.

Linguists have held out the promise that the key to identifying the topic of discourse lies in the classification of the linguistic distinctions and devices noted above. We suggest that, while it is necessary to do so, it is not sufficient. Purely linguistic analyses are about as much use in discourse as in word-meaning analyses. Take for example a simple declarative of transparent meaning: 'The cat is climbing into the fridge.' What does it mean? Since the subject is 'cat' and the predicate ' . . . . fridge', is the topic the cat and the comment its undesirable location? It could be, but one would like to go beyond linguistics and say that the case would be stronger *if background knowledge were presupposed*: the fridge is on and contains tonight's dinner. The conjunction between linguistic analysis and some formalization of knowledge structures might hold the key. Let us reveal the true state of affairs: the fridge is indeed open and contains tonight's dinner, but it had been left open over the weekend and the kippers have gone mouldy. The cat is only one more disaster: the overall topic is the state of the fridge. The fact that the cat is climbing in is only a comment upon the parlous state of affairs obtaining within a wider frame than the single utterance. The proper study of topicalization procedures is the relationship between conventional rules of delivering linguistic information, the background knowledge credited to the interlocutors and the presuppositions which are triggered as antecedents of the target utterance. How far can one get by dividing the information in the utterance into what can be taken as already given and what is genuinely new?

Bates (1976) cuts the gordian knot by legislation: the topic/comment distinction maps onto the given/new distinction of Haviland and Clark (1974), not to mention the new/old distinction of Chafe (1976), the figure/ground distinction of MacWhinney (1974) *et tutti quanti*. Miller (1979) also collapses some of these. Hornby (1972) is more circumspect: topic is 'the part of the sentence which constitutes what the speaker is talking about, the rest of the sentence – the comment – providing new information about the topic'. But packing down dichotomies is not the same as integrating them, as we now show by unpacking the relation between devices previously thought of as having a topicalizing function and theories of information-processing in sentence-comprehension.

Haviland and Clark (1974) and Clark and Haviland (1977) in formulating the 'given/new contract', analysed the information content of an utterance in terms of the use made by a cooperative speaker of syntactic devices for conveying the difference between (a) knowledge presumed to be known by the listener and (b) knowledge provided by the speaker as presumed to be currently unknown to the listener. Bates (1976) assumes that topicalization procedures are equivalent to devices for highlighting new information. Clark and Haviland, however, did not suggest that an utterance *in isolation* conveys the sense of given and new information, but rather that the listener is able to gain access to the essential antecedent information by building inferential links from an existing knowledge-base. Hence, given and new information are interpreted within an *extended* representation of knowledge having the status of a presuppositional structure. Clearly then, topic, while being strongly related to given information, is not to be equated with it, nor with the subject slot which may realize both. We make the entirely formal proposal that topic be conceived of as *that particular frame of reference which (a) is accessed by the given information, (b) instantiates a set of presuppositions enabling the listener to integrate the new information with the antecedents of the linguistically-given information.*

This is close to the proposal of Keenan and Schieffelin (1976) that topic be defined as a propositional representation, but diverges on one crucial point. Keenan and Schieffelin locate topic as the (set of) proposition(s) about which the speaker is giving or requesting information. We propose that topic does two jobs: (a) delimits the appropriate presuppositional pool, i.e. those aspects of the context which the given information refers to, in such a way that new information can be added to the pool, and (b) linguistically encodes the given information itself. Formally, the topic frame itself organizes the links by making default assignments (inferential bridges) which complete its internal construction.

So topic is a big concept upon which others converge. What saves it from thereby being analytically useless in generating evidence? There are three answers to that. The first will be left to the rest of this chapter on a 'proof of the pudding' basis. The second is that there are a number of powerful formalisms which describe knowledge macro-structures and which can be focused. These include Reiter's (1980) logic for default reasoning to formalisms for how a knowledge-base can be used to pair mental representations with functional processes: the episodes of Schank (1975), the plans and scripts of Schank and Abelson (1977), and the frames of Minsky (1974 and 1975), Kuipers (1975), Goffman (1974) and Winograd (1975). All the above accounts attempt to produce models for the extended representation of knowledge, and hence address a common problem area. Finally, it is in itself advantageous to have a clearing-ground for related phenomena:

1 Contrastiveness

Chafe (1976) points out that devices of stress and syntax often mark a contrast between what is explicitly stated and what has been left unstated, so that relevant presuppositions can be contrastively defined – hence implicating the set of applicable distinctions as in the beverage example. The device of foregrounding consists in the selection of a *particular* referent from a set of plausible options.

2 Extended discourse sequences

If topic is to be treated as the extended representation to which a current input is assimilated, this makes sense of the wide variety of devices above the single-utterance level identified by Keenan and Schieffelin (1976). Devices such as collaborative topic-maintenance in question/ answer sequences, topic-incorporation by shifting topic to update a frame of reference under the impact of new information, and the like, need a formalism of background knowledge.

3 Representing linguistic and nonlinguistic information in a common format

Minsky (1975) supplies a frame analysis for the organization of information from disparate input sources. The concept of topic draws attention to the need for a common format for integrating information, and permits the scaling of linguistic and nonlinguistic cues in cases where the sense and reference of a linguistic unit may not seem easily relatable one to another (Stedmon and Freeman 1980b).

4 Plausibility of relations within a topic frame

Canonical relations amongst objects being referred to may bias representation (Freeman 1980), perhaps via the operation of circumscription rules upon the set of predicates used to express the facts (see McCarthy 1980). Again, what is given linguistically may well have a central organizing function in leading the listener to access stored knowledge, and may serve as an expectancy cue. But successful communication demands that salience should be assigned to the new information that is to be incorporated. We conclude with a formal definition: topic frame is an organized and structure for representing knowledge from the immediate linguistic and contextual input, such that a presuppositional background can be activated which assigns maximum salience to the new information.

The rest of the chapter is devoted to giving concrete examples and new evidence on these rather abstract points.

4 A case of children's miscomprehension – produced by their word-use or utterance-use problems?

Now we have the necessary tools to analyse an intriguing study. Donaldson and Lloyd (1974) showed 14 4-to-5-year-olds' collections of cars and garages like those in Table 3.3. There was a spare car or an empty garage, and the task was to verify whether 'all the cars are in the garages' or, on other occasions, whether 'all the garages have cars in them'. Five children always assented to both statements with four garages and five cars, thus in effect ignoring the spare car. These and a further one always dissented from both statements given a spare garage. 'Watching children and listening to them, one had the powerful impression that the empty garage was somehow salient for them, and that they interpreted everything in ways affected by this salience' (Donaldson 1978, 67).

So a spare car is not salient enough, and a spare garage is too salient. In itself this cuts out one formal linguistic explanation. Suppose that the children obey a rule that 'a universal affirmative quantifier in the subject slot generalizes to the predicate'. So 'all the cars are in the garages' is processed as 'all the cars are in [all] the garages', leading to over-exhaustive search for one-to-one relations between the sets. This would account for the extra-garage salience, but obviously not the lack of extra-car salience. So let us go to the other extreme of explanation. Assume that the only function of the utterance is to trigger background knowledge. Children might think to themselves that a garage's customary job (canonical function) is to contain cars, and all utterances get referred to that single criterion. Therefore, there might be a bias towards expecting words like 'some' or 'most' rather than the 'all' with which they have to deal.

Indeed this point, in more analytic form, will become relevant shortly. For the present, all we need to note is that many studies show how powerfully expectations about object-relations and usage can operate in 'word-comprehension tests' (Baldwin 1975, Grieve *et al*. 1977, Freeman, Sinha and Condliffe 1981, Wilcox and Palermo 1975; see also the chapter by Bridges in this volume). So will the concept of canonical function give the key to the problem? Are children really construing the situation as one in which the topic is the rules of use of garages, thus falling prey to adventitious cognitive 'human sense'?

4a A study of canonical relations between sets

The obvious step is to make clear that the objects will often *not* be put to customary use, in a systematic replication of the Donaldson-Lloyd study. Thus one can arrange cars on top of garages, make tables have vases under them, etc. Table 3.1 shows the design: for each canonical relationship of *in*, *on*, or *under*, there is a contrasting noncanonical relationship. This is important in case the garage-salience be specific to containment (*in*-ness) more than canonicality. So we can check the Donaldson-Lloyd study of spatial relations, to see whether it is really a fragment of the study of canonicality, containment or whatever.

The garages, fireplaces, tables and bridges can be thought of as the *fixed objects* (FO) in relation to which the smaller *moveable objects* (MO) can be placed. This distinction has psychological reality: it is more natural to describe a moveable car as being near a fixed garage than the reverse. Fixed objects are landmark reference objects: see Bowerman (in press) and Macrae 1978 for an analysis of semantic, syntactic and pragmatic considerations. At the moment we shall use FO and MO as a notation, and later analyse its role in the evidence.

Table 3.1 Combinations of objects and spatial relations about which the children were questioned.

Fixed objects	Moveable objects	Implicit spatial contrast	Canonical relation	Non-canonical relation
garages	cars	IN/ON	IN	ON
fireplaces	clocks	IN/ON	ON	IN
tables	vases	IN/UNDER	ON	UNDER
bridges	boats	ON/UNDER	UNDER	ON

The procedure was always that four FOs were put on the table, then either three or five MOs were placed at the FOs, leading to one spare + FO or one spare + MO, respectively. On each trial we explained that the rest of the objects were 'not in the game', so that it was only what was on the table that was 'being talked about'. On each trial the child was asked, 'Are all the MOs [at] the FOs?' *or* 'Have all the FOs got MOs [at] them?' Each child had 32 trials, to cover the whole matrix of possibilities, in counterbalanced order.

The results from 32 5-year-olds were particularly clear. The frequency of correct answers was unaffected by canonicality (compare the columns in Table 3.2) or by particular spatial relations (compare each row in Table 3.2). Minute breakdown of the data gave no different pattern. Neither did replication of the study on another 59 children in the two-year age-bands above and below 5 years. So the children's judgement-error has impressive generality over categories which could provide explanations which would compete with the one shortly to be promoted. But this is only a start: now to reconsider the data.

One needs data at the individual level: 'the sheer numbers of right answers is much less informative than the pattern of their occurrence' (Donaldson and Lloyd 1974). Add another step (from a study of spatial

Table 3.2 Classification of the data in terms of canonicality and spatial relationship. Maximum number of possible correct responses per cell is 128.

Implicit spatial contrast instantiated by array	Spatial relation instantiated by array items	No. of correct responses for canonical instantiations	No. of correct responses for non-canonical instantiations
IN/ON	IN	72	78
	ON	72	69
ON/UNDER	ON	73	71
	UNDER	66	73

Table 3.3 Evidence for identifying stable strategies. Key: ☐ = fixed object (FO); X = moveable object (MO); ☒ = MO at FO.

Strategy	Array		Code	Response to either question
Topicalizing fixed	☒ ☒ ☒ ☒	X	+ MO	Yes
elements	☒ ☒ ☒ ☐		+ FO	No
Topicalizing moveable	☒ ☒ ☒ ☒	X	+ MO	No
elements	☒ ☒ ☒ ☐		+ FO	Yes
Joint Topicalizing both fixed and moveable elements	☒ ☒ ☒ ☒ ☒		+ MO	No
(mismatch strategy)	☒ ☒ ☒ ☐		+ FO	No

relations): treat 'all the patterns as legitimate variants. . . . it is impossible to score single responses as correct or incorrect' (Tanz 1980). We shall employ two shorthand notations: response-patterns will be referred to as 'strategies', and individual responses will be referred to as 'correct/incorrect' to mean 'like/unlike adult responses', the notation to be unpacked in a study shortly to be discussed. We tabulate the children's patterns of 'yes/no' in terms of the relative salience accorded to the FO or MO sets of referent items. Three easily-identifiable strategies emerged, according to an arbitrary criterion of accounting for 90 per cent of the individual's responses. The first strategy is that of providing information about whether all the FOs are paired with MOs, i.e. topicalizing FOs. Table 3.3 shows how this and the other strategies were identified. The reverse strategy is that of topicalising MOs. Finally, some answers were about the mismatch between the sets: a joint topicalization strategy. Always saying 'yes', whatever the question, and 'random' strategies also occurred, as usual.

The results are shown in Table 3.4 for all 91 subjects studied, from 3–8 years of age. We feel reasonably confident that the characterization is accurate, from post-test discussions with the individuals. The empty-garage-salience strategy is here labelled 'topicalization of FOs' and clearly, as in the Donaldson-Lloyd study, is stronger than the MO strategy: 42 children compared with 12. It is the dominant response mode. But topicalizing MO *did* occur, and presumably it was their small sample size which prevented Donaldson and Lloyd from noticing it.

It is now clear that the salience of the empty garage does not derive from its spatial role as a cavity-bearer nor from its canonical function. Instead, most children seem to use a general-purpose strategy cutting across a wide variety of object-pairs and spatiofunctional relations. Two questions are now raised. The first is what it is in the situation

Table 3.4 Number of children falling into each strategy group, for our results and those of Donaldson and Lloyd (1974).

Strategy	Results of Experiment 1	Results of Donaldson and Lloyd's (1974) experiment reanalysed
Responding yes to all questions	7	2
Topicalizing the fixed object	42	5
Topicalizing the moveable objects	12	0
Joint topicalizing both sets of objects	11	1
Alternative 'random' strategies	19	6
Total	91	14

which leads statistically to a modal bias towards fixed objects. The other is − to hark back to an earlier briefly-made point − whether some of the answers are *really* wrong in adult terms. A useful step would be to find a situation in which adults too used similar strategies. This we now do as the first step in the long process of solving the modal-response puzzle.

4b Topicalization processes underlying adults' comprehension of quantifiers

All that needs to be done is to find a situation in which adults find it natural 'erroneously' to reply 'yes' to the question, 'Are all the MOs [at] the FOs?', even given an extra MO; and 'no' when there is an extra FO (cf. Table 3.3). Again Donaldson (1978, 66) gives a lead: if we say, 'Have you put all the knives and forks on the table?' we are at least as likely to mean 'all the knives and forks that are going to be needed' as 'all the knives and forks that are kept in the drawer': the choice of meaning will depend upon the total context. Responsiveness to a perceived purpose will provide the listener with *appropriate reasons* for an answer which is only wrong according to timeless context-free criteria of the logic of truth-values. These reasons, *grâce à* John Locke, are ingredients of topic-setting processes in the listener's mind.

We drew two naively realistic pictures. In one, four saucepans served as FOs relative to four saucepan-lids plus one lid lying next to the cooker amongst vegetables and a knife. In the other, four saucers served as the FOs, with three of them having a cup on. Twenty non-psychology students were accosted in a public place and spun an almost-true tale. In effect, they were told that the experimenter was designing a language comprehension test for children, but had been surprised at their performance. In view of this, she was seeing whether adults found the situation clear. The two pictures they would be shown came from test batteries concerned with domestic scenarios of mother either cooking or laying the table for tea. They were then shown the pictures and asked: (1) 'Are all the lids on the saucepans?' (2) 'Are all the cups on the saucers?'

The results were clear. Sixteen subjects replied 'yes' to question 1 (P .006, Binomial) and 17 replied 'No' to question 2 (P .001). Only one subject expressed any feelings of ambiguity but still gave the modal responses. So the results replicate the 'errors' of children. Since adults can reasonably be credited with comprehension of the formal semantics of the questions, it must be concluded that their interpretation of quantified expressions depends upon conventional rules of use which encompass the perceived purposes and intentions of the speaker. This is very like the Glucksberg *et al.* study (1976), outlined in section 2, on the semantics of 'same'.

Adults did not interpret the referring expression 'all the cups' to mean 'all the cups visible in the picture', rather to mean 'all the cups which ought to be present'. Similarly, a nonfunctional lid is not assumed to be a member of the referent set encoded in the phrase 'all the lids'. The hypothesis to be evaluated is that children could conceivably understand the formal semantics of, say, 'all the cars' but still have to rely upon conventional rules to decide *which* set of cars the speaker had in mind. But there is a huge gap between the cookery lesson and the 'garage-salience' data. If we are to appeal to conventional rules to bridge it, we have next to describe some of these rules, then to find out whether that leads us to gain an analytic grip on the 'garage-salience problem' so as to predict a new effect. To anticipate, it does.

5 Conventional rules for interpreting quantified expressions

When a speaker asks a question about the presence of 'all the Xs', he is implicitly requesting the hearer to carry out an exhaustive search to check that no X is missing. Asking someone such a question is only legitimate 'socio-dialogically' if there is at least a possibility that some X is (or some Xs are) in actuality missing. The conventions underlying asking such a question therefore presuppose not only that the size of the intended referent set is potentially larger than the contemporaneously present set of Xs, but that such knowledge is potentially available to both interlocutors.

If the hearer's task is to check the context for cues which might indicate the absence of one of the items, then there is a conventional discourse bias towards giving a negative reply. *Effectively the situation provides a context for plausible denial (Wason 1965) in view of the speaker's apparent concern that nothing is missing.* Furthermore, if the children thought that the search was instigated for a particular purpose it would hardly be relevant for them to mention any extra referents lying outside the set identified within the discourse context. Hence answering a question about 'all the Xs' is likely to entail ignoring irrelevant Xs and searching for cues which indicate a missing X. Both the empty garage in Donaldson and Lloyd's experiment and the unpaired saucer in the adult experiment could be taken to show that an item of the intended discourse referent set must be missing. Again, when an item referenced by 'all the Xs' is ignored, clearly the quantifier does not operate with the logical scope of embracing a universal set of Xs: rather, 'all the Xs' is taken to mean 'all the Xs which ought to be present' or 'all the Xs which the speaker intends to be present'. In other words, adult comprehension is guided by the listener's assumptions about the speaker's temporary interests, which may be *inferred by default*, from real-scene knowledge, including knowledge of what have come to be called event-scripts and scenarios. In the child experiments, this leads to the testable alternatives that the children are construing the experimental situation in such a way that either (a) a purpose can be attributed to that particular experiment, as in Locke's argument outlined early on, or (b) it can be taken for granted that *any* speaker would naturally be topicalizing the garages. Since the garages are fixed, four in number in a row, this forms the natural set for checking that nothing is missing. This is, at the moment a guess: data come shortly.

Now there is a gap between the adult and the child studies. In the former, real-world knowledge is obviously called up in the subjects' minds, and gives a rational basis for their replies. In the child study, we cannot be sure, yet, whether this holds true. So the next step is to 'naturalize' the artifical child task, taking care to set the topic in such a way that we can be reasonably sure that the children understand that we are attempting to share a common purpose (a temporary interest) with them. In the Donaldson-Lloyd, and our first, experiment, the speaker was attempting to use the rather unconventional rule of employing a quantified expression to refer solely to the immediate visible array. This runs foul of the 'context of plausible denial' effect. In the next study we deliberately provide two differing plausible contexts for conventional rules of 'reasoning to attain a conclusion'.

6 The effect of setting a topic with children

There is a useful analysis of establishing a topic set out in the Keenan and Schieffelin (1976) model: in our terminology, the referents which are intended to be talked about should be included in the topic frame triggered by the utterance. It was shown in section 4b that adults' procedure for finding the referents of quantified noun phrases depends on the interlocutors constructing the same background knowledge schemes for interpreting the target utterance. When the context instantiates a highly familiar event or set of activities, utterances may be quite economical: many of the referents involved will already be incorporated into a scripted knowledge-frame (Nelson and Greundel 1979), and so need not even be mentioned. It can safely be assumed that the listener knows the ingredients of a cookery scene. If children, like adults, can interpret quantified expressions as referring to a set of items other than those immediately present, they must somehow have constructed a topic frame which includes either a larger or smaller set of items than those present in the array. As yet we have no real idea of the cues by which children make the fixed objects the salient entry in a topic frame, nor the cues which might lead them to swing over to entering the moveable object into this slot instead. Yet if the rules of interpretation set out in the previous section are anywhere near the mark, it ought to be easy to do so.

Here is a simple experiment which feeds children with a great deal of knowledge and thereby swings the strategy of individuals from topicalizing fixed objects to topicalizing moveable objects. The arrays were exactly as in the Donaldson-Lloyd study, only using cows and cowsheds. The experimenter, Tony Fehler, told 9 4-year-olds a story focused either upon the naughtiness of cows or upon the propensity of cowsheds to burn down. At crucial moments in the story, acted out with the toys, the child had to verify the quantified expressions. The results, scored for strategy as in section 4a, were unambiguous. When the cows (MOs) were topicalized by the experimenter, 8/9 children topicalized them in an answering strategy. When the cowsheds (FOs) were topicalized by the experimenter, 7/9 children topicalized them in their answers.

So the 'garage-salience effect' − the FO salience effect noted in the big experiment − can be reversed in the same individuals. It should also be recalled that adults too could be led to give entirely reasonable 'wrong' answers. So we have found a rational basis for the Donaldson-Lloyd effect and reversed it under conditions predicted by discourse analysis. But it is not yet a very satisfactory state of affairs. It is one thing to demonstrate theoretically that the problem of quantifiers is not primarily one of word-meaning but conventional discourse rules and topic-setting procedures, and it undeniably helps to get adults to give child-like answers and children to reverse their strategies; but it is another thing to demonstrate that this is what went on in the simple 'garages tasks'. Yet this is now easy to do: let us scrutinise the 'garages study' for potential topic-setting cues, then manipulate them to reverse the children's strategies. This brings the evidence together over quite a wide range.

7 Numerical invariance as a topic-setting cue for children

The Donaldson-Lloyd results appeared as an *unadultlike* pattern induced by *fixed objects* acting as *containers* in *canonical* mode. We now know that none of the italicized ingredients is essential, though we do not know the conditions under which any or all may assume importance. The strongest case for the adequacy of a theory would be to find the simplest condition under which none of those variables exerted any effect. It is daunting to try to do so all in one swoop. What seems an easier option is to scrutinise the arrays in terms of these few concepts which have come out as theoretically the most basic ones, and this should lead us to the unique variable underlying the action of those we have investigated. Thence manipulation of the variable should enable us to reverse individual strategies.

At the risk of being repetitious, the argument which follows applies a discourse analysis to the task. This means that it is not regarded as a test of language comprehension but of children's problems with a shared topic. The children's answers to the experimenter's questions indicate that they seem to have identified the garages as that aspect of the array which is topicalized by the experimenter's utterance. Possibly our previous guess that numerical invariance might mark the intended topic set is on the right lines. If the experiment be repeated with an invariant set of four MOs and a variable set of three or five FOs, the children ought to switch to topicalizing the MOs.

From the 5-year-olds in the big canonicality study, we selected 23 who had on 90 per cent of their trials topicalized the fixed objects in each array (as set out in Table 3.3). After a fortnight's interval we retested them with the moveable objects now held invariant in number, as shown in Table 3.5, bottom two rows (the top two rows contain the configurations used in the canonicality test, for ease of comparison). In this study, only 24 trials were given, since we held back the cars and garages. After the 24 trials were over, the four garages and three/five cars were reintroduced as a post-test to see whether the children would swing back to fixed-object topicalization when the invariance cue was returned to the fixed objects.

With the moveable objects invariant, only 5/23 stuck to this fixed-object topicalization strategy. Five gave 'random' patterns, leaving 13 who now did take account of the moveable objects: 6 switching to topicalizing them and 7 adopting a joint-topicalization (mismatch cue) strategy. It was noteworthy that 11 of these 13 then reverted to fixed-object topicalization with the post-test of invariant garages. What seems to be happening is that the invariance cue does work, but against the background of some bias towards fixed objects, rather than moveable. Of course this might be due to the selection of previously-biased subjects for the strategy-reversal experiment; or there may be an inherent bias towards topicalizing fixed objects. Either account is

Table 3.5 Comparison of the arrays from the canonicality study and the invariance-cue study on 5-year-olds. Key: □ = fixed object (FO); X = moveable object (MO);   ⊠ = MO at FO.

Task structure over trials	Array type	Array structure
Experiment 1 Fixed objects invariant in number for all 32 trials	+ MO + FO	⊠ ⊠ ⊠ ⊠ X ⊠ ⊠ ⊠ □
Experiment 2 Moveable objects invariant in number for all 24 trials	+ MO + FO	⊠ ⊠ ⊠ X ⊠ ⊠ ⊠ ⊠ □

reasonable in view of the analysis offered here, but needs further testing. We have done experiments in which the child handles either the fixed set or the moveable set, when each set in turn is made invariant, and it is possible to scale a number of cues for topic-setting within this general paradigm. These studies will be written up separately, from the report by Stedmon and Freeman (1980a).

This is straightforward work. The more challenging task is to alter the referential form of the utterances to provide varying degrees of information about the referents, and to check these forms to see if they operate as linguistic topic-setting cues. Our discourse analysis provides a way of formalizing relations amongst different cues. Karmiloff-Smith (1979) has presented an analysis of child language which provides an empirical basis for scaling the identifying strengths of various linguistic forms. Accordingly Stedmon and Freeman (1980b) amalgamated one of Karmiloff-Smith's designs with modifications of the Donaldson-Lloyd design, and showed that scaling linguistic and non-linguistic topic cues against one another led to very orderly data. In the next section we analyse the role of just the nonlinguistic cues in order to generalize the account beyond quantifiers.

8 How the context supplies topic-setting cues

There are two rather different but related ways in which context and utterance jointly supply information about topic. First, cues from context and utterance may help the listener to identify the intended referent-set to which the speaker is apparently addressing his or her concerns. This can range from a disordered refrigerator to unhoused cars, from a chessboard to an apparently faulty taperecorder. Through this *referential* function of topic-setting, listener and speaker can negotiate a common frame of reference, and a common set of interests with respect to that frame. Second, cues from utterance, external context, and internal frame of reference may help the listener to identify what particular information must be added to their current representation, if they are to give an informative reply. This *informative* function of topic-setting enables the listener to update his or her topic frame to bring it into line with that apparently held by the speaker.

Linguistic devices for signalling both the referential and informative aspects of topic-setting are well documented. Nonlinguistic cues have been grossly neglected. A consequence of this neglect is that we are still in the dark as to the relative salience of linguistic as opposed to nonlinguistic cues for young children. In the absence of previous comparative data over a wide range, miscomprehension of linguistic form has been attributed to children in cases where a ready alternative explanation consists in positing a rational use of nonlinguistic information in a discourse context.

There are now two ways in which one can recognize cases of misidentification of the topic – cross-purposes between the interlocutors. It would occur either through inadequate decoding of the adult utterance at a semantic-syntactic level, or through the rational application of alternative discourse conventions by the child. This enables one easily to dig out premises for a purely linguistic account of the Donaldson-Lloyd study. One would have to assume that when the syntax of the utterance is altered from 'all the cars. . . .' to 'all the garages. . . .', the surface change in grammatical subject from the moveable to the fixed objects is enough to mark a change in discourse topic.

However, it is critically important to note that marking implicit topic-changes by linguistic means will ensure a change in the truth value of the response if, and only if, the items referred to in the utterance have been identified by the listener as those which are momentarily present in the physical array. Any psychological bias on the part of the child towards widening or narrowing the identified set (remember the cookery experiment in section 4b, and the 'cowshed' one on section 6) will upset the experimenter's calculations.

Let us now compare two analyses of the evidence. The first is in terms of faulty semantic processing. Children fail to decode the syntactic distinction which conventionally assigns the topic to the grammatical subject. They therefore cannot make use of the subject-predicate construction to identify the topic, and search for some nonlinguistic, perceptually salient cue to 'make human sense' of the utterance. They do not notice the error of this procedure, and will defend their verdicts because they fail to recognize the syntactic constraints for restricting the scope of the quantifier to those precise items referred to in the noun phrase in which it occurs. This failure is equivalent to failure to comprehend a quantifier.

The second is a discourse analysis which captures the general tenor of Donaldson's more recent work (e.g. Donaldson 1978), that children try to understand what people mean, not only what words mean. This is the 'context of plausible denial' sort of approach. With simple declaratives, the subject-predicate distinction is certainly the canonical device for linguistic encoding of the topic-comment distinction (for the referential use of language). By convention it is also the canonical device for encoding the distinction between given and new information (for the informative use of language). But herein lies the rub. As we noted earlier, when the subject-predicate distinction is used to encode a given/new distinction, nothing entails that this has to map onto an underlying topic/comment distinction. Rather, topic may be *identified by inference* from that part of the utterance which is the syntactic realization of the given information. So there are two distinctions which the surface form of the utterance, subject-predicate, can encode; and one needs pragmatic rules for relying on one or other distinction as being communicatively more reliable. It may well be the case that adults would often tend to treat subject-predicate as the surface realization of topic-comment, and there is a set of studies on linguistic intuition in parsing waiting to be done. (The work of Bock (1977) and Hornby (1972) provide a lead here.) But children might regard the informative use of language − the request for information from the controller of the situation − as a more reliable discourse-maintenance function, and thereby apply a pragmatic rule for identifying topic. Their replies provide information about this construed topic, rather than the referential content of the subject noun-phrase in the adult utterance. The adult *thinks* that she is requesting information about cars in the array because she has taken care to start off by saying 'all the cars', but the child *knows* that garages are the topic. *Once garages have been established within the topic slot, the topic frame assigns by default a numerical value to the variable set. This value is precisely the number of items needed to match the topic-set in accordance with the conventional meaning of the word 'all'.* Under such a condition even adults will reliably ignore an extra lid or concentrate upon a spare saucer. To be sure, they understand the restrictive nature of 'all', but they have to look to the array to make up their minds about which set of referent items is intended, and this may be taken to be more or less than those physically present. Whenever a situation gives a listener access to background knowledge, whether in the form of scripts or knowledge frames about themes such as cookery, or in the form of noticing what the speaker has apparently taken care to make perceptually salient, or to keep invariant, in the situation, a frame of reference is set up. Making reference to a set of items within a frame is never enough to establish *joint* reference between two people unless the different conventional rules of discourse coincide.

Whenever children give strange answers in such studies, it is up to the psychologist to *prove* that he or she has really established joint reference with the child in the way that was intended, if faulty semantic/syntactic comprehension is to be invoked as an explanation. It is essential to work towards independent evidence of this, and it is not sufficient to say that children must have miscomprehended the semantics *solely* on the grounds of a context-free truth-value violation some-where. As Locke showed so long ago, truth-values can be relative things – relative, surely, to the set of distinctions one is trying to get the listener to draw. Collaborative focus on a topic is the children's key to the world of communication. They may not always find the lock for themselves. Only if there is independent evidence that the relevant frame of reference has been set up, and the relevant distinctions have been drawn, and that *still* the answer is wrong, are we on safe ground in producing a purely linguistic analysis. It is an uphill task, and one in which few research lines have managed to achieve enough altitude for a bird's-eye view to be possible.

References

Baldwin, P. 1975: *On the acquisition of the meaning of In, On and Under*. MA thesis, University of Stirling.

Bates, E. 1976: *Language and context: the acquisition of pragmatics*. New York: Academic Press.

de Beaugrande, R.A. 1980: The pragmatics of discourse planning. *J. Pragmatics* **4**, 15–42.

Bennett, J. 1976: *Linguistic behaviour*. London: Cambridge University Press.

Bock, J.K. 1977: The effect of pragmatic presupposition on syntactic structure in question answering. *J. Verbal Learn and Verbal Behaviour* **16**, 723–34.

Bowerman, M. (in press): Starting to talk worse: clues to language acquisition from children's late speech errors. In S. Strauss (ed.), *U-shaped behavioural growth*. New York: Academic Press.

Chafe, W.L. 1976: Givenness, contrastiveness, definiteness, subjects, topics, and point of view. In C.N. Li (ed.), *Subject and topic*. New York: Academic Press.

Clark, H.H. 1970: The primitive nature of children's relational concepts. In J.R. Hayes (ed.), *Cognition and the development of language*. London: Wiley.

Clark, H.H. and Haviland, S.E. 1977: Comprehension and the given/new contact. In Freedle, R.O. (ed.), *Discourse production and comprehension*. Hillsdale, NJ: Erlbaum.

Donaldson, M. 1978: *Children's minds*. London: Fontana.

Donaldson, M. and Lloyd, P. 1974: Children's judgements of match and mismatch. In Bresson, F. (ed.). *Problèmes actuels en psycholinguistique*. Paris: Presses Universitaires de France.

Donaldson, M. and Wales, R. (1970). On the acquisition of some relational terms. In J.R. Hayes (ed.). *Cognition and the development of language*. London: Wiley.

Finn, G. 1979: Social context, social interaction and children's interpretations of class inclusion and related problems. PhD thesis,

University of St Andrews.

Freeman, N.H. 1980. *Strategies of representation in young children: analysis of spatial skills and drawing processes*. London: Academic Press.

Freeman, N.H., Sinha, C.G. and Condliffe, S. 1981: Collaboration and confrontation with young children in language comprehension tests. In W.P. Robinson (ed.), *Communication in development*. London: Academic Press.

Freeman, N.H., Sinha, C.G. and Stedmon, J.A. 1981: The allative bias is almost proof against task naturalness. *J. Child Language* **8**, 283–96.

Frege, G. 1892: Uber Sinn und Bedeutung. *Zeitshrift für Philosophie und Philosophische Kritik* **100**, 25–50.

Gazdar, G. 1979: *Pragmatics: implicature, presupposition and logical form*. London: Academic Press.

Goffman, E. 1974. *Frame analysis*. Harmondsworth: Penguin.

Glucksberg, S., Hay, A. and Danks, J. 1976: Words in utterance contexts: young children do not confuse the meaning of 'same', and 'different'. *Child Development* **47**, 737–41.

Grice, H.P. 1968: Utterer's meaning, sentence meaning and word-meaning. *Foundations of Language* **4**, 225–42.

— 1975: Logic and conversation. From Grice's William James Lectures, Harvard University, 1967, reprinted in P. Cole and J. Morgan, (eds.), 1975, *Syntax and semantics* **3**, *Speech Acts*. New York: Academic Press.

Grieve, R., Hoogenraad, R. and Murray, D. 1977: On the young child's use of lexis and syntax in understanding locative instructions. *Cognition* **5**, 235–50.

Haviland, S.E. and Clark, H.H. 1974: What's new? Acquiring new information in memory representations of meaning. *J. Verbal Learning and Verbal Behaviour* **16**, 119–36.

Hornby, P.A. 1972: The psychological subject and predicate. *Cognitive Psychology* **3**, 632–42.

Hughes, M. 1978: Selecting pictures of another person's view. *B. J. Educational Psychology* **48**, 210–19.

Jacoby, L.L., Craik, F.I.M. and Begg, I. 1979: Effects of decision difficulty on recognition and recall. *J. Verbal Learning and Verbal Behaviour* **18**, 585–600.

James, W. 1892: *Psychology*. New York: Harper and Brothers.

Karmiloff-Smith, A. 1979: *A functional approach to child language*. London: Cambridge University Press.

Keenan, E.O. and Schieffelin, B. 1976: Topic as a discourse notion: a study of topic in the conversations of children and adults. In Li, C.N. (ed.), *Subject and topic*. New York: Academic Press.

Kuipers, B.J. 1975: A frame for frames. In D.G. Bobrow and A. Collins (eds.), *Representation and understanding*. New York: Academic Press.

Langendoen. D.T. 1971: Presupposition and assertion in the semantic analysis of nouns and verbs in English. In D.D. Steinberg and L.A. Jacobovits (eds.), *Semantics*. London: Cambridge University Press.

Light, P. 1979: *The development of social sensitivity*. London: Cambridge University Press.

Locke, J. 1690: An essay concerning human understanding. London.

Lyons, J. 1977: *Semantics*, vol. I. London: Cambridge University Press.

McCarthy, J. 1980: Circumscription – a form of nonmonotonic reasoning. *Artificial Intelligence* **13**, 27–40.

McGarrigle, J. and Donaldson, M. 1975: Conservation accidents. *Cognition* **3**, 341–50.

McGarrigle, J., Grieve, R. and Hughes, M. 1978: Interpreting inclusion: a contribution to the study of the child's linguistic and cognitive development. *J. Experimental Child Psychology* **26**, 520–50.

Macrae, A. 1978: Use and understanding of locative prepositions by nursery school children. (Unpublished ms, University of Edinburgh).

MacWhinney, B. 1974: How Hungarian children learn to speak. Unpublished doctoral dissertation, University of California, Berkeley.

Miller, G.A. and Miller, K. 1979: Critical notice – John Lyons on semantics. *Q. J. Experimental Psychology* **31**, 711–36.

Miller, M.H. 1979: *The logic of language development in early childhood*. Berlin: Springer.

Minsky, M. 1974: Frame systems. MIT: AI Laboratory Memorandum.

— 1975: A framework for representing knowledge. In Winston, (ed.), *The psychology of computer vision*. New York; McGraw-Hill.

Nelson, K. and Greundel, J. 1979: From personal episode to social script: two dimensions in the development of event knowledge. Paper presented at biennial meeting of Society for Research in Child Development, San Francisco.

Oh, C.K. and Dinneen, D.A. 1979: *Syntax and semantics: Presupposition 11*. New York: Academic Press.

Reiter, R. 1980: A logic for default reasoning. *Artificial Intelligence* **13**, 81–132.

de Saussure, F. 1966: *Course in general linguistics*. New York: McGraw-Hill.

Schank, R.C. 1975: The structure of episodes in memory. In D.G. Bobrow and A. Collins, (eds.), *Representation and understanding*. New York: Academic Press.

Schank, and Abelson, R. 1977: *Scripts, plans, goals and understanding: an enquiry into human knowledge structures*. Hillsdale, NJ: Lawrence Erlbaum.

Searle, J. 1975: Indirect speech acts. In P. Cole and J. Morgan (eds.),

Syntax and Semantics **3**: Speech Acts. New York: Academic Press.

Sinha, C.G. and Carabine, B. 1980: Interactions between lexis and discourse in conservation and comprehension tasks. *J. Ch. Lang.* **8**, 109–29.

Sinha, C.G. and Walkerdine, V. 1978a: Conservation: a problem in language, culture and thought. In N. Waterson and C. Snow (eds.), *The development of communication*. London: Wiley.

—— 1978b: Children, logic and learning. *New Society* **43** (January), 62–4.

Stedmon, J.A. and Freeman, N.H. 1980a: All the cars: which cars? Conditions under which children understand what you say but not what you say it about. Paper given at the BPS Developmental Section, Edinburgh, September 1980.

—— 1980b: When reference fails: the use and misuse of quantified referring expressions to make identifying reference. Paper given at European Psycholinguistics Association Meeting on Background Knowledge, October, Gothenburg, Sweden. To appear in J. Allwood and E. Hjelmquist (eds.), *Foregrounding background*. Stockholm: Doxa.

Strawson, P.F. 1950: On referring. *Mind* **59**, 320–44.

Tanz, C. 1980: *Studies in the acquisition of deictic terms*. London: Cambridge University Press.

Walkderdine, V. and Sinha, C.G. 1978: The internal triangle: language, reasoning and the social context. In I. Markova (ed.), *The social context of language*. London: Wiley.

Wason, P.C. 1965: The context of plausible denial. *J. Verbal Learning and Verbal Behaviour* **4**, 7–11.

Wilcox, S. and Palermo, D.S. 1975: 'In', 'on' and 'under' revisited. *Cognition* **3**, 245–54.

Winograd, T. 1975: Frames and the declarative-procedural controversy. In D.G. Bobrow and A. Collins (eds.), *Representation and understanding*. New York: Academic Press.

4
Propositional attitudes[1]

James Russell

From earliest times the principal means of studying how children think has been to ask them questions − there is every reason to believe that its popularity will continue. But what happens when we have the answers? In particular, how do we deal with the two related problems: does the child understand me? and how do I interpret what he says? Specifically, what does it mean to believe the child when he says that we only have snow for children to play in, that clouds move because pedestrians drag them along as they walk, that quantity changes with visual appearance?

The topic of this chapter is the way children acquire the ability to make basic logico-mathematical judgments, how they come to move from giving the wrong answer to giving the right answer. The way I want to approach this topic is by consideration of what we should do with the wrong answers. Some would focus on the child's deficiencies as an information processor (e.g. Klahr and Wallace 1976, Klausmeier 1979). But the approach I will be adopting here begins by asking whether the incorrectness resides in the way the child construes the question and in the principles on which he frames his judgment. Without wishing to become involved at this point in the wrangle about whether one is an epiphenomenon of the other, let me just say that concentrating on this latter, linguistic-interpretive question is at least as sensible as making models of the child's 'information' handling.

Let us consider the possibility that the younger child's judgment is divergent because he does not possess a notion of 'correctness' versus 'incorrectness' that is sufficiently like our own. He may indeed not have fully distinguished language in imaginative play from language in the communications of publicly corrigible fact. Perhaps he is giving something that we would call an opinion when we would like him to make an attempt at 'the answer'. The child, in short, may be regarding verbal propositions in a radically different way to the way we do. It is not that

[1] The research described here was supported by a project grant from the Social Science Research Council. I am very grateful to Mary McMurran and Pamela Lyon for their assistance.

his semantics or syntax is primitive — although they may be — rather it is his attitude to the implicit criteria which sustain the truth of such judgments that is radically divergent. We do not have to look very far for a term to describe this divergence. The philosophical literature contains the term 'propositional attitude', and it is used there in a way that is analogous to how I will be using it here. The term is derived from Brentano's concept of the 'propositional act', our attitude of mind towards propositions such as thinking, fearing, doubting, hoping, expecting *that*. This is sometimes known as the 'dyadic-relation' theory of propositions, because a distinction is made between the act of proposing and the statement itself. J.M. Baldwin (1901) elaborated such a view and Gilbert Ryle (1929) argued that there can be a notion of 'the proposition' which is the neutral invariant against which different 'propositional attitudes' can be taken by different people and by the same person at different times.

Let me provide an illustration of how successful verbal communication depends on the listener and speaker sharing an appropriate propositional attitude *as the term will be intended here*. Two people are discussing a film. A says, 'I enjoyed *The Fiend without a Face*.' B says, 'You can't have enjoyed it because it isn't an enjoyable film.' If A does not (implausibly) interpret this answer as mere boorishness and if A is (almost as infuriatingly) of an analytical turn of mind, he may reply in the vein that saying he enjoyed the film is making a statement about his own experience, not essentially about the film; that although some films can be said to be more enjoyable than others nobody can tell him that he did *not* enjoy a film; that when we are considering enjoyment there is always the possibility of being in a minority of one — some kinds of masochist probably are . . . . and so on. That is, B does not know that the appropriate propositional attitude is 'subjective'. In contrast, what if A says, 'I saw *The Terror of Tiny Town* at the Rialto last Thursday evening' and B says, 'You can't possibly have seen it, it was only shown on Wednesday/it was on at the Plaza/I saw you at the match that evening/it's The *Tenor* of Tiny Town . . . .'? Here the two will be arguing about objective fact. If A says that it does not matter to him whether the film really had been shown and the main thing is that he *thinks* he saw the film and that's where the issue should rest, then it is now he who lacks the appropriate propositional attitude-of objectivity.

There is a steadily growing body of evidence that young children *do* have propositional attitudes which are divergent from ours. The work of Martin Braine has much the same pioneering status here as in the field of language development. In two ingenious experimental studies (Braine and Shanks 1965a and b) he showed that the natural interpretation which 5- to 7-year-old children give to questions about shape and size is a phenomenalistic one. That is, when asked whether a stick which appears bent by light refraction when placed in water has changed its shape, or whether a cube is larger under a magnifying glass, they will answer affirmatively, despite the fact that most *can* frame a realist interpretation by age 5 given a sufficiently unambiguous context. And of course Bruner (1966) made a similar point about the nonconservation judgment a little later, claiming that the nonconserving child is telling us about 'how things look to him' rather than 'how they are really'.

A related point about interpretations is made by the work of Margaret Donaldson and her associates (see Donaldson 1978). For many years now Donaldson has been insisting that any judgment a young child makes in an experiment is a function of both his construal of what is expected of him by the experimenter and the way that the materials support different construals. Some recent examples of the Donaldson approach developed in interesting directions are to be found in Sinha and Carabine 1980 and Light *et al*. 1979. The orientation that these workers share is that the child's thought is labile (c.f. Werner 1948) relative to our own: it is coloured by the insertion of a single adjective in the instructions and canalized by the smallest manipulation of experimental materials. It is, in short, determined by what linguists call 'pragmatics' – communicative intent within the practical context. Needless to say, other workers (notably Rose and Blank 1974) have produced comparable data.

My own approach has differed from this only in emphasis. It has been to try to tease out pragmatic-interpretive failure by employing non-Piagetian problems in order to study directly the variable of instruction interpretation (Russell 1975, 1976) and by presenting Piagetian problems nonverbally rather than modifying the instructions or materials (Russell 1979). About conservation at least my conclusions have been that: (a) nonconservers can fail by linguistic misinterpretation *prior* to witnessing any transformations of the materials; (b) nonconservers may use conservation language to describe their own performance, but its use by the experimenter distorts their judgments in the direction of nonconservation; (c) nonverbal competence in conservation can be found as early as 4 to 5 years if an appropriate transfer of learning design is used. (Other nonverbal tests of conservation have found only small effects with children who are in any case practically or actually within the concrete operational age range (e.g. Miller 1979, Weldall and Poborca 1980).)

Why, in particular, does a nonconserver, when asked why he chose the (correct) pair of transformed pencils on a transfer condition, say that he chose the ones that were 'the same size' but then perform like a nonconserver again on the standard (verbal) post-test. In the Russell 1979 experiment, the only essential difference between the two situations was that it was the *experimenter* who used the phrase in one case. My speculation was that the nonconserving child cognizes length equality through transformation in a 'subjective' or 'private' manner. He cannot appreciate that when *another* person uses a phrase such as 'the same size' he and that person can hold a common reference not only to the simple perceptual fact of protrusion, but to a length identity which is manifest in the covariance of two dimensions[2] (one pencil protrudes but another trails, therefore length constant). He does not know that length judgments, at least, can refer to this privately-cognized invariance. Public criteria for invariance of physical properties can, he thinks, only be one-dimensional and 'perceptual'.

The picture which begins to emerge before those who are at all sympathetic to this line of thought is that of the young child having a propositional attitude that is phenomenalist/labile/pragmatic/subjective/private/perceptual. (All these words are, of course, more or less unsatisfactory because this is not a state of mind that adults have to refer to – by definition.) On this model the main developmental task is the progressive socialization of the child's judgments, their tuning in with those of the adult by means of the appropriate public criteria. The attainment of intersubjectivity is the *necessary* (but of course not sufficient) condition for the objectivization of thinking. As I have indicated elsewhere (Russell 1978), although such a conception gained philosophical currency by way of Wittgenstein and the Pragmatists and has recently been elaborated by David Hamlyn (1978), it was J.M. Baldwin (1861–1934) who first spelled out the implications of such an assumption for developmental theory.

But how does all this accord with Piagetian theory? Of course, Piaget is a notoriously protean and eclectic thinker – some might find in Piaget's famous notion of egocentrism a conceptualization akin to that being sketched here. But, that said, I believe the attempt to explain judgmental deficiencies by divergence of propositional attitudes is fundamentally opposed to the Piagetian orientation. This incompatibility comes into sharp relief when we consider the Piagetian account of how *social* processes are supposed to function in the equilibration of mental structures. This is best seen in Piaget's book *The psychology of intelligence* (1950). In a fascinating penultimate chapter Piaget compares 'intellectual' interaction between individuals to 'a vast game of chess, which is carried on unremittingly and in such a way that each action carried out with respect to a particular item involves a series of equivalent or complementary actions on the part of the opponent; laws of grouping are nothing more or less than the various rules ensuring the reciprocity of the players and the consistency of their play' (165). Piaget is here drawing something far stronger than a mere analogy between preoperational children as individuals and the individual centrations of preoperational children. Just as centrations are equilibrated through reciprocal *intra*-individual cognitive conflict, so judgments are

---

[2] Those that stress the importance of identity knowledge (e.g. Acredolo and Acredolo 1979) would have to concede that knowledge of covariance is at least an additional necessary condition. Is it even possible to dissociate knowledge of *quantitive* identity from that of covariance, as each seems to entail the other?

socialized by the equilibration of reciprocal *inter*-individual cognitive conflict. The empirical implication is there to be extracted: social inter-action between cognitive *equals* (e.g. fellow preoperational children) can be the *sufficient* social experience for the objectivization of thought.

The theory is that egocentrism is dissolved through the child's having to cooperate with other children who necessarily adopt different pers-pectives from his own: the reciprocal coordination of mental perspec-tives. Piaget had introduced a similar conception much earlier in his work on moral development; in any event it is a notion absolutely at the heart of his theory. According to equilibration theory knowledge is not transmitted to the child, it is constructed by him both individually and in concordance with others (the two processes are indissociable). In principle, therefore, preoperational children do not require *exposure* to the concrete operational judgments to construct them — the equilibra-tion machinery will see to that. My crucial (Gedanken!) experiment here would be to ship a group of healthy preoperational children to a desert island and leave them there for about four or five years; if Piaget is correct they should have constructed a system of concrete operations by then out of the exigencies of social cooperation.

The critical point that I want to make is this: for such a process to function, the preoperational children who find themselves making conflicting judgments must be capable of regarding these judgments *as* conflicting. What if they do not? What if their pragmatic/subjective/ etc. propositional attitudes direct that they will be like two film fans who have the *appropriate* propositional attitudes and are reporting to each other whether they enjoyed the film rather than discussing who directed it? To illustrate, within equilibration theory two non-conservers may come to coordinate liquid conservation by the follow-ing kind of dialectic. They are sharing out a drink: one child boasts that he has more because the liquid in his (thinner) glass comes higher up; the other child counters with the claim that *he* has more because his drink is wider. Eventually they come to agree that neither of them is correct and fall back on the fact that both drinks came out of (say) full glasses of the same shape: they hit upon the principle of identity via that of the necessary incompatibility of unidimensional judgments. Naturally, this is a gross characterization of a process which Piaget would regard as having a much finer grain than this. But my point is that, on the non-Piagetian approach being developed here, if such a conversation ever took place it would not be about reality and truth, it would be about something more akin to appearance and opinion. The children would not engage in a dialectic at all: the conversation over their glasses would have more in common (in logicality if not style) with that of two wine tasters considering whether 'tart' or 'piquant' is the appropriate adjective. Two children with such propositional attitudes would never attempt to coordinate their perspectives, any more than adults ever really discuss whether a film is 'enjoyable' – yes or no.

We cannot ship children off to desert islands to test the implications of the equilibration model, but we can test dyads to see whether such conversations and such coordinations do indeed take place. And fortunately we do not have to rely on Piagetian exegesis for the framing of this 'cognitive conflict hypothesis'. Willem Doise (see especially Doise 1978) of Geneva and his associates have been performing experiments since about 1974 as demonstrations of just this thesis. Principally they have been concerned with the facilitatory effect of having two spatially 'egocentric' children cooperating on a model landscape reconstruction task based on Piaget and Inhelder's (1956) tasks. They report (e.g. Doise *et al.* 1975) that conflicts of centration between children result in performance at a higher cognitive level than either child is capable of when performing solo. Despite this, it was Piaget's formulation which motivated our research project on dyadic interaction, which began in 1978. (In fact it could not have been otherwise, because I did not come across Doise's work until after that phase of the project was complete!)

The aim of the project was to pair children whose performance was preoperational on a specific task in such a way that they would approach the problem from (sometimes literally) different perspectives. We also paired children who succeeded on the pre-test with such children in order to examine the possible transmission of the principle from one child to another. Altogether we tested around 150 dyads in the age range of 4 to 8 years. In those dyads who contributed to the grouped data the children were of the same sex, within 6 months of age and (usually) from the same class at school. All were tested in the department's developmental laboratory, being left alone in a room containing a remote-control video camera which filmed their reflection in an observation mirror. Speech was recorded by a ceiling microphone. Each dyad performed either 5 or 6 tasks together in one half-day session, which gave us around 22 hours of tape by the end. Two check lists were drawn up from pilot tapes which were meant to be applicable to any dyadic performance of a concrete operational task: an 'epistemic' list which scored behaviour in terms of its correctness and logical characteristics, and a 'pragmatic' list which descriptively recorded events in the stream of social behaviour (questions, counters and so on).

Conservation

Figure 4.1 represents the arrangement of two children who have to decide on an answer to the standard length conservation question. The post-transformation display is shown here. If both are nonconservers than a direct perspective mismatch is virtually guaranteed, because child A will judge pencil x to be bigger and child B will judge pencil y to

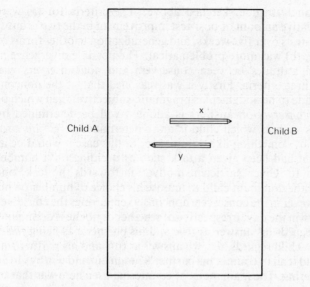

Figure 4.1 Diagram of the post-transformation display in the conservation study.

be so. We can then compare this kind of dyad with one which contains a conserver and a nonconserver. Additionally, because the resolution of disputes is to a greater or lesser degree a function of what is loosely known as social dominance as well as of certainty about the answer, all children were given a task which was supposed to indicate something about the relative dominance of the partners. This task employed the 'Etch-a-Sketch' toy which is like a miniature TV screen containing a drawing stylus that can be guided by two dials: one dial moves the line horizontally and the other dial moves it vertically. The partners took a dial each and were instructed to copy a step-like figure. As pilot tapes had shown, in this situation one of the children tends to take charge and instruct his partner to 'turn', 'stop' and so on. Therefore we employed the (admittedly crude) measure of which child gave the more task-relevant instructions as the index of relative dominance. We also used a story completion task for the same purpose, on the assumption that the suggestion for finishing the story of the more dominant child would tend to be adopted. The procedure in the conservation study was that the experimenter would pose the conservation question after trans-formation, tell the children that they had to agree on *one* answer, and that they should shout 'ready' when they had finished, and then leave the room.

Two kinds of question were asked by means of this design:
(a) does the pairing of nonconservers result in success by virtue of perspective coordination as compared to nonconserver/conserver dyads? (b) does the dyadic behaviour of nonconservers evince the kind

of propositional attitude sketched above? The criteria for (a) were simply the relative amount of post-test improvement in the two groups, on three post-tests over five weeks, and generalization to other forms of conservation; (b) was more problematical. The possible divergence in propositional attitudes between conservers and nonconservers was assessed by three criteria. Firstly it was reasoned that, if the nonconserver's attitude to his judgment is pragmatic-subjective, then which of the two *nonconservation* answers is adopted will be determined by social factors such as which child is more determined to get his own way, that is, by something like dominance. In this case it would be as if the children had been given a task such as deciding on a number between 1 to 10. Given sufficient motivation towards the task, one would expect the dominant child to impose his choice of number on his partner. However in the conserver/nonconserver pairings the conserver should often win the day, irrespective of whether or not he is dominant, because he regards his answer as *true* and his partner's as being *false*. Secondly, if a child regards his own answer as true and his partner's as false he should tend to counter his partner's judgment and win by virtue of this countering. The main index of countering used here was that of the frequency of giving judgments opposite to the partner's judgment. Finally, a child who regards his answer as true and logically so should tend to produce more rule-bound justifications for it. However, if a child's orientation to his judgment is pragmatic-subjective he should produce fewer justifications, and what he does produce should be of a social and situational nature.

Typically the conserver's answer was adopted; thus replicating comparable nonconserver-conserver dyad studies such as those by Miller and Brownwell (1975) and Silverman and Litman (1979). In those few cases where nonconserver pairs did produce conservation answers, this was due to one of the children spontaneously judging conservation *before* the partner had made his judgment. Overall, the evidence for perspective coordination was practically nonexistent, and the degree of post-test gain and generalization after the nonconserver pairings was very slight indeed compared to that of the conserver/nonconserver pairings (see Russell, in press (a) for full details). Although it is difficult to make unqualified statements on the basis of these kinds of data, it is fair to say that cognitive change was not facilitated in the nonconserver dyads.

Turning to the criteria for propositional attitude it could be seen that this lack of facilitation was due to the fact that nonconservation dyad members did not appreciate the fact of cognitive conflict. The child whose incorrect answer was adopted in nonconservation dayads tended ($p < .05$) to be the child who had instructed his partner more on the Etch-a-Sketch task, whereas no such relation was found when it was a conserver whose answer was adopted. This latter (conserver + nonconserver) finding replicated Miller and Brownwell 1975. However, only in the case of the conserver/nonconserver dyads did the winner (i.e. conserver) give more opposing judgments than his partner. This seems paradoxical: how could the 'dominant' child have had his answer adopted in the nonconservation pairings if he did not tend to oppose his partner's judgement? The paradox is resolved by the fact that, as more detailed analysis of the checklists showed, it was not that the *dominant* child won by what he did but rather that the more *compliant* child gave in without any opposition. Quite frequently one saw sequences such as: 'That one's bigger', then hesitation by the partner before he says, 'OK then'; or 'That one', 'That one', 'That one . . . oh we'll take yours'. As regards justifications, these were far less frequent in nonconservers than in conservers. More significantly *all* conservation justifications were in terms of rule-bound principles (reversibility, irrelevance of movement etc.); whereas 10 of the total 24 nonconservation justifications were by reference to pragmatic-situational factors (e.g. 'My brother is good at these and he told me . . .'; 'I got this right when I did it at school'). Indeed some of the nonconservers actually used phenomenal and perspective arguments in *support* of their answers. Two children said 'It *looks* bigger' as a justification. Two said something of the kind . . . 'that one's bigger to you and that one's bigger to me' with the implication being: 'as there is no right answer we may as well pick mine.'

Our data *are* highly interpreted. However, it does not demand much interpretive skill to justify the following claim on the basis of these data: children regard their nonconservation judgments as pragmatic and subjective relative to the way conserving children regard their judgments. But can this notion explain why some nonconservers adopt the conservation answer after mere exposure to it in a session that may last less than 20 seconds and go on to maintain it throughout three post-tests over five weeks? To explain this we would require the additional assumption that the transitional nonconserver is aware that his judgment is subjective-perceptual but that he regards logico-mathematical judgments that are not thus perspective-relative as inherently preferable. Exposure to the correct judgment makes him aware that *it is possible to make objective judgments about length relations*. The speculation is that changes in propositional attitude set the scene for, or canalize, changes in what actual propositions come to be expressed.

Spatial egocentrism

It is in the field of spatial judgments that the cognitive conflict view of dyadic interaction carries most force, because it is here that perspective clashes may be quite literal. Not surprisingly it is spatial tasks that Doise and his associates (Doise *et al.* 1975, Doise and Mugny 1979, Mugny and Doise 1978) have employed to elaborate the conflict of centration model. What motivated our study of allocentric placement was again a deep scepticism about the view that in a situation where two children from the preoperational age range are manoeuvred into adopting different perspectives we have the conditions for conflict-fuelled cognitive change. The important difference between the logic of this and the conservation study was that incorrect responses were not verbal judgments about physical properties but placements (or judgments about placements) of items. Moreover the claim was not being pressed that these placements actually reflect the subjective-pragmatic propositional attitude itself. The assumption was that, as preoperational thought is as it is because of the child's inability to frame the right kind of propositions, then any preoperational phenomenon that does not involve the child in framing propositions is either produced by faulty interpretation of the instructions or by 'performance' errors. (See the review by Helene Borke (1978) for studies showing allocentric abilities in very young children.) This claim will become clearer when the data are discussed. The general relevance of this study to the issue of propositional attitudes was in predicting that reciprocal egocentrism which engenders conflicts of centration does *not* characterize dyadic interaction in spatial tasks between children from the preoperational age range.

Figure 4.2 illustrates the task. As before, the children sat across from each other at the table. To one side was a photograph representing a

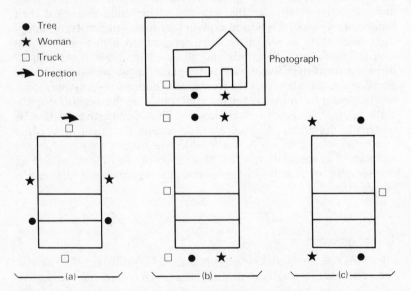

Figure 4.2 Schematic diagram of the allocentric placement task. In the lower portion are three cases of the house facing the child on the left.

lego house with a lego woman and tree stationed in front and a toy truck parked at the side. Before the children on the table were all the pictured items. The house was turned to face one of the children. In the lower portions of the figure the house is facing the child on the left. The children were then told to cooperate in placing the three items (truck, woman, tree) in the same positions that they were in on the photograph. When they had done that the experimenter returned and reoriented the house to face the *other* child and instructed them as previously. Four possible kinds of error were framed on the basis of a pilot study. First there was the standard egocentric error where the child places the items as if the house were facing himself rather than facing his partner. Secondly there was the reverse case of the child placing the items vis-à-vis his partner when the house faces himself – called here 'perspective-other' errors (see Figure 4.2(a) for egocentric and perspective-other errors). Thirdly there were errors that resulted from placing the items in 1:1 correspondence with their representations on the photograph (Figure 4.2(b)). In this case the child would either place items directly below their counterparts (as shown in the upper part of (b)) or in 1:1 correspondence below or beside (in the case of the truck) the house. Finally there were unclassifiable errors (Figure 4.2(c) shows some cases of these). Others might be bizarre responses such as placing items on the roof of the house.

As some previous workers have found when using the more standard technique of photograph selection (Fishbein *et al*. 1972, Houssidas 1965, Laurendau and Pinard 1970), the proportion of errors that were egocentric actually *increased* between the ages of 4 and 8 years. Thus, contrary to Doise's position, the probability of an error being in the egocentric category was *lower* in the preoperational age range: only 26 per cent in the 4- to 5-year-olds and 50 per cent in the 8-year-olds. Perspective-other errors were somewhat less common but took a similar developmental course. Conversely, 1:1 photographic errors became less frequent with age (from 35 per cent of total errors to 6 per cent). Unclassifiable errors were infrequent overall but somewhat more common in the youngest children.

Not only were egocentric errors only one kind among others, but they were explicable as errors of *performance* rather than as indices of a deep epistemic egocentrism. The picture which emerges from considering the relative frequency of the actual placements in the egocentric category was that of children trying to do the right kind of thing but not doing it well enough. They rarely made what is the most obvious egocentric error, that of placing the woman or tree on their own side of the house when it was facing their partner. In the five cases where this error was made it was very clear from the child's conversation with his partner that he thought the experimenter expected them to ignore the house's direction. Secondly, what of the substantial proportion of perspective-other errors? Surely the parsimonious interpretation of both kinds of perspective error ('egocentric' errors could be referred to as 'perspective-self') would be the claim that they simply reflect tendencies to put the truck the wrong side of the house, to reverse woman and tree etc., which happen to be somewhat more pronounced when the house is facing away from the error-maker. We did not test anyone over the age of 9 years, but I am sure that such errors would not be unknown in an adult population. Additionally, the dyads seem to believe – despite what we said to them – that speed was of the essence, thus creating the perfect conditions for performance errors.

Conflict of centration was assessed by recording the incidence of one child countering a placement or judgment of his partner and the resistance of this counter by the child. The resulting profile was not that of two spatially egocentric children coming into conflict over placements. Quite simply the egocentric responder did not contest his placement: he passively accepted counters of it and rarely countered correct allocentric placements. But the picture was entirely different for the children who made 1:1 photographic errors. Counters of these *were* resisted – sometimes hotly – in 50 per cent of cases. Here at least the children seemed to have been adopting a radically different construal of the task from the allocentric construal. Indeed these children may have been adopting a topological conception of spatial location in terms of proximity and spatial succession (see Piaget and Inhelder 1956).

In fact some primitive tendency towards 1:1 correspondence may be responsible for the apparently 'egocentric' errors in the three-mountains task where the child selects his own photograph when asked to find that of what another can see: here the child is selecting a photograph where the items are in 1:1 correspondence with the modelled items. As to why egocentric errors proportionally increase with age, it is possible to consider this, as I have argued elsewhere (Russell, in press (b)), as a form of 'growth error' determined by the second phase of rapid development of the frontal cortex during this age period (Luria 1973), given that the frontal cortex may control egocentric responding in primates (Pohl 1973).

But explaining how the errors come to be made is not our major concern here. What relevance to the issue of propositional attitudes is there in the finding that the child's spatial judgments vis-à-vis another child's perspective were essentially allocentric, apart from an early tendency towards a topological interpretation of the instructions? The relevance arises from the consideration that, if the child's orientation to his judgments is, let us say, subjective in the sense of being perspective-relative, this not only fails to exclude the possibility that he should be able to appreciate other perspectives, but actually suggests that this appreciation of perspectives is part and parcel of the kind of propositional attitude which we have been considering. His problem, on the present account, is that he is *too ready* to accept 'perspectivism' and believes that 'objective' facts about the physical world should indeed be judged on the perspectivist pattern. Of course such a view may appear needlessly paradoxical and even to go directly against the tide of developmental studies which have plotted the slow and painful increment in 'perspective-taking' abilities with age as related to moral development (Fehr 1978), individual differences (Light 1979) and general cognitive level (Asher 1979). I merely wish to state – because I do not have space to argue the proposition – that perspective-taking studies may well be measuring something other than the ability to, as it were, 'get inside another's head'. There is, after all, another theoretical framework which regards the child as developing away from a primordial self-other empathy (Hoffman 1976) and fusion with the other's consciousness (Werner and Kaplan 1963).

Transitivity

The previous studies both demonstrated that the incorrect child is less certain of his judgment than the correct child (c.f. Scott Miller's copious studies of certainty in conservation, e.g. Miller 1973) and will typically not contest his judgment against the correct one nor justify it logically. The first of our dyadic studies of transitivity reinforced this finding as a kind of spin-off from its main aim, which was to examine the issue of premise memory (see Russell 1981). In this task dyads cooperated on a transitive measurement problem ($A > B, B = C, \therefore A > C$). The room contained a tower of small lego bricks on the floor (A) and one of large wooden bricks on a table (C); and the dyad was given a stick (B) the same height as the table tower with which to measure. The incorrectly ($C > A$) inferring children were less likely to justify their answers spontaneously, and almost inevitably gave way when their partners produced the correct answer. However, other factors suggested that the incorrect answer was not a mere performance slip. First, a separate study had shown that a third of incorrect inferrers will, when asked, justify their incorrect inference by reference to the *correct* premises; and in the present study 15 per cent of incorrect inferrers spontaneously did likewise (though mostly to the experimenter). Moreover, nearly 70 per cent of the incorrect children who were challenged by their correct partners reiterated their answers. All this makes it difficult to extract any conclusions about the incorrect inferrer's propositional attitude. On the one hand he is uncertain of the judgment relative to the correct inferrer [other studies have shown the logical necessity with which the transitive inferrer regards his judgment (Miller *et al*. 1977; Somerville *et al*. 1979)]. But on the other hand it appears that incorrect *strategies* have to be implicated in some way. The terms 'subjective' and 'pragmatic' are too strong to describe the apparent propositional attitude, and yet it does not appear that the child regards his as *the* answer in the way that the transitive inferrer typically does.

We carried out a further study of transitivity in an effort directly to encourage perspective clashes. Here, as before, two children faced each other across a table on which there was a large cardboard sheet this time. Before each child was a black, vertical (to his view) line, one of which was a little longer than the other. They were instructed to cooperate in the drawing (with a pen on a piece of paper stuck temporarily to the cardboard) of a line intermediate in length between the two lines. Each was told to 'make sure the line is longer/shorter than the line on your own side of the table'. To aid them they were given a cardboard strip on which they could mark the extent of each line as well as rule the to-be-drawn line.

At present the checklists have yet to be analysed in any systematic way. But one conclusion is clear: there were a number of ways in which children failed (drawing a line before measuring the original lines, drawing a line equal to one of them, inappropriate marking on the strip etc.) but none of them involved an 'egocentric' mismatch. By this I mean a situation in which each child tries to draw a long or short line merely to ensure that he has fulfilled his part of the instruction. For this reason there were no perspective clashes. There were cases where children happily drew *two* lines in this way but none in which they tried to end up with one line on this principle. The only clashes we witnessed were tugs-of-war over the felt-tip marker. There was, however, evidence of what could be described as a pragmatic orientation to the task on the part of the younger children. They tended first to draw a line, sometimes freehand, that they estimated to be somewhere between the two lengths, then make some rough comparisons with each of the original lines, and finally add to or scribble out a little from the drawn line. Unlike the older children who could not extract the correct measurement procedure, they were perfectly happy with their productions. The younger ones did not appear to be distinguishing between rough estimation and an accuracy that was founded on an appropriate procedure. The older children who failed did appreciate this difference and they were dissatisfied. This is comparable with the finding of Harris and Singleton (1977) that 4-year-old children will rely on their own perceptual *estimations* of the relative size of towers sufficiently separated as to make such estimates unreliable, whereas 6-year-olds will either say nothing or that they are unable to judge. Harris also showed that the younger children do nevertheless realize that side-by-side comparisons are more accurate. There is a tenuous analogy here with our finding that incorrect inferrers will tend to adopt the correct inference when presented with it.

Class inclusion

In this final dyadic task our aim was not to pair children whose strategies were likely to be both wrong in order to see if this produced perspective coordination via cognitive conflict. Instead, the rationale was to pair children whose approach to the problem was preoperational but in a situation in which they could both be *partially correct*. Would this partial correctness lead to complete correctness through a kind of coordination that did not necessarily involve conflict, or would the dyad adopt some infralogical strategy as a pragmatic compromise (rather as the younger children had done on the previous task)?

The problem was one of class inclusion. Six pencils were placed before the dyad: three yellow and three green (Russell, in press (c)). Each child was instructed in turn. One was told to 'take more yellow pencils than [the partner]'. The other child was told to 'take more pencils altogether than [the partner]'. Thus, the first child should finish up with two yellow pencils and the second with one yellow and three green. To produce jointly a correct solution here neither child need understand the class inclusion principle (as the term is employed by Piaget at least). The 'more yellow' child has to focus exclusively on the subclass and there is no need to cognize the relation of subclass of yellow pencils to the total class. Conversely the child choosing 'more altogether' need pay no attention to the 2 subclasses: he has to ensure that he ends up with at least 4 pencils, by focussing on the class. However, we did perhaps have a somewhat uneven division of labour in that there is only one way in which the 'more yellow' child can succeed, but a number of ways in which the 'more altogether' child can do so. Success must therefore come through negotiation but with the 'more yellow' child being more responsible for this success. Clashes of perspective could come about either by the 'more altogether' child ignoring the other child's demands, or by the 'more yellow' child wanting *all* the yellow pencils.

I shall only mention data for the children who failed the class-inclusion pre-test. As regards success of outcome first of all, the equal sharing of the pencils was very much the predominant strategy of the younger children: all the yellows for one child and all the greens for the other. Two thirds of the 4.5 to 5.5 years age-group did this and (as in the drawing task) with evident confidence in their correctness. Of the oldest children (in the 7.6 to 8.5 year age-group) 44 per cent of dyads shared the pencils. Although there was a steady increase in correct outcomes throughout the age range, equal sharing was the predominant outcome overall. The propositional attitude which might have been producing such an outcome is again that of satisfaction with something that is just about right and not particularly unfair to either partner, which we saw in the drawing task. 'Pragmatism' is again an appropriate term.

Turning to the question of inter-child conflict, there were no cases of the 'more altogether' child just picking more pencils irrespective of their colour. He or she invariably 'took perspective' sufficiently to take all the greens, at least initially. Conflict was engendered through the 'more yellow' child wanting to have *all* the yellow pencils, and much less frequently by the 'more altogether' child pressing the third yellow pencil on his partner. Thus, conflict was not a function of the adoption of what could be called different perspectives, but rather of the consistency with which children pursued the half-each strategy. Within 'conflictual behaviour' we included (a) countering, (b) snatching a pencil, and (c) resisting the attempt to take a pencil. Twenty-eight per cent of children showed some form of this; and it was over twice as pronounced in the 'more yellow' children.

However, the notion of pragmatic propositional attitude does not fit terribly well with the conflict data. The 'more yellow' child's insistence on having all the yellow pencils often resulted in some veritable battles, and we cannot lightly dismiss the charge that 'more' may have meant 'equal' (as well as 'less'!) for some children − and this despite the care that was taken with the instructions (each child had to repeat his instructions correctly before the trial began).

What of the 38 per cent of these class inclusion *failers* who ended up with the correct division? Do we not here have evidence for something like the Doise viewpoint that two heads are better than one if the two heads are located at different logical perspectives? In order to answer this question we tested children *individually* on the same kind of task. They were presented with a model policeman and a model fireman either side of a table with six plastic bricks between them, three of which were yellow and three green. The instructions were to give more yellow bricks to the policeman and more bricks altogether to the fireman. Twenty-seven percent of the group (who had been distributed in similar age-groupings to dyads in the 4−8 year age range) succeeded. If we compare dyads with individuals there was a slight overall superiority on dyadic performance, but it was one which fell well short of statistical significance. As before, the predominant incorrect strategy was equal sharing, and again the younger the child the more likely it was that he or she would respond swiftly and with evident certainty. Almost all the children in the oldest group who were incorrect knew they were incorrect and yet did not know what they could do about it.

Understanding logical distinctions

The dyad studies provide some suggestive support for the notion that preoperational thought expresses subjective, pragmatic . . . etc. propositional attitudes. But the question has yet to be tackled of how the child is able to change his propositional attitude towards 'concrete operational' judgments to one that is objective, necessary, general and stable. In order to work towards a solution to this problem I would want to make the working assumptions that the child *potentially appreciates* something about how necessity and objectivity grow out of the conceptual system, and that interaction with others brings him round to the application of necessary and objective propositional attitudes to his own logico-mathematical judgments. Such a change is a necessary condition for the acquisition of what Vygotsky called the 'scientific concepts'.

But where does this appreciation of necessity come from in the first place? Actually, I do not have to answer this to make the point about propositional attitude change. But I might say that we can regard (with Vygotsky (1934) and Baldwin (1908)) the child's notion of necessity as emerging from his being led to 'reflect' on the structure of the conceptual system as expressed in language, as an alternative to the Piagetian viewpoint that the notion of necessity is a *result* of the process of equilibration.

We were searching, therefore, for a basic level of competence in cognizing the logical characteristics which distinguish between 'preoperational' and 'concrete operational' modes of thinking. It is this basic competence of which the child becomes progressively more aware. The criterion we used to assess this competence was teachability; in fact we asked whether a child understands what an adult is talking about when the adult tells the child that some judgments must be true no matter what whereas some only *may* be true. I want here to briefly mention three teaching studies which we carried out: (a) on necessarily true versus contingent judgments; (b) on absolute versus relative, general versus particular, objective versus subjective, causal versus intentional judgments; and (c) on necessarily *false* versus contingent judgments.

The rationale and procedures for all three studies were identical. Thirty pairs of sentences were presented to the child (e.g. 'That rose is a flower' plus 'That rose is a present'), one of the sentences was repeated, and then the child had to make the appropriate response for either necessity or contingency. We then plotted errors and trials to criterion (9 out of 10 correct in a run, or 30 trials) in the usual manner. In order to study the efficacy of teaching the principles on which these distinctions rested, we compared the performance of a 'teaching' group with that of a 'non-teaching' group. Also, in order to make the situation as gamelike as possible the sentences were spoken by a 'talking teddy';[3] that is, they were recorded on a cassette and played through a speaker in the bear's head. The child sat in front of the bear and between them (in addition to the experimenter) was a response box on the table. This consisted of a metal box with a light on top and a lever at each side which could be depressed. The child's task was to respond by depressing either the left or the right-hand lever, depending on which sentence had been repeated. A correct choice made the light come on and a chime sound in the box. On all studies the children were grouped into three age levels: 5-to 6-year-olds; 7- to 8-year-olds; 9- to 10-year-olds.

In the non-teaching condition the child was told that his task was to

[3] I am glad to acknowledge my debt to Peter Lloyd, who used a similar creature in his work on communicative perspective-taking in young children.

find which sentence worked which of the levers, and that he had to find the 'clue' about the difference. The child had to repeat both sentences after the pair had been presented, and was then asked how he thought they were different. When one was repeated by the bear and the child had responded, the experimenter drew his attention to its being a 'left' or 'right' kind of sentence. In the teaching condition of the necessary/contingent experiment the child was told that it was a game about finding the difference between 'things that must always/had to be true and things which may or may not be true'. The child was also told which lever was for the necessary and which lever was for the contingent sentences. After each pair was presented the child was asked which one he thought had to be true and which he thought did not. One of the sentences was repeated and the experimenter told the child to respond appropriately. Then, irrespective of his choice, the experimenter explained why he had been correct or incorrect with reference to the actual sentences.

We separated the necessary/contingent sentences into five relatively distinct sets of 30 pairs as follows: (1) *definitionally necessary* sentences were those in which the predicate held by virtue of the subject's definition (e.g. 'John's dad is a man' versus 'John's dad is a farmer'); (2) *situationally necessary* sentences were those where a description of a situation had to be true (e.g. 'There are people in the crowd' versus 'There are children in the crowd'); (3) *relationally necessary* sentences were those within which two terms necessarily had to be related in the way expressed (e.g. 'My green shirt is the same colour as my green tie' versus 'My green shirt is the same material as my green tie'); (4) *informationally empty* sentences were similar to the definitional ones, except that the necessity was less strong because it was possible though unlikely for the negation to hold (e.g. 'That zebra has stripes' versus 'That zebra has babies'); (5) *negated tautologies* were those where the predicate was the equivalent in negative form of the characterizing adjective in the subject (e.g. 'The fat man is not thin' versus 'The fat man is not well').

The main findings of this study were that even the youngest group (mean age 5.10 years) clearly benefited from the teaching; and that what improved with age was the ability to benefit from teaching rather than the ability to find the 'clue' about the difference (a significant interaction between age levels and teaching/non-teaching). As regards necessity versus contingency, therefore, the child in the late preoperational age range at least (4-year-olds did not adapt to the experimental procedure) seems to possess a basic competence in cognizing such distinctions as elaborated in speech. There was a very steep increment in performance in the teaching group between the first two age levels and hardly any improvement between the latter two (a 'floor' effect may have been operating for some subgroups). Thus the ability to benefit from such instruction appears to be something that improves during the preoperational/concrete operational transition period. Moreover, although the discernment of when a necessary or tautologous truth as implied *by an instruction* may not be manifest until adolescence (Osherson and Markman 1978), the cognizing of a speaker's description of this logical property seems to be present long before then.

However, to distinguish preoperational from operational propositional attitudes on the ground of necessity/contingency alone is somewhat crude because these distinctions subsume and, to some extent, grow out of others. We studied these finer-grain distinctions next. I hope the descriptions carry their justifications: (1) *objective-subjective* (e.g. 'That liquorice sweet is my last' versus 'That liquorice sweet is my favourite'); (2) *general-particular* (e.g. 'Zebras have legs' versus 'Zebras have stripes'); (3) *absolute-relative* (e.g. 'The bat is a wooden one' versus 'The bat is a long one'); (4) *causal-intentional* (e.g. 'The rain made us wet' versus 'The rain made us stay home'). The only difference in procedure between this and the previous experiment was that there was no real attempt to describe the general demands of the task in the teaching condition before presentation began. Subjects were different children in the same age groupings.

The results also were similar. Teaching was highly successful even in the youngest age group, and what improved with age (between the first two age levels at least) was the ability to benefit from teaching rather than to extract the basis of the distinction without teaching. In contrast to the necessary/contingent subgroups some distinctions were much easier to teach than others: teaching of causal/intentional and general/particular was more successful than that of the other two types. This was, to some extent, because the other two distinctions were more difficult to put into words; but then the difficulty of teaching is not likely to be *contingently* related to that of learning. For it is well to consider that in some languages there is a single word for both learning and teaching. Sutton (1979) has shown how the lack of such a differentiation in the Russian language must bear on our reading of Vygotsky.

Our final study using this methodology was an exact parallel to the first, except that it was sentences that were all necessarily *false* rather than necessarily true which were contrasted with the contingent ones. Here are some examples in the same five groupings as before: 'The cat is an insect' versus 'The cat is a mother'; 'The man in the car is walking' versus 'The man in the car is waving'; 'The boy who is six is younger than the boy who is two' versus 'The boy who is six is fairer than the boy who is two'; 'These cups of tea are to eat' versus 'These cups of tea are for sale'; 'This water is not wet' versus 'This water is not dirty'.

The same story can be told about the results except that this was a far easier task overall than the other two. Children's perception of a priori nonsense is very good indeed. But is this not what we would expect, given that the child is far more likely to focus on what is verbally funny than what is verbally obvious? Very often the children would laugh at the sentences, although this laughter was by no means a guarantee of successful discrimination. We are dealing here with a very primitive competence: the ability to discriminate between what is conceptually inappropriate and conceptually appropriate with the corresponding propositional attitudes of the playful and the serious. Here is a typical example of the early appearance of this ability. Chukovsky (1976) tells how at 23 months his daughter came up to him 'looking mischievous and embarassed at the same time . . . She cried to me even when she was at some distance from where I sat: 'Daddy, doggie-miaow' − that is she reported to me the sensational and to her incorrect view that doggie, instead of barking, miaows. And she burst out into somewhat encouraging, somewhat artificial laughter, inviting me, too, to laugh at this invention' (601). Piaget's (1951) famous observations show still earlier forms of incongruity humour in object play.

Reluctant as I am to burden the world with yet another theory of the cognitive function of humour (and being still more reluctant to claim any originality for it), might it not be that, by appreciating the conceptually inappropriate via that most distinctive propositional attitude of the humorous, the child − maybe even from the time of his first peekaboos − is led to construct the category of the appropriate and eventually that of the objectively true? At least one theorist of humour (Rothbart 1977) has claimed that jokes share the property of suggesting incongruity.

So by a peculiar detour we are brought back to our starting point: that of conflict models of cognitive development. For implicit in the preceding analysis is the view that the child has to appreciate the contradictory, indeed conflictual, nature of the relationships between certain propositional attitudes − that the child must see the basic opposition, for example, between the necessary and contingent, the objective and the subjective. And out of this realization of conflict should evolve the higher knowledge that notions can be located somewhere on a continuum between these two extremes (e.g. 'Was it a *good* film?'). I am suggesting that the child's sense of humour and playfulness is the first move in a process whereby conceptual congruity is sculpted by the chisel of conceptual incongruity.

Of course Piaget's conflict of centration model is hardly uninfluenced by the Hegelian dialectic,[4] and the previous remarks on the importance of the sense of contradiction in cognitive development express the same source. (See Lawler 1975 for an informative analysis

---

[4] In his recent book on Piagetian theory Charles Brainerd (1978) makes the important point that Piaget's earliest concern with the part-whole problem and his resultant concept of 'structures-of-the-whole' was framed by Hegelian philosophy.

of the relationship between Hegelian contradiction and Piagetian theory.) But the sense of contradiction which is here being emphasized is not that between propositions but between attitudes to these propositions.

References

Acredolo, C. and Acredolo, L.P. 1979: Identity, compensation, and conservation. *Child Development* **50**, 203–17.

Asher, S.R. 1979: Referential communication. In G.J. Whitehurst and B.J. Zimmerman (eds.), *The functions of language and cognition*. London: Academic Press.

Baldwin, J.M. 1901–5: *The dictionary of philosophy and psychology*. New York: Macmillan.

— 1908: *Thought and things*, vol. 2, *Experimental logic*. New York: Swann and Sonnenschein. 1908.

Borke, H. 1978: Piaget's view of social interaction and the theoretical construct of empathy. In L.S. Siegel and C.J. Brainerd (eds.), *Alternatives to Piaget*. New York: Academic Press.

Braine, M.D.S. and Shanks, B.L. 1965a: The conservation of shape property and a proposal about the origin of conservation. *Canadian J. Psychology* **194**, 197–207.

— 1965b: The development of the conservation of size. *J. Verbal Learning and Verbal Behaviour* **4**, 227–42.

Brainerd, C.J. 1978: *Piaget's theory of intelligence*. New Jersey: Prentice-Hall.

Bruner, J.S. et al. 1966: *Studies in cognitive growth*. London: Wiley.

Chukovsky, K. 1976: The sense of nonsense verse. In J.S. Bruner, A. Jolly and K. Sylva (eds.), *Play: its role in development and evolution*. Harmondsworth: Penguin.

Doise, W. 1978: *Groups and individuals*. Cambridge: Cambridge University Press.

Doise, W. and Mugny, G. 1979: Individual and collective centrations in cognitive development. *European J. Social Psychology* **9**, 105–7.

Doise, W., Mugny, G. and Perret-Clermont, A.N. 1975: Social interaction and the development of cognitive operations. *European J. Social Psychology* **5**, 367–83.

Donaldson, M. 1978: *Children's minds*. Glasgow: Fontana.

Fehr, L.A. 1978: Methodological inconsistencies in the measurement of spatial perspective-taking ability: a cause for concern. *Human Development* **21**, 302–15.

Fishbein, H.D.S., Lewis, S. and Keiffer, K. 1972: Children's understanding of spatial relations: co-ordination of perspectives. *Developmental Psychology* **7**, 21–33.

Hamlyn, D.W. 1978: *Experience and the growth of understanding*. London: Routledge & Kegan Paul.

Harris, P.L. and Singleton, W.M. 1977: Children's understanding of measurement. In A.M. Lesgold, J.W. Pellegrino, S.D. Fokkema and R. Glaser (eds.), *Cognitive psychology and instruction*. London: Plenum.

Hoffman, M.L. 1976: Developmental synthesis of affect and cognition and its implications for altruistic motivation. *Developmental Psychology* **11**, 607–22.

Houssidas, L. 1965: Coordination of perspectives in children. *Archiv fuer die Gesamte Psychologie* **117**, 319–26.

Klahr, D. and Wallace, J.G. 1976: *Cognitive development: an information processing view*. Hillsdale, N.J.: Erlbaum Associates.

Klausmeier, J.H. 1979: *Cognitive learning and development*. London: Harper & Row.

Laurendau, M. and Pinard, A. 1970: *The development of the concept of space in the child*. New York: International Universities Press.

Lawler, J. 1975: Dialectical philosophy and developmental psychology: Hegel and Piaget. *Human Development* **18**, 1–17.

Light, P.H. 1979: *The growth of social sensitivity*. Cambridge: Cambridge University Press.

Light, P.H., Buckingham, N. and Robbins, A.H. 1979: The conservation task in an interactional setting. *British J. Psychology* **49**, 304–10.

Luria, A.R. 1973: *The working brain*. Harmondsworth: Penguin.

Miller, S.A. 1973: Contradiction, surprise, and cognitive change: the effects of disconfirmation of belief on conservers and nonconservers. *J. Experimental Child Psychology* **15**, 47–62.

—— 1979: Candy is dandy and also quicker: a further nonverbal study of conservation of number. *J. Genetic Psychology* **134**, 15–21.

Miller, S.A. and Brownwell, C.A. 1975: Peers, persuasion and Piaget: dyadic interaction between conservers and nonconservers. *Child Development* **46**, 992–7.

Miller, S.A., Brownwell, C.A. and Zukier, H. 1977: Cognitive certainty in children: effects of concept, developmental level and method of assessment. *Developmental Psychology* **13**, 236–45.

Mugny, C. and Doise, W. 1978: Socio-conflict and structure of individual and collective performances. *European J. Social Psychology* **8**, 181–92.

Osherson, D. and Markman, E. 1978: Language and the ability to evaluate contradictions and tautologies. *Cognition* **7**, 13–27.

Piaget, J. 1950: *The psychology of intelligence*. London: Routledge & Kegan Paul.

—— 1951: *Play, dreams and imitation in children*. London: Routledge & Kegan Paul.

Piaget, J. and Inhelder, B. 1956: *The child's conception of space*. London: Routledge & Kegan Paul.

Pohl, W. 1973: Dissociation of spatial discrimination deficits following frontal and parietal lesions in the monkey. *J. Comparative and Physiological Psychology* **82**, 227–39.

Rose, S.A. and Blank, M. 1974: The potency of context in children's cognition: an illustration through conservation. *Child Development* **45**, 499–502.

Rothbart, M.K. 1977: Psychological approaches to the study of humour. In A.J. Chapman and H.C. Foot (eds.), *It's a funny thing humour*. Oxford: Pergamon.

Russell, J. 1975: The interpretation of conservation instructions by five-year-old children. *J. Child Psychology and Psychiatry* **16**, 233–44.

— 1976: The nonconservation of area: do children succeed where adults fail? *Developmental Psychology* **12**, 367–8.

— 1978: *The acquisition of knowledge*. London: Macmillan.

— 1979: Nonverbal and verbal judgments of length invariance by young children. *Br. J. Psychology* **70**, 313–17.

— 1981: Children's memory for the premises in a transitive measurement task assessed by elicited and spontaneous justifications. *J. Experimental Child Psychology* **31**, 300–9.

— in press (a): Cognitive conflict, transmission and justification: conservation attainment through dyadic interaction. *J. Genetic Psychology*.

— in press (b): Why 'socio-cognitive conflict' may be impossible: the status of egocentric errors in the dyadic performance of a spatial task. *Educational Psychology*.

— in press (c): Dyadic interaction in a logical reasoning problem requiring inclusion ability. *Child Development*.

Ryle, G. 1929–30: Are there propositions? *Proceedings of the Aristotelian Society* **30**, 1–20.

Silverman, K.W. and Litman, R. 1979: Two tests of Piaget's equilibration model: a replication and an extension. *Int. J. Behavioural Development* **2**, 225–33.

Sinha, C. and Carabine, B. 1980: Interactions between lexis and discourse in conservation and comprehension tasks. *J. Child Language* **8**, 109–29.

Somerville, S.C., Hadkinson, B.A. and Greenberg, C. 1979: Two levels of inferential behaviour in young children. *Child Development* **50**, 119–31.

Sutton, A. 1979: Vygotsky and the dialectical method. Paper presented to the annual conference of the Developmental Section of the British Psychological Society, University of Southampton.

Vygotsky, L.S. 1934: *Thought and language*. Reprinted 1962, Cambridge, Mass.: MIT Press.

Weldall, K. and Poborca, B. 1980: Conservation without conversation? An alternative nonverbal paradigm for assessing conservation of liquid quantity. *British J. Psychology* **71**, 117–35.

Werner, H. 1948: *The comparative psychology of mental development*. Chicago: Follett.
Werner, H. and Kaplan, B. 1963: *Symbol formation*. London: Wiley.

5

The contribution of nonvisual communication systems and language to knowing oneself

Cathy Urwin

> Seeing comes before words. The child looks and recognizes before it can speak . . . . Soon after we can see we are aware that we can also be seen. The eye of the other combines with our own eye to make it fully credible that we are part of the visible world.
>
> John Berger, *Ways of seeing*

The nature of preverbal communication has recently roused a good deal of interest amongst developmental psychologists, the impetus for which appears to have come from two directions. On the one hand, a new wave of mother-infant interaction studies has grown out of empirical and theoretical objections to Attachment Theory and to traditional approaches to socialization (see Bullowa 1979 and Schaffer 1977 for representative examples of work in this tradition). This has been parallelled by a line of investigation more concerned with the origins of language, and which has argued that language as a system of communication is grounded upon modes of relating already functioning prior to speech (see, for example, Bates *et al.* 1975, and the collection edited by Lock, 1978).

Though the opening quotation was not taken from either of these research traditions, it shares with them three assumptions which I hope to question in this chapter. Firstly, it assumes the primacy or dominance of the visual system as the means through which the child comes to know the world and other people in it. Secondly, it implies that language is built on what the child already knows. Thirdly, it assumes a unified preexistent subject, which is aware of itself before it is aware that it is seen by others, and which is identifiable with a particular 'point' in space. To anticipate a future objection with a question addressed to Berger's statement: What and where is the source of the 'I' which combines with the 'Eye' of the other, and how can we conceptualize its development?

In the developmental work, the priority implicitly or explicitly assumed for vision is evident from the amount of emphasis which has been placed on the role of visually-based communication systems in the regulation of mutual attention and in the signalling of communicative intent. Thus, despite their differing priorities, both the mother-infant interaction studies and the studies explicitly concerned with the origins of language have concentrated on a strikingly similar range of phenomena. These include the play exchanges observable between mothers and infants in the first three months, in which eye-contact is given a central role in the regulation of the tempo of the interaction (Brazelton *et al*. 1974, Stern 1974, Bruner 1977, Trevarthen *et al*. 1975); the role of gaze direction in the monitoring of mutual attention to objects, a capacity which is said to provide a basis for establishing a shared frame of reference (Bruner 1977, Collis and Schaffer 1975); and the use of gestures, such as indicative pointing and reaching in demand, which, along with offering objects and 'give and take' games, first emerges in the last quarter of the first year (Bates *et al*. 1975, Sugarman-Bell 1978, Trevarthen and Hubley 1978). Initially accompanied by distinctive prosodic marking, gesturing persists once the child begins to use words, and conveys the particular communicative effects which he or she intends (Bates *et al*. 1975, Bruner 1978, Carter 1978, Dore 1975). This persistence is taken as evidence for continuity between preverbal and verbal communication, and as support for the general assumption that the 'very nature' of the child's prelinguistic communicative system may be such as to 'aid the passage from prespeech communication through to language' (Bruner 1978).

While the use of gesture and other nonverbal communicative means is assumed to provide the origins of illocutionary force in language, (Bates *et al*. 1975, Bruner 1978), the notion that language is built on what the child already 'knows' is drawn in to account for the propositional component and for the origins of semantics. This notion is articulated explicitly in the principle of cognitive primacy, which proposes that 'language development is guided by and is the result of cognitive development' (Snow 1977a). It generally takes the form of appealing to Piaget's theory of a general representational process to account for, say, what 'lifts' the child out of preverbal communication into language proper (Bates *et al*. 1975, Dore 1978, Sinclair 1971), the ability to use words in an arbitrary sense (Bloom 1973, Morehead and Morehead 1974, Sinclair 1971), and the origins of the conceptual relations underlying the first word combinations (Bowerman 1973, Brown 1973, Edwards 1973). From this position, the task of language acquisition thus becomes one which involves grafting selected aspects of the input onto preexisting conceptual structures, such as concepts of agents and objects and the relations between them.

As far as the origins of the subject are concerned, much of this developmental work adheres to the prevailing ideology of western psychology as a whole, which preserves a distinction between the individual within and the social world outside. Following in the tradition of the *cogito*, this assumes a unified, rational subject which either exists prior to entry into society, or which is formed over the course of development such that the individual becomes the source of all perception and experience. This position is perhaps most obvious in the ways in which the problems of accounting for subjectivity and knowledge of other people have been disposed of by proposing that infants are 'born social' (Ainsworth *et al.* 1974), or that they possess an innate capacity for 'intersubjectivity' (Trevarthen 1975). It is also apparent in the way the cognitive primacy hypothesis, described above, has been applied. Less obviously perhaps, it is implicit in Piaget's own theory, since this neglects the important sense in which rationality is itself a social product (Venn and Walkerdine 1978, Ingleby 1980a). Affectivity and social interaction do, of course, contribute to cognitive development in Piaget's theory. But the relationship is entirely functional; they provide the 'energetics' or speed up the necessary coordinations, but they do not enter into the structure of cognition itself.

Limitations in this philosophical stance have recently been recognized by a number of investigators who have followed what Ingleby (1980a) has described as a shift from an Enlightenment to Romantic world view, which recognizes that it is not in the nature of the individual but in the 'ensemble of social relations' (Marx) that the human essence resides (e.g. Lock 1980, Newson and Newson 1976, Newson 1978, Shotter 1974, 1978). Drawing particularly on G.H. Mead's (1934) theory of the social construction of the self and the writings of Vygotsky (1962, 1966), these investigators have argued that both intelligent activity and ourselves as subjects are produced and perpetuated through relationships with other people. Developing a new approach to the study of socialization and language acquisition in this light, they stress that the particular significance of the early negotiations and shared activities between parent and child lies in their providing opportunities for establishing such specifically 'human' qualities as the capacity for intentionality, the origins of agency and meaning, and the child's ability to interact on the basis of rules.

This appears to provide the beginnings of an account both of the social production of subjectivity and of rationality. However, the account is severely limited by the fact that the chief mechanism put forward is that of the mother 'interpreting' the child's actions. These interpretations are said to play a crucial role in helping the child learn the significance of his or her actions, and in providing a 'structure of motives' (Shotter 1978) which is then in some way internalized. As in Mead's theory from which these ideas are derived, this kind of process may contribute to the production of socially appropriate behaviour; but it cannot by itself account for reflexiveness and conscious subjectivity. Since the initial status of the child's actions is discounted or left unexplored, the only recourse is to assume that subjectivity is already formed, or that it develops elsewhere. (See Ingleby 1980b and Giddens 1976 for similar objections to Mead's theory.)

Both the cognitive primacy hypothesis as usually formulated and the assumption that subjectivity is pregiven present crucial barriers to our fully appreciating the relations between different spheres of development in the child's acquisition of language. The notion of cognitive primacy is an example of a more general view of the relation between language and thought which assumes that language is a 'reflection' of thought, or that the two processes are separate but in some way isomorphic. If the relationship is posed in this way, then it becomes very difficult to conceive of the acquisition of language playing a progressive role in the child's thinking, since the opposite of the cognitive primacy hypothesis implies that the child gets 'something' from 'nothing'. Paradoxically, the same problem applies in reverse with the linguistic relativity hypothesis (Slobin 1979, Cromer 1974), which proposes that language is the 'mould' into which thought is poured.

The assumption of a preformed rational subject precludes an account of the development of the totality of cognition as a social product. It is perhaps for this reason that none of the approaches which aim to give social processes a guiding role in the development of language have been able to deal with the question of cognitive change within the same account. Bruner (1978), for example, bypasses the problem altogether, and restricts his attention to describing changes in communicative function. Alternatively, elsewhere he makes uneasy references to Piagetian schemes, which reinforces the traditional distinction between 'social' and 'cognitive' development (Bruner *et al.* 1979). Other investigators regard cognition as a separate topic which may be dealt with at a later point, (Lock 1980), or admit that the reconciliation of cognitive and social processes is a problem which has yet to be solved (Newson, pers. comm.).

If we are to investigate the possibility that, apart from directing behaviour and aiding memory, language may actually play a useful or influential role in the child's thinking, then it may be necessary to find some way of realigning the traditional conception of the thought-language relationship. And if we are to develop an approach which allows social interaction into the structuring of cognition, such that it may contribute to the propositional component of language as well as to its communicative function, then it is necessary to view the individual subject/social world relationship in a new way.

On both these counts, perhaps the most promising developments have occurred outside empirical developmental psychology, in the work of the psychoanalyst Jacques Lacan and in the branch of linguistics known as semiotics, which deals with the workings of systems of signs. What is so striking about this work is that it recognizes as problematic exactly what psychology takes for granted, and poses many of its traditional questions from the other way up. That is to say, rather than assuming the pregiven subject as the starting point, and the 'individual' as the atom of explanation, it gives priority to specific social practices, as perpetuated through systems of signification, and regards subjectivity not as preexistent but as constituted through the appropriation of signs. This view is espoused most explicitly by Lacan (1949, 1966, 1973) for whom the 'I' of the *cogito* is illusory or forever unattainable. He argues that it is only in and through signs, which are by definition social, that conscious subjectivity is possible. That is, it is only through signs which represent things but which are not those things in themselves that we can ever achieve autonomy over immediate experience. And since we can only be conscious of ourselves with reference to something which is not-self, for Lacan conscious subjectivity is founded upon the 'I' – 'You' dialectic in language, which defines subjects by their mutual opposition.

In developing a theory as to how this occurs, Lacan uses both psychoanalytic concepts and formulations drawn from Jakobson's theory of the nature of the linguistic code (Jakobson and Halle 1956). This stresses that the processes of selection and combination are fundamental to the formation of linguistic signs, and that movement through the code operates not simply through a relationship between 'thought' and 'language' (as in the 'reflection' view described above) but also through thought's relationship to itself, set into play through relations between signs (see Lemaire 1977). He uses the principle of *metaphor* to refer to contiguous, synchronic relationships, or the vertical aspects of the code, and *metonymy* to refer to the diachronic aspects, or the successive, linearly progressive relationships between signs. (See Walkerdine, this volume.)

For Lacan the energetics for the child's entry into language are both affective and cognitive, and come through the parent-child relationship which is initially an essentially unequal one. Through the parent's preparations and expectations from· before the child's birth, and through the assignation of a name, the social world creates a place for the child. But the child's own subjectivity must be constructed through its active participation in signifying practices. For Lacan, a crucial step in this process occurs in the preverbal period at around six months when the infant first delightedly discovers his own image in a mirror. This experience provides the child with his first glimpse of a unified self, which obeys his every movement, and which serves as a matrix for all future identifications. But this image is itself an ideal, which compensates for the infant's real state of dependence, immobility and fragmentation. The mirror stage thus marks the inception of two distinct orders of meaning, the 'real' and the 'imaginary', and introduces a structural change in the dynamics of power within the parent-child relationship. This proceeds through a series of identifications and conflicts engendered by the experience of difference and absence. The child's precipitation into language allows the child some mastery over and detachment from immediate reality, and initially resolves a contradiction between desire for the mother and for control over her, and the need for autonomy.

In the first instance, the mediating links between experiences and signs are metaphoric, and are established through processes of repression and displacement. In the sense that there is always a disjunction between lived experience and the sign which replaces it, this entry into language thus involves something of a 'cost'. However, this is to some extent redressed through the fact that entry into the common linguistic code makes reflective self-awareness possible and provides the child with a purchase point, from which he or she enters into all future signifying relationships.

Thus for Lacan, the entry into language both marks the beginnings of the child's apprenticeship into the signification practices which perpetuate the social world, and at the same time founds his own subjectivity. The signs which realize the social also realize the individual, thus cutting across the traditional distinction between the individual and society. Though not specifically concerned with language development, the utility of some of Lacan's ideas has been demonstrated by Walkerdine and Corran (1979; see also Walkerdine, this volume) in their study of children's learning mathematics in a school situation. Emphasizing that the child is required to enter into a specific code which is at first remote, they have used the notions of metaphor and metonymy to show how the teacher makes new signifying relations comprehensible to the child by relating them to what is already known. They have also shown how the connections or sign-sign linkages made by different children vary, arguing for the importance of considering subjective processes in any learning situation.

For the study of language acquisition Lacan's account as it stands cannot be readily translated into empirical predictions. The theory also has many questionable assumptions, including an unjustified phallocentrism which appears to reflect Lacan's own prejudices (e.g. Irigaray 1977). Nevertheless, the philosophical position put forward by Lacan and the broad features of his developmental account suggest the beginnings of an approach which in principle allows affective processes into the structuring of representation, and which avoids the sharp dichotomy between 'social' and 'cognitive' development. If the kind of processes which Walkerdine and Corran describe also apply at younger ages, then it is also possible that through investigating the kinds of sign-sign linkages made by the child in the early stages of language acquisition, one might develop a less deterministic view of the relationship between language and thought than that offered by the cognitive primacy hypothesis or by its counterpart, the notion of linguistic relativity.

The purpose of this chapter is not to develop such an approach, but to indicate its potential value by considering children who themselves problematize what is taken for granted about the nature of development in infancy − (even by Lacan) − and about the transition from preverbal communication to language in particular. These are children who are congenitally blind. Such children must of course progress through infancy without the advantages of vision, and cannot view themselves in a mirror. Yet, as is perhaps self-evident, for them language must play a particular crucial role in their developing knowledge of the world around them, in their coming to know it as others know it, and in their coming to know themselves.

Literature dealing with the sighted child leads to certain predictions concerning the consequences of lack of vision for development in infancy and the emergence of language. The next section explores the extent to which these predictions are supported by the available evidence on the early development of blind children. This is followed by an account of three children whom I followed longitudinally through a large part of the preverbal period into the early stages of language development (Urwin 1978a, 1979). The concluding section of the chapter discusses how far the findings of this study are comparable with the theoretical scheme which may be drawn from Lacan's work, and the implications for further research into preverbal communication and language development in sighted children.

Some implications of blindness for development in infancy and early language

The dominance assumed for vision in literature on the sighted child leads to the prediction that congenital blindness will pose considerable problems for development in infancy, and that this will have consequences for both communicative and semantic aspects of early language. Broadly speaking, these assumptions are given considerable support in the available literature on the early development of blind children, which emphasizes that lack of vision imposes severe constraints on the development of social relations in infancy, and on the construction of an object world beyond the infant's immediate sphere of action (e.g. Burlingham 1961, Fraiberg 1977, Wills 1970). Though language development is invariably encouraged by the blind infant's parents, since it promises them a form of contact which they have missed (Burlingham 1961), many blind children are delayed in acquiring words and do not always use them in spontaneous communication immediately (Wood 1970, Wills 1979). Substantial delays in making requests, particularly for objects, are also reported, and although there are children who acquire words more rapidly, they generally show a marked bias towards acquiring words and phrases associated with caretaking and familiar routines, apparently at the expense of acquiring words for referring to objects and the inanimate environment (Burlingham 1961, Fraiberg 1977, Wood 1970, Wills 1979). The tendency to rely on readymade phrases is prolonged in some cases, and delays in the production of word combinations can go hand in hand with a marked propensity to imitate. There is also one development which it has been claimed is universally delayed in blind children: the acquisition of 'I' as a stable pronoun, and by implication the ability to use 'you' to refer to the other party in interaction (Fraiberg and Adelson 1975, Fraiberg 1977). Since she has found a concomitant delay in self-representation in fantasy play, Fraiberg (1977) has argued that this delay represents a lag in a more general developmental process – the capacity for self representation. Again assuming a unified subject, Fraiberg also suggests that delays in mastering 'I' and 'you' in language are an inevitable consequence of blindness, testifying to 'the extraordinary problem posed by blindness in constituting a self and an object world and in representing the self as an "I" in a universe of "I's" ' (Fraiberg 1977, 249).

However, in the majority of cases this and other language difficulties are resolved by the end of the nursery school period. In other children, initial restrictions persist, such that at a comparable age their speech is stilted, limited in content and/or highly imitative. These kinds of difficulties are not infrequent in children whose mobility and object skills are apparently developing well (Wood 1970, Wills 1979), and may persist in some form into the early school years or even into adult life (see Urwin 1978b for a fuller review of this evidence).

Investigating the origins and consequences of such marked indivi-dual differences might ultimately prove extremely useful in elucidating general developmental processes, as Lieven (1980, and this volume) has argued for sighted children. Overall, however, the difficulties appear to be most marked in the early stages, and seem to support many of the predictions which may be drawn from the sighted child literature. With the exception of Bruner (1975), the preverbal communication-to-language studies have not speculated on the origins of the 'I'/'you' distinction explicitly (see Clark 1978). But there are good historical grounds to suggest that it is no accident that 'I' and 'eye' sound just the same in our language (see Henriques 1978) and within psychology itself, the equating of 'sight' and the 'self' is strongly implicated in some of its terminology – from 'self image' to 'self perception' and 'self disclosure'.

But for the children concerned, it is extremely unhelpful to assume that these kinds of delays and difficulties are inevitable, and the blind child's situation poses many questions which the literature on the sighted child cannot answer. For example, in line with the cognitive primacy hypothesis, one kind of explanation is to assume that 'cogni-tive delay' accounts for, say, the paucity of references to objects and the delays in the production of word combinations, and that cognitive change underlies the later progress in language. This has been put forward by Fraiberg (1977) in the context of a longitudinal intervention study of 10 totally blind infants, the largest and most comprehensive study of blind infants' development to date. Fraiberg was able to demonstrate that in most areas of development these children were relatively advanced compared to the blind child population as a whole. But she argues that they all showed substantial delays in the development of object permanence and in the capacity for representation. This conclusion is based on the fact that none of the children initiated sustained searching for objects in alternative locations in the absence of prior sound or tactile information. She explains the later improvements in language solely in terms of the increased 'experience' of objects, made possible through the development of independent mobility, a development which the literature suggests is generally delayed in blind children (see also Burlingham 1961).

However, how the two spheres of development – language and the general representational process, which are supposed to proceed in parallel – actually interrelate is left unspecified, as in Piaget's own account (Karmiloff-Smith 1979, Sugarman 1979). Cognitive problems are undoubtedly at issue for some blind children. But the absence of particular conceptual structures deemed important for sighted children does not explain why the apparent anomalies and characteristic biases reported for blind children, such as the pre-ponderance of routine phrases and imitation, should take the form that they do. Moreover, the assumption of a simple unidirectional relationship between cognition and language is thrown into question by the not infrequent reports of language delays which still persist once object skills and mobility are firmly established.

But perhaps the major inadequacy of the sighted child literature is that it contains nothing which could explain how the *absence* of particular communication systems in infancy, such as the use of gesture to make requests, the capacity for registering other people's attention to oneself and for monitoring their attention to objects can ever be overcome.

To answer these questions, it is necessary to question the priority given to vision, and to examine the possibility that other communication systems may play a role in the child's transition from preverbal communication to language. If, as I have argued, it is not the communication systems themselves but the appropriation of signs which brings about the child's awareness of itself in relation to others, then it is possible that language use can itself provide a route through which blind children may appreciate the objects of other people's attention, become aware of independent perspectives, and are constituted as part of the same world. The ability to use language to gain access to what is unknown is clearly evident in some blind children by the end of the nursery school period. As Burlingham (1961) has put it, such children 'find uses for speech which sighted children do not require.' They may make extensive use of questioning, for example, to keep in contact with other people, to aid their own mobility, and to collect characteristics of objects which will enable them to place them in relation to their own experience. They may even begin to use language to seek information about aspects of the sighted world to which they can have no immediate access themselves (Urwin 1978a). In this way language serves to make knowable what is unknown to them, and gives them a handle on the sighted world. Since this development is of crucial importance in their acceptance within the sighted community, it is imperative to know how early and in what way this process may begin.

To consider these questions and possibilities further, the next section describes the development of three congenitally blind children who have progressed extremely well compared to that of the blind child population as a whole, showing parallels with sighted children's developments which challenge the assumption that lack of vision necessarily results in developmental delay.

A longitudinal study

The three children, Steven, Jerry and Suzanne, are all registered as blind[1] and have no additional neurological damage. Steven and Jerry are first born children, but Suzanne has an elder sister, Elaine, who is sighted. Suzanne and Jerry are totally blind. Steven, however, has a little sight in one eye. Though extremely limited, this gave him considerable advantages, particularly in the development of object skills. Nevertheless, his early language showed many characteristics differentiating him from fully sighted children.

The three children were observed, video and audio recorded in interaction with one or other of their parents in their own homes at regular intervals. Steven was first visited when he was 18 days old, and at weekly intervals until the 7 month. A series of videotapes was made over this time. From the age of 7 months, both he and Jerry were visited every fortnight until they were 20 months old, by which time they were both producing their first word combinations. Suzanne's development was followed through the first year by Michael Tobin, from the Institute of Research into the Visually Handicapped, Birmingham, and he has made his video and other records available to me. I began following Suzanne when she was 15 months old, and made monthly visits until the twenty second month. Two further visits were made at two years and at two years three months. At the close of the investigation, syntactic criteria placed her at the onset of Brown's (1973) stage III. A fuller discussion of the research methods used may be found elsewhere. (Urwin 1978b and c).

---

[1] In England and Wales, functional rather than solely opthalmological criteria are used in defining blindness, the statutory definition of blindness in children being 'requiring education by methods not involving the use of sight'. That is, children defined as blind have insufficient sight to allow them to read print, or to be totally reliant on this medium, and have to be taught braille. This definition encompasses a wide range of visual defects and degrees of visual loss. There are only about 2000 children registered as blind in England and Wales altogether, and very few of these children are totally blind.

The children's home environments differed considerably, and the parents held rather different views on how they thought that they themselves could or should contribute to their children's development. This contributed to contrasting characteristics of interaction between each parent and child, and ultimately to different biases in the children's early use of language (see Urwin 1978b, 1979 for a fuller account of these differences). But there were also many similarities in each child's course of development; and overall there were striking parallels with sighted children.

As has already been implied, these children's relatively satisfactory progress was largely because the parents found ways of using alternative communication systems. But it is misleading to assume that it was simply a question of the mothers' using 'more' speech or 'more' physical contact than they might have done with fully sighted children. Their ability to use these systems depended on their being able to find some alternative sign of attention or responsiveness from their babies; and this itself depended crucially on the context in which the behaviour occurred.

One of the most striking characteristics of these mothers was the extent to which they came to rely on the ways in which things were 'usually done', both in responding to and interpreting the children's behaviour and eventually in eliciting cooperation from them. Putting themselves at their children's disposal in episodes of play in the mid-months of the first year, for example, the mothers would 'work' to find some sign of attention or responsiveness which they could take as a 'reply' to their initiatives. And once they discovered particular procedures which 'worked', they would use them again and again. As a consequence, particular forms of interaction became regularized, some of them persisting and evolving throughout the study.

Some of these regularized forms of interaction involved vocalization. Here the parents would elaborate rituals by imitating and building on new sounds as the children began to produce them. Other routines were adaptations of well known nursery games, such as 'Patacake' and 'Ride-a-cock-horse'. Grosser forms of body play were particularly marked for the two totally blind children. In Jerry's case this was outstanding for its roughness, vigour and provocative teasing and contributes to the fact that, in contrast to the position of inevitability put forward in the literature, he was not delayed in becoming mobile (see Urwin 1978b for fuller descriptions of some of these games).

There were, however, some basic similarities in the forms of play recorded for each child. At first the interaction sequences were comparatively short, were simple and repetitive and appeared to be regulated through the mother adjusting to or 'absorbing' herself into some rhythm underlying the child's actions. In spite of the fact that the babies could not see them, the mothers would watch their faces intently, 'mirroring' fluctuations of attention and expressions of affect in their speech. All the mothers showed a marked tendency to imitate or dramatize the infants' preverbal vocalizations. Using many questions and prompts, they would encourage them to imitate themselves or to vocalize in turn. Jerry's parents appeared to be particularly attuned to the child's body movement. Seeing it as communicatively significant, they would mark excitement, anticipation and gross changes of position in their speech, feeding back to the child something of the effects of his actions on those who watched him.

In this 'matching' or 'mirroring' of the children's actions, the mothers' contribution to the interaction appeared similar to that described for mothers of younger sighted infants, where adaptation to the infants' response tendencies paradoxically results in the adults' producing behaviour which is very similar to the child's own (Stern 1974, Trevarthen *et al.* 1975, Sylvester, Bradley and Trevarthen 1978). Here, since the mothers were actively seeking ways of behaving which would prolong the infants' attention, it is very tempting to speculate that the observed interaction sequences bore some relation to a sighted infant's captivated performance in front of a mirror at a similar age, which Lacan has made much of in his theoretical account.

But here, the fact that the interaction was sustained by the mothers rather than through a mirror had particularly important implications. Coming to rely on predictable procedures for making the babies smile, vocalize or in other ways respond, they effectively maximized opportunities for mutual expectancies to become established. As a consequence, over the second half of the first year the babies showed increasing evidence of anticipation and control. But in response to these signs, the mothers began to introduce new variations into the routines, so that the interaction could continue to hold the child's attention and remain interesting to them both. For example, since many routines were initially based on synchronized action and repetitive speech, they began to use elements separately, or substitute an element of one routine for another. Alternatively, they might extend the game into new contexts. By introducing objects into social play, for example, they both marked the object as significant and at the same time drew the child's attention to the fact that, despite the variability, this was still the same game.

These predictable forms of interaction thus introduced principles of substitutability and detachment crucial to the development of the metaphoric axis in Lacan's account. But as important developments occurred within the familiar interaction frames themselves. Taking advantage of what the babies already knew, here the parents began to tease their infants, to introduce conflict, and to push them towards making their intentions explicit. As a consequence an initial 'mirroring' gave way to an assertion of the difference between the roles of adult and child and their mutual interdependence.

Something of these dynamics is illustrated in the following examples.

In the first case, Steven and his mother are playing 'Patacake'. She uses the fact that the clapping procedure has a significance which they now both share to draw his attention to the relation between his body parts and her own, and to the effects of his actions in relation to hers.

STEVEN (Eleven months, thirteen days).
The child on her lap, the mother introduces the clapping routine. Appealing to his 'knowing all about it', she introduces new variations, varies her role to emphasize the child's, and simultaneously requires him to recognize hers. 'Are you going to clap my hands for me?' She puts her hands up in front of him. 'Clap my hands.' S. takes hold of her hands, and she claps, one, two, three, one, two, three. She speeds up her clapping. S. takes control, smiling, and speeds up her claps. 'There!' S. lets go, and claps his own hands on the outside of hers, pushing them together. He manipulates her fingers. She pinches his nose, 'Boo! Cut his nose' and repeats it. 'Boo!' S. pulls his mother's hands apart; she resists. S. laughs. His mother laughs, and claps. The child reaches for her hands, and pushes them together, lets go, and flaps them. The mother claps. S. lets go and swings his hands hard at the mother's. She leads him into 'Patacake'.

Sitting astride his father's leg at a comparable age, Jerry can now restart a game initially based on simple repetitive synchronized action. To some extent he can respond to his father's teasing as he varies the pace and prompts the child to produce some sign which would confirm his active participation.

JERRY (Eleven months, sixteen days)
Jerry's father has been giving him rides, holding the climax through 'Ready, Steady, Go'. The father calls a halt, removing his hands. 'And no more. No more. No more. ALL STOP.' J.'s head is down. He clenches his fist. Teasing him, his father jerks his leg three times and pauses. J. bounces three times and pauses. J. then bounces four times and pauses. His father does the same. His father jerks his foot to make a noise three times, and pauses. J. smacks his legs three times, and lifts his hand out. His father takes it, and J. begins bouncing and vocalizing: his father cooperates in restarting the procedure.

Thus by the end of the first year, within well established routines, each of these children was able to reinitiate and in some measure control the actions of the parent. In this they showed a level of competence akin to sighted children of a similar age, who reproduce social performances to make adults laugh and to manipulate their actions (Bates *et al*. 1975, Sugarman-Bell 1978). In addition, for these children these kinds of

routines provided the groundwork through which they acquired particular communicative procedures for controlling the actions of the other
partner.

As the following example suggests, the emergence of clear communicative initiatives on the child's part both added a new dimension into
the interaction, and also had consequences for the demands made by
the parent. Again with Jerry and his father, the parent acknowledges
that the child has specific intentions, encourages his persistence, and
prolongs the dialogue by creating a 'gap' which will eventually be filled
with the insertion of words. Completing the utterance for the child, he
then thwarts the child's expectations, thereby asserting his own
authority.

> JERRY (One year, twenty days)
> Jerry now uses prolonged demand-vocalizations to request more
> play. Standing holding his father's knees, he whines. 'Do you want
> to come up?' J. whines. 'Do you want to come up more?' J. whines
> again. The father continues in this vein, and then apparently gives
> way to the child's frustration. 'Alright then. Just once more, yeah?'
> J. whines quietly, and his father puts his hands round his waist.
> 'Ready?' as if to lift him. Then he drops his hands, sitting back. 'No,
> I've changed me mind, I've decided not to.' J. protests vigorously,
> then shows distress, and laughing the father picks him up.

From this age onwards, all three children began to acquire standard
words. As is consistent with the evidence of continuity between preverbal and verbal communication described for sighted children, these
were first accompanied by previously established communicative procedures. In the blind children all of these early words clearly originated
in predictable forms of interaction which were highly affective, and in
which the child had already gained some measure of active control,
such as situations involving greetings, caretaking, and the kinds of play
routines described above. Thus social interaction provided the origins
of the children's lexical development as well as allowing the continuity
between preverbal and verbal communicative function.

Throughout the course of the single word period there were further
similarities with sighted children's developments as they extended
words initially based in social action into new contexts, including those
involving objects. Using the same word to serve a number of communicative functions in interaction, the totally blind children also showed
a particularly marked tendency to repeat these words to themselves in
their own play. Over the same period they began to 'run off' elements of
well established routines without support from an adult, clapping their
hands on their own, for example, or stamping out the rhythm of 'ring-
a-ring-a-roses'. At around 18 months, each child's vocabulary began to

expand rapidly, and at this time they also began to produce their first word combinations. The majority of these involved words which the children had been using in a variety of contexts in preceding months. Thus the contiguous relations between the words in combination lifted the principle of substitutability to a new level of explicitness.

These developments cooccurred with the beginnings of representational play and changes in the way the children searched for objects, indicating that they knew of their continued existence independent of their own actions and specific locations. Such parallels are of course consistent with the Piagetian position put forward for sighted children. Though they do not necessarily testify to the adequacy of that position, these children's developments clearly challenge the assumption that the emergence of representation is necessarily delayed in blind children. But besides the broad similarities with sighted children, these children also showed uses for speech which are unlikely to be observed so early or so extensively in children who can see, and which is many ways are comparable to the adaptive uses for speech described in the literature for older blind children. These developments themselves originated in the preverbal period.

Earlier it was mentioned that ritualized forms of vocal imitation evolved between these mothers and children. Imitation games are of course not uncommon between sighted infants and their mothers (Sachs 1977, Snow 1977b). But as Jerry's mother put it at the end of the first year, 'you can have, like, a conversation with him'. These quasi dialogues might last up to 15 minutes at a time. As the following example suggests, the mother might provoke the child through marking the distinction between his turn and her own.

JERRY: 0.11.8
Mother: Are you poor babba? Yeah?
Child: Er
Mother: Mm (*following the child*)
Child: Er
Mother: Mm
Mm (*taking the lead*)
Jerry: Er
Mother: Hm
Jerry: Er
Mother: Hm
Jerry: Er
Mother: Hmm!
Jerry: Er! . . .

And sometimes the child would vary the form of stress himself as if 'experimenting' with controlling the mother's response.

JERRY: 0.11.14
Jerry: Huh.
Mother: Huh.
Jerry: HUH!
Mother: Huh
Jerry: Er – uh
Mother: Au – Aa
Jerry: Huh
Mother: Hm . . .

Comparable preverbal dialogues have been described by Fraiberg (1968), though she emphasizes that many mothers find it difficult to 'talk to' their blind infants. She and other observers have also noted that in contrast to these children, many blind infants are remarkably silent during the first year (Fraiberg 1977, Wills 1979, Wood 1970). Here the vocal system not only provided the children with a way of keeping in contact with their mother's presence over greater distances; they also paved the way for a particularly early mastery of basic procedures for allocating 'turns' and for asserting a differentiation of roles in language. This was particularly marked in the two totally blind infants, who rapidly began to use rising intonation to elicit replies from their parents, mirroring the parents' own tendency to prompt with questions. Indeed, one of Suzanne's first 'words' and most frequently produced single word utterances was 'Ay?', a highly effective acquisition since, whatever the context, it was virtually guaranteed to induce her mother to speak again. This acquisition was followed by a standard conversation opener, 'Mummy?'; and by 21 months she was beginning to throw the onus back to her mother again with, 'Where are yer?' Similarly, Jerry would use 'Hello' and 'Bye-bye' to open and close interactions, generally turning his body towards and away from the mother as he did so.

With the predominance of vocal imitation in the preverbal period, it is not surprising that the totally blind children's early speech was highly imitative. But this served many functions. In Jerry's case, for example, it appeared to aid mobility, as the child used the parent's voice as a reference point. It also helped to consolidate the basic dialogue procedures themselves. In addition, the use of the same words by both mothers and child, where the child had active control, may have been particularly important to the child's becoming aware of his mother's attention, and of his own attention to her.

From calls and acknowledgements, questions and answers to greetings and farewells, these simple procedures carry with them a basic reversibility, suggesting the potential for representing the self in opposition to the role of the other. Earlier it was mentioned that the first word combinations emerged at around the same time as the beginnings of representational play. But here there were important differences between Steven and the two totally blind children. The majority of recorded examples of Steven's early pretend play involved objects and were clearly based on things which he had seen and which had been marked as significant by the mother. (Urwin 1978b). For the two totally blind children, at this stage, I could find few episodes of pretence involving objects. Instead, their representational play involved language itself. At a time when sighted children begin to engage in role play with dolls and other animated objects, these children began to reconstruct 'conversations' centring round past or habitual events. Through using questions and answers, varying tone of voice and other prosodic features, they would represent a distinction between self and other.

The following example shows Jerry reconstructing an episode which had taken place some two hours previously. It is based on a game which I have called 'Are you sure?' This game began before the end of the first year, and evolved as the father attempted to promote the child's mobility. At the time when this episode was recorded, Jerry was just beginning to use language to control the initiation of the game. Shortly afterwards he began to resist his father's teasing by shouting back. Here, using his own voice for himself and a 'gruff' voice for his father, Jerry represents the two roles in mock dialogue.

JERRY: .1.6.2
(Jerry is rambling round the room while both parents are elsewhere).

| *'Father's voice':* | Are you sure? |
| *Jerry's voice:* | I sure Dad. |

| *'Father's voice':* | Are you sure? |
| *Jerry's voice:* | I sure Dad |

'Father's voice':	You sure?
Jerry's voice:	I sure Dad
	I sure Dadda

(and bursts of hysterical laughter.)

Thus, through identifying with the parent's role and appropriating his language, Jerry expresses his own subjectivity in terms of their mutual opposition. Even if in the context of phrases acquired whole-sale, his use of 'I' and 'you' in this example clearly questions the assumption that vision is necessary for the early emergence of this distinction.

However, it was not the case that lack of sight posed no problems for these children. During the preverbal period, in particular, the fact that they could not look towards their mothers placed the onus for initiating interaction fairly heavily on the parent. Thus the competence displayed in the play routines at the end of the first year depended on physical contact, and on the parents' already having decided to put themselves at their children's disposal. For the two totally blind children, requests for particular forms of play, independent of physical support, eventually emerged in language after a period in which they used the elements of body play routines, first produced in their own play, to initiate and control their parents' responses across the space between them.

In spite of this use of their bodies, these children did not use gesture or other nonverbal means to draw attention to objects and events outside their immediate sphere of action, in the way that sighted children do with pointing and reaching-in-demand from the end of the first year. Along with the appearance of 'give-and-take' games, this behaviour is taken to indicate changes in the child's ability to coordinate interaction with people with action on objects (Sugarman-Bell 1978, Trevarthen and Hubley 1978). At a comparable age, these children showed evidence of such coordination. Jerry for example, would prolong long sequences involving banging on objects to produce sounds in mutual imitation. Suzanne would sustain her mother's frequent comments on the objects she was investigating by vocalizing in 'reply'. But none of the children, apparently, began to offer objects spontaneously. This was achieved through deliberate training, and in Suzanne's case not until the third year.

The lack of these particular forms of initiative and communicative means on the part of the blind infants cannot be disassociated from the fact that there were aspects of the immediate context to which their access was inevitably limited. This resulted in some constraints on how they used words in the early stages, when compared to sighted children. For example, their extensions of early acquired words showed the multiplicity of function which is perhaps one of the most significant characteristics of the period. But there were some relative restrictions in their use of the particular 'function' words, such as 'no', 'there', 'more' and 'gone', delineated by Bloom (1973). All the children acquired these words relatively early. But by the time they had begun to combine words, Steven was the only one of the three to use 'more' or any equivalent to comment on objects as distinct entities, and to refer explicitly to the 'nonexistence' of things where expected. This was in spite of the fact that their search behaviour indicated that they 'knew' of the continued existence of objects.

Related constraints were also implicated in the children's use of object names and references to other people. Though they had each acquired a number of object names by the end of the single-word period, by and large their production was confined to situations in which they were in physical contact with the object in question, or in Steven's case when it was within his limited visual range. Similarly, Steven was the only child to make requests for objects with any degree of frequency by twenty months. These were restricted to particularly familiar things, when he could see them, and none of the children referred implicitly to the place of things outside their own sphere of action.

By the twentieth month, all the children had amassed large numbers of names of familiar people which the totally blind children used particularly frequently. Here, of course, the children were learning names for those objects in their environment which were capable of answering back. Suzanne, for example, would call out to her mother or her sister, or to the children next door when she heard them playing in the street. But none of the children had by this time produced either a single word or two-word combination which could be construed as a spontaneous comment on another person's actions. Though· this is not an early development for sighted children, Greenfield and Smith (1976) report the two children in their study using words in this way before the end of the single-word period.

The relatively late appearance of requests and the restricted use of object names are characteristics found in the blind child population as a whole, as described in the previous section. But for these children, it is clearly inadequate to view these relative restrictions as a consequence of the delayed emergence of some general capacity for representation. As I have argued elsewhere (Urwin 1979) they are better explained in terms of the blind children's relation to the ongoing context, and their different ways of gaining access to it. These children, of course, lacked access to just those contrasts or markers of change which are potent elicitors of comment in sighted children, such as objects disappearing from the field of view, or the simultaneous presence of members of the same class of objects; and at this stage of development, sighted children's references to and requests for objects are largely if not entirely elicited by the things which they see (Huxley and Urwin: unpublished data).

Yet it is precisely in the areas where at first these children showed some restrictions that language can be invaluable to the blind child: to express communicative functions carried by gesture and other visual means in sighted children, to become aware of distinctions which are instantaneously available to the sighted child, and to extend their appreciation of the activities of other people and their independent access to the environment. Since Suzanne was followed to an older age, it was possible to examine how this was achieved, and the extent to which early biases in her use of language contributed to this process.

Suzanne's later development

By the close of the investigation, at 2; 3, the restrictions in Suzanne's use of language, relative to sighted children, had apparently been resolved. She was referring to distant objects and locations, marking recurrence and frequently making requests for objects. She was now beginning to comment explicitly on the actions of other people when those actions were familiar to her, and she had begun to use both 'I' and 'you' appropriately. Exact imitation appeared to have given way to a strategy whereby she would continue a conversational theme by incorporating part of her mother's utterances into her own following utterances, building upon them. While this kept alive a topic of conversation between the two of them where cues from the surrounding context were minimal, through such means she was beginning to reconstruct her mother's explanations about past or habitual events. She was also showing the extensive use of questions observable in some older blind children.

Of factors contributing to this development, independent mobility was particularly important, as Fraiberg's (1977) evidence suggests. But here, this was not simply a question of the child's increasing experience of objects. More important were the new kinds of social activities made available to her, and the fact that mobility opened new contexts in which talk could take place. This had immediate implications for the expression of locative relations, as a large proportion of her utterances referred to places outside her own body, the kitchen, 'upstairs' or the bedroom next door, and to her determined efforts to take herself there, the new location standing as the goal of her intended action.

Along with increasing proficiency at categorizing objects, the ability to sustain a goal over space and time was also evident in her object play, and particularly in her requests for objects. Cues from the surrounding context were of course still minimal. But she would now demand objects necessary to complete some plan of action already underway; or playing with one toy she would demand another toy related to it or of a similar sort. Playing with one farm animal, for example, she might demand another, or the farm to put them inside. Compared to the earlier months she appeared to make use of the sounds going on around her. Hearing her sister, Elaine, go into the adjoining room, for example, she could recognize what she was doing, where she was going, and would demand to go there too.

Cognitive changes were clearly integral to these developments. But they cannot in any simple sense be regarded as the determining 'source' underlying related developments in language. The child's plans were produced through predictable forms of social interaction, in which developments in the discourse mode itself played a particularly crucial role. Here there were ways in which the mother's own use of speech appeared particularly suited to extending the child's access to the surrounding context and to providing a backdrop against which she could interpret the significance of distal sounds.

In describing the development of social play in the preverbal period, examples were given to illustrate how each child's increasingly active control over predictable forms of interaction was accompanied by changes in the parent's demands, leading to an increasing emphasis on social appropriateness and a simultaneous requirement that the child appreciate the difference in roles. Similar principles applied to the way in which Suzanne's mother adapted her use of language to the increasing competence displayed by the child. For example, as the child began to acquire names for objects towards the end of the single word period, the mother elaborated naming games using the toy farm animals, for example, in the way that mothers with sighted children use picture books. This procedure was soon reversed by the child, such that she herself began to draw the mother's attention to objects close at hand.

The appropriation of names provided a basis from which the child could become aware that the objects in question were accessible to them both. But once the child had acquired names for things, the mother knew that the child knew of the objects to which they referred. The names could then be used to refer to objects beyond the range of touch. With the emergence of independent searching for objects, for example, the mother would prompt the child with 'where's X?' questions, encouraging her to explore the space around her. This form was appropriated by the child in expressing her first requests for objects, as in, 'Where train?' or 'Where car?'. These requests initially occurred in cases where the child searched for objects with which she had recently been in contact, such that her accompanying behaviour was similar to that which the mother's use of the question form had previously initiated.

But again, the ability to make requests itself added a new dimension to the interaction. In conjunction with the onset of independent mobility in the third year, this brought further demands from the parent. She would no longer willingly respond to the child's requests for objects by providing them herself. More often she would specify their location relative to the child, or to the now familiar object within the room. 'It's by the door', 'This way', 'That way', 'Over there', or 'It's on the table'. Thus by building on what the child already knew, the mother was able to make links for the child to what was distant or unfamiliar to her. In this way the mother's language prefigured developments in the child's, and discourse itself established a shared world.

Apart from contributing to the child's ability to talk about objects, discourse also provided the route through which Suzanne became capable of referring explicitly to other people as agents of their own actions. In the final sessions many of Suzanne's explicit references to others occurred in conversations about past or habitual events. As the following example suggests, reconstructing her mother's explanations and prompts occasioned her referring to the activities and whereabouts of other people.

SUZANNE: 2.3.0
Suzanne: Where's Nanny gone, Mum?
Mother: Where's Nanny gone?

Suzanne:	Yes.
Mother:	She's gone home now.
Suzanne:	Home to her flat.
Mother:	Yes.
Suzanne:	In the car?
Mother:	Mm? No. Nanny went on the bus.

While these kinds of conversations lifted interaction out of the here and now, in the immediate context the majority of Suzanne's explicit references to others' activities occurred with respect to her sister Elaine. Here, too, the mother's own speech played a significant role. Throughout the second year she consistently referred to Elaine in her speech to Suzanne, keeping her utterances within the kinds of things the child was likely to understand. But increasingly these references came in response to initiatives from Suzanne as she began to call out to her sister by name. From the end of the second year, the kinds of activities in which the two children engaged, such as playing with particular toys, for example, became closer. As a consequence, in the mother's speech statements about Elaine's state, such as 'Elaine's tired, Suzanne', or 'Elaine wants a cuddle', gave way to statements about Elaine's actions on objects. By the third year the mother was obliged to sort out some competition between the two of them. Many of Suzanne's requests for objects, for example, were elicited by her hearing Elaine play with a particular toy, which she could identify, or through her recognizing the significance of what she was saying.

The following example shows how with language Suzanne was able both to establish mutual attention to objects, and also to distinguish her own and others' access to them. Reconstructing one of her mother's ways of 'keeping the peace', she marks the relation of possession, and perhaps comes to terms with notions of sharing.

SUZANNE:	2.3.0
Suzanne:	Elaine's got the case
Mother:	Elaine's got the case, yes
Suzanne:	And *I* got the hairdrier.
	Naughty ole hairdrier!

The ability to refer to Elaine and her actions related to the fact that the sister's activities were predictable and were very similar to her own. At the same time, through drawing attention to this relationship the mother's language helped to provide the bridge. The affective basis through which Suzanne took over her mother's language is indicated in the following instance of fantasy play, as she reconstructs an episode which took place shortly before hand. Here Suzanne identifies with both her mother and her sister, and in doing so produces both 'I' and 'you'. The example also reveals something of the relationship between herself, her mother and her sister, and the dynamics of power and control, empathy and affection through which it has been established.

> SUZANNE: 2.3.0
> (*Elaine is bouncing and jumping off the settee. Suzanne apparently appreciates something of what her sister is doing and, in her own way, attempts to copy her.*)
> *Suzanne:* I'm 'Laine (*laughing*)
> Whoops! (*She deliberately throws herself on the floor*). I fell over!
> (*The mother intervenes and warns Elaine, and then smacks her to discourage her exuberance. Shortly afterwards, Suzanne laughs and apparently reconstructs the scene for herself*).
> *Suzanne:* You's fall over! (*In her own voice*)
> (*Using a severe intonation, she then goes on to reproduce something of her mother's language.*)
> *Suzanne:* Now watch it!
> You asked this!
> (*The episode ends with a mock cry, presumably as a representation of Elaine, and further laughter from Suzanne.*)

Thus, through acquiring language Suzanne's position as a subject within the family is established. Though she was not followed for long enough to plot the emergence of the I/You distinction in all its grammatical manifestations (this is not normally expected in sighted children before the middle of the third year (Clark 1978)) at the close of the study Suzanne was clearly on the way to achieving what poses considerable problems for most blind children. At that time she was still producing utterances which actually required her to use 'you' comparatively infrequently. But as I have suggested elsewhere (Urwin 1978a), this must change with further opportunities for cooperative action involving objects, and with the emergence of questions of the form 'What are you doing?' Each of these seemed a particularly likely candidate for development in Suzanne's case.

Concluding discussion

It is generally assumed that research into the development of children with such an apparently clearcut handicap as lack of vision will contribute to our understanding of 'normal' development. Very often such research uses differences in the performance of normal and handicapped groups to substantiate the importance of what the handicapped child lacks to the child who has it. In contrast, by describing children who problematize what the recent studies of preverbal communication have taken for granted, I have aimed to challenge the priority given to vision, and to draw attention to inadequacies in the ways in which the relationships between 'social' and 'cognitive' development and 'language and thought' are usually presented.

The close parallels between the developmental progress of these children with that of sighted children does not, of course, mean that vision is not important to sighted children. Rather they suggest that there is a problem in the way in which its role is generally conceived. It is not for example, simply a question of redressing a balance by doing further research into the use of touch, hearing, or any other communication/sensory systems that one cares to think of, as if these systems constitute separate faculties. Rather, these children's development suggests that the crucial questions concern the interrelations between different systems, their separability, and their potential substitutability. While this potential for a multiple encoding of reality ultimately makes it possible for the child lacking aspects of sensory experience to appropriate the language used by all, it may also be a crucial component to symbolic functioning in general.

In illustrating the use of nonvisual communication systems between these mothers and children, I have described the evolution of predictable forms of social interaction in which principles of substitutability were integral. These interaction frameworks provided the conditions through which these children both mastered communicative procedures which expressed communicative intentions and also appropriated their first words. As I have described elsewhere (Urwin 1978a and c), each child's use of words and growth of vocabulary through the one-word stage showed a clear bias related to differentiating characteristics of social interaction. This argues for the social origins of representation in language. It also makes questionable the assumption that social and cognitive processes make separable contributions to the emergence of language.

Problems in the ways in which the relationship between language and cognition is usually conceived, such that one underlies or determines the development of the other, are seen particularly clearly in Suzanne's case. Here, on the one hand further developments in language were realised through predictable forms of social action; and at the same time gains in her ability to relate to and represent her environment were made through the functions of discourse itself.

I have suggested that each of these limitations in theories of development in sighted children is related to the philosophical/ideological stance which presumes the pregiven, individual subject. As an alternative, Lacan's account of the social production of subjectivity was put forward as a possible starting point for future theorizing. From the initial meshing or 'mirroring' of mother and child actions, to the inception of conflict and marking of difference, and the processes of identification through which these children appropriated the parents' language and thereby defined themselves, in many respects the developments observed for these children are highly compatible with Lacan's account. They also suggest, however, that we do not need to interpret the 'mirror' of the mirror stage literally, and that what constitutes a significant difference may depend on what is marked as such in the child's environment.

That the constitution of subjectivity in blind children depends on their appropriating the language used by those around them is perhaps self evident. Since language is obviously particularly important to blind children, it might be argued that the processes observed in these three children are of no relevance to sighted children. On the other hand, one might also argue that these children's development clarifies processes which are in fact at issue for normal children. If this is so, then the dynamics through which these children entered language should have their counterparts in sighted children.

There is already some evidence in the literature which suggests this. For example, the routinized interactions which developed between these children and their parents are in many respects similar to what Bruner (1975, 1977) has described as 'formats': predictable forms of interaction which provide a stable framework within which mutual intentions can be read. Though Bruner has emphasized their contribution to illocutionary force in language, his data also show that these interactions provide the basis for the first words. Similarly, studies of children's word usage through the single-word stage also suggest that sighted children's early words originate in predictable forms of interaction which are highly affective and in which the child has already gained some measure of active control. As for the blind children, these situations include greetings, caretaking situations and ritualized games, and also situations involving prohibitions (Bowerman 1978, Edwards 1978, Ferrier 1978). There are also studies of individual differences which show a relationship between characteristics of word usage and lexical development in the early stages and differentiating styles of parent child interaction (Lieven 1978, Nelson 1973, Rosenblatt 1977).

Each of these lines of research suggest that the inception of representation in language is social. Once language use is well established, the detachment from the 'here and now' evidenced by Suzanne in the final phase of the study may again be observed in sighted children at a comparable age, as they begin to sustain their first discourses about events in the past, or which occur predictably without recourse to concrete props (Greenfield and Smith 1976, Snow 1978). Where these discourses depend on relating signs to signs, the strategies through which Suzanne's mother made the unknown accessible to the child through using signs to relate it to what was already known are not in principle disimilar from those used by the teachers described by Walkerdine and Corran (1979) in promoting the children's entry into the 'mathematical code'.

But despite these broad compatibilities, evidence for some of the most crucial contributory processes in these children's developments is not available in the sighted child research, either in the field of child language or in the study of early social relations. In particular, these children's development suggests that affectivity may play a significant role in the marking of distinctive contrasts or points of change which are realized as semantic distinctions in language. It also suggests that processes of identification are integral to the child's appropriation of language and to its entry into signification systems in general. It is a consideration of the origins of such active processes on the child's part which is missing in the recent Meadian based accounts of social development, and which is essential to any account of the development of conscious subjectivity.

It is thus perhaps time that development research took seriously those processes which have historically been regarded as the province of psychoanalysis, and also questioned its own philisophical basis. However useful Lacan's theory ultimately proves in elucidating such questions as the child's entry into language and the relation between language and thought, its major advantage is that it allows subjective, social and cognitive processes to be theorized as a unity, rather than as separate, interactive or additive forms of knowledge. Such a position both promises an enrichment of psychology's own field, and also raises the possibility that the study of development may contribute empirical material which is relevant to theories of ideology.

References

Ainsworth, M., Bell, S. and Stayton, D. 1974: Infant-mother attachment and social development: 'socialization' as a product of reciprical responsiveness to signals. In M.P.M. Richards (ed.), *The integration of a child into a social world*. Cambridge: Cambridge University Press.

Bates, E., Camaioni, L. and Volterra, V. 1975: The acquisition of performatives prior to speech. *Merrill Palmer Quarterley* **21**, 205–26.

Berger, J. 1972: *Ways of seeing*. Hardmondsworth: Penguin.

Bloom, L. 1973: *One word at a time: the use of single word utterances before syntax*. The Hague: Mouton.

Bowerman, M. 1973: *Early syntactic development: a cross-linguistic study with special reference to Finnish*. Cambridge: Cambridge University Press.

——1978: The acquisition of word meaning. In E.N. Waterson and C.E. Snow (eds.), *The development of communication*. Chichester: Wiley.

Brazelton, T.B., Koslowski, B. and Main, M. 1974: The origins of reciprocity: the early mother-infant interaction. In M. Lewis and L. Rosenblum (eds.), *The effect of the infant on its caregiver*. New York: Wiley.

Brown, R. 1973: *A first language: the early stages*. Cambridge, Mass.: Harvard University Press.

Bruner, J.S. 1975: The ontogenesis of speech acts. *J. Child Language* 2, 1–19.

— 1977: Early social interaction and language acquisition. In Schaffer 1977.

— 1978: From communication to language: a psychological perspective. In I. Markova (ed.), *The social context of language*. Chichester: Wiley.

Bruner, J.S., Roy, C. and Ratner, N. 1979: The development of requests. In K. Nelson (ed.), *Children's language*, vol. 3. New York: Gardner.

Bullowa, M. 1979: *Before speech: the beginning of interpersonal communication*. Cambridge: Cambridge University Press.

Burlingham, D. 1961: Some notes on the development of the blind. *Psychoanalytic Study of the Child* 26, 121–45.

Carter, A. 1978: From sensori-motor vocalizations to words: a case study of the evolution of attention-directing communication in the second year. In Lock 1978.

Clark, E. 1978: From gesture to word: on the natural history of deixis. In J.S. Bruner and A. Garton (eds.), *Human growth and development (Wolfson College Lectures 1976)*. Oxford: Oxford University Press.

Collis, G.M. and Schaffer, H.R. 1975: Synchronization of visual attention in mother-infant pairs. *J. Child Psychology* 16, 315–20.

Cromer, R. 1974: The development of language and cognition: the cognition hypothesis. In B.M. Foss (ed.), *New perspectives in child development*. Harmondsworth: Penguin.

Dore, J. 1975: Holophrases, speech acts and language universals. *J. Child Language* 2, 21–40.

— 1978: Conditions for the acquisition of speech acts. In I. Markova (ed.), *The social context of language*. Chichester: Wiley.

Edwards, D. 1973: Sensory-motor intelligence and semantic relations in early child grammar. *Cognition* 2, 395–434.

— 1978: Social relations and early language. In Lock 1978.

Ferrier, L. 1978: Some observations of error in context. In N. Waterson and C.E. Snow (eds.), *The development of communication*. Chichester: Wiley.

Fraiberg, S. 1968: Parallel and divergent patterns in blind and sighted infants. *Psychoanalytic Study of the Child* 23, 264–300.

— 1977: *Insights from the blind*. London: Souvenir Press.

Fraiberg, S. and Adelson, E. 1975: Self representation in language and play: observations of blind children. In E. Lenneberg and E. Lenneberg (eds.), *Foundations of language development: a multidisciplinary approach*, vol. 2, New York: Academic Press.

Giddens, A. 1976: *New rules of sociological method*. London: Hutchinson.

Greenfield, P. and Smith, J. 1976: *The structure of communication in early language development*. New York: Academic Press.

Henriques, J. 1978: *Perception, cognition and group relations: a critique of cognitive social psychology*. Unpublished manuscript.

Ingleby, D. 1980a: Freud and Piaget: the phoney war. Paper presented at the First World Congress on Infant Psychiatry. Coscais, Portugal.

— 1980b: Review of Lock 1980. *European J. Social Psychology* **10**, 319–28.

Irigaray, L. 1977: Women's exile. *Ideology and Consciousness* **1**, 62–76.

Jakobson, R. and Halle, M. 1956: *Fundamentals of language*. The Hague: Mouton.

Karmiloff-Smith, A. 1979: *A functional approach to child language*. Cambridge: Cambridge University Press.

Lacan, J. 1949: *The mirror-phase*. Tr. Jean Roussel. Reprinted in *New Left Review* **51**, 71–7.

— 1966: *Ecrits*. Paris: Seuil. Selection tr. Alan Sheridan, *Ecrits: a selection*. London: Tavistock, 1977.

— 1973: *Les quatre conceptes fondamentaux de la psychoanalyse*. Seminaire XI. Paris: Seuil. Tr. Alan Sheridan, *The four fundamental concepts of psychoanalysis*. Harmondsworth: Penguin, 1979.

Lemaire, A. 1977: *Jacques Lacan*. Tr. David Macey. London: Routledge & Kegan Paul.

Lieven, E. 1978: Conversations between mothers and children: individual differences and their possible implications for the study of language learning. In N. Waterson and C.E. Snow (eds.), *The development of communication*. Chichester and New York: Wiley.

— 1980: Different routes to multiple word combinations? Paper presented at Stanford Child Language Conference, April.

Lock, A. (ed.) 1978: *Action, gesture and symbol: the emergence of language*. London: Academic Press.

MacNamara, J. 1972: Cognitive basis of language learning in infants. *Psychological Review* **79**, 1–13.

Mead, G.H. 1934: *Mind, self and society*. Chicago: University of Chicago Press.

Morehead, D.M. and Morehead, A. 1974: From signal to sign: a Piagetian view of thought and language during the first two years. In R.L. Schiefelbusch and L.L. Lloyd (eds.), *Language perspectives: acquisition, retardation and intervention*. London: Macmillan.

Nelson, K. 1973: Structure and strategy in learning to talk. *Society for Research into Child Development Monograph* **149**, 38, Nos. 1–2.

Newson, J. 1978: Dialogue and development. In Lock 1978.

Newson, J. and Newson, E. 1976: On the social origins of symbolic functioning. In U.P. Varma and P. Williams (eds.), *Piaget, psychology and education*. London: Hodder & Stoughton.

Rosenblatt, D. 1977: Developmental trends in infant play. In B. Tizard and D. Harvey (eds.), *The biology of play*. Clinics in Developmental

Medicine 62. London: Heinemann.

Sachs, J. 1977: The adaptive significance of linguistic input to prelinguistic infants. In C.E. Snow and C.A. Ferguson (eds.), *Talking to children: language input and acquisition*. Cambridge: Cambridge University Press.

Schaffer, H.R. (ed.) 1977: *Studies in mother-infant interaction*. London: Academic Press.

Shotter, J. 1974: The development of personal powers. In M.P.M. Richards (ed.), *The integration of a child into a social world*. Cambridge: Cambridge University Press.

— 1978: The cultural context of communication studies: theoretical and methodological issues. In Lock 1978.

Sinclair, H. 1971: Sensorimotor action patterns as a condition for the acquisition of syntax. In R. Huxley and E. Ingram (eds.), *Language acquisition: models and methods*. London: Academic Press.

Slobin, D.I. 1979: *Psycholinguistics*. 2nd edition. Illinois: Scott-Foresman.

Snow, C. 1977a: Mothers' speech research: from input to interaction. In C. Snow and C. Ferguson (eds.), *Talking to children: language input and acquisition*. Cambridge: Cambridge University Press.

— 1977b: The development of conversation between mothers and babies. *J. Child Language* **4**, 1–22.

— 1978: The conversational context of language acquisition. In P. Smith and R. Campbell (eds.), *Recent advances in the psychology of language*. London: Plenum.

Stern, D.N. 1974: Mother and infant at play: the dyadic interaction involving facial, vocal and gaze Behaviors. In M. Lewis & L. Rosenblum (eds.), *The effect of the infant on its caregiver*. New York: Wiley.

Sugarman, S. 1979: *Scheme, order and outcome: the development of classification in children's early block play*. Unpublished doctoral dissertation, University of California, Berkeley.

Sugarman-Bell, S. 1978: Some organizational aspects of preverbal communication. In I. Markova (ed.), *The social context of language*. Chichester: Wiley.

Sylvester-Bradley, B. and Trevarthen, C. 1978: Baby talk as an adaptation to the infant's communication. In N. Waterson and C.E. Snow (eds.), *The development of communication*. Chichester: Wiley.

Trevarthen, C. 1975: Early attempts at speech. In R. Lewin (ed.), *Child alive*. London: Temple Smith.

Trevarthen, C. and Hubley, P. 1978: Secondary intersubjectivity: confidence, confiding and acts of meaning in the first year. In Lock 1978.

Trevarthen, C., Hubley, P. and Sheeran, L. 1975: Psychological actions in early infancy. *La Recherche* **6**, 447–58.

Urwin, C. 1978a: *The development of communication between blind infants and their parents: some ways into language*. Unpublished. PhD. thesis, University of Cambridge.

— 1978b: Early language development in blind children. *British Psychological Society Occasional Papers* **2**, 73–87.

— 1978c: The development of communication between blind infants and their parents. In Lock 1978.

— 1979: Preverbal communication and early language development in blind children. *Papers and Reports on Child Language Development* **17**, 119–28. Dept. of Linguistics, Stanford University.

Venn, C. and Walkerdine, V. 1978: Critique of Piaget. *Ideology and Consciousness* **3**, 67–94.

Vygotsky, L.S. 1962: *Thought and language*. Cambridge, Mass.: MIT Press.

— 1966: Development of the higher mental functions. In *Psychological Research in the USSR* Moscow: Progress Publishers.

Walkerdine, V. and Corran, G. 1979: Cognitive development: a mathematical experience? Paper presented at BPS Developmental Section Conference on Social Cognition. Southampton, September 1979.

Wills, D. 1970: Vulnerable periods in the early development of blind children. In *Psychoanalytic Study of the Child* **25**, 461–80.

— 1979: Early speech development in blind children. In *Psychoanalytic Study of the Child* **34**, 85–120.

Wood, H. 1970: *Problems in the development and home care of pre-school* blind children. Unpublished PhD thesis, University of Nottingham.

6

From context to text: a psychosemiotic approach to abstract thought

Valerie Walkerdine

The production of rational and abstract thought is considered to be central to the technological society in which we live. Yet abstract reasoning is notoriously difficult, and is seen as the culmination of the developmental process by many psychologists. This chapter will address the problem of the nature and origins of abstract thought within the context of debates within developmental psychology, examining particularly those explanations put forward by Margaret Donaldson (1978). I shall consider the ways in which young childrens' thinking can be said to be initially tied to familiar contexts and then, in Donaldson's words, has to be 'prised out of the old primitive matrix in which all thinking is contained' (76) in order to approach formal reasoning.

Typically, abstract reasoning is considered to be a property or quality which develops in the mind of the child. I wish to argue rather that it is a mistake to envisage the problem in these terms, and I want to replace Piaget's abstract epistemic subject, a shadowy and always disembodied figure, with the notion of human subjects as created through the incorporation, through the medium of signs, of children into the social practices which make up our everyday life.

I will argue that young children are able to reason in familiar contexts not because they possess reasoning 'skills' which are contextually bound, but because their learning involves being able to adopt positions in discourse in relation to familiar practices and to operate accordingly. 'Abstract' reasoning, on the other hand, requires conscious reflection on the linguistic structure of the discourse itself.

The social context of thinking

There have been many recent studies of cognitive development and of language acquisition which have highlighted the influence of context on the performance of children (Walkerdine and Sinha 1978, Wells 1981). The point has been pertinently made by many researchers that children are neither 'abstract epistemic subjects' nor 'ideal speaker-hearers', but grow up in real contexts, facing real problems and so on. However, it has become an increasing problem to attempt to move beyond mere assertions that context is important towards actual attempts to understand how to theorize this term and therefore more clearly to understand its effect. I want to challenge that assumption that context can be seen as an effect which can be 'welded on' to a Piagetian edifice left almost entirely intact. I believe that Margaret Donaldson searches for the answers to important problems in precisely the right places, but is hampered by a retention of certain basic psychological assumptions. For example, reasoning is placed firmly within the mind of the child, while context is placed firmly on the outside : the context/cognition problem becomes one of how the social impinges upon the preexisting individual. In psychology the problem is conceived in terms of the 'internalization' of social features, that is by relating the 'external' social dimension to the 'internal' individual dimension. This approach gestures towards a social developmental psychology (as in the approach towards intersubjectivity (Bruner 1975) social cognition, roles and scripts (Nelson 1980)). My position is that this approach, though useful up to a point, is radically unable to provide the breakthrough which is required. Although the present context is not appropriate for an examination of the theoretical problem posed for psychology itself, I want to begin to search for a way out of the impasse by utilizing and developing certain notions from semiotics and from discourse analysis (Foucault 1972) – to cut across the inside/outside, context/cognition distinction.

I shall begin by sketching out my line of analysis and then go on to relate this to data discussed by Donaldson and to my own work. I shall elaborate certain concepts which are familiar to linguists, but will examine them from a rather different perspective than that normally applied in child language. The question is what, in specific concrete cases, do children take to be the context? What processes do they use for working this out? These are not simply theoretical issues but are crucial to educational practice, especially to mathematics, as I shall point out later. It is a basic notion within the Piagetian formulation that the origin of conceptualization lies in the formation of schema from the internalization of action upon objects. Piaget proposes the possibility of a separate and primary theory of the child's appropriation of the world of objects, of signifieds, and a secondary process in which concepts formed at this level are represented by signifiers. Thus in Piaget's terms the production of the sign happens in terms of grafting of signifiers onto existing concepts. The primacy of cognition is asserted by the possibility of the prelinguistic but cognate subject.

Urwin (this volume) argues cogently against the necessity of such assertions. Those who would propose a subject created through significations would not limit their formulation of signs to 'language' but – as we shall see later – argue against the limits set on what counts as 'language' within the limits of the discourse of linguistics. Although I am not dealing with studies of young babies, my concern is to show that young children, at least of nursery school age, do not first 'know' objects and then graft signifiers as representations on to their knowledge. Rather I intend to develop the theme that children are engaged in a process in which the crucial moment of understanding lies in a specific relation of signified to signifier. However, I do not wish to be seen as debating the primacy of language. Rather, I wish to relate my argument to developments within the field of semiotics, which stress that the relation between signs cannot be understood as a purely linguistic relation but rather as a social one. This split between linguistic and social relations is to some extent produced by categorizations proposed by Saussure in which a distinction is made between 'langue' and 'parole'. Theoretical linguistics has widened the gap in terms of assertions that 'langue' is the object of a proper science of linguistics, with 'parole' separate and subsidiary. Thus, when in developmental research we talk about language, we do not refer to the insertion and relation of signs in actual social practices. This leads us to have to 'graft on' context rather than being able to theorize it as a criterial feature of signification itself. Adlam *et al.* (1977, 48) remark:

> F de Saussure's distinction between langue and parole. . . . has perpetuated the notion that the proper science of linguistics is an abstracted system of signs, of lexical and grammatical relations which may, indeed must, be considered outside the concrete instances of their implementations in speech (Saussure 1974). Saussure's influential structuralism informs a concept of discourse which, as well as being separated from a realm of nondiscursive practices, can be apprehended independently of discursive practices themselves. That is the concept of discourse becomes the Saussurian langue in motion, and thus cannot escape the criticism of the separation which was required to form this concept. The outcome of one strand of thought based upon this position was that, to a proper science of linguistics, meaning is quite subsidiary. Moreover, this particular theory (Chomsky's early work) which rigidly maintained the langue/parole distinction also purported to be a theory of 'mind'. Saussure's distribution can be found in many other theories of consciousness, and where representation is considered a central question the implication usually is that we can understand the relation of language to thought without consideration of the social practices within which the relation is effected.

My argument in relation to the context-specificity and later disembedding of children's reasoning hinges on a critique of the notion of 'context' as something which is external to, and exists in an additive relation to, thinking. If we change the terms of the discussion, referring not to language, thinking and context as separate systems but to processes of signification, understood without reference to the langue/ parole dichotomy, we do not need to understand contextual processes as external to signification but as regulated signifying relations themselves. In this way we can account for the linguistic marking of systematic differences, but we do not have to seek the origin of that marking within language itself.

Let me exemplify the need to go beyond the linguistic in order to account for behaviour and understanding. Imagine the following situation. A young couple have just had their first baby. The baby cries and the parents variously try feeding, changing its nappy, rocking and so forth — they consult baby manuals, they wonder if the child is getting enough milk and so on. Now, how can we account for the sequence of words and actions on the part of the parents which accompany the baby's cries? We could agree that the baby has certain biological needs and the important thing is for the parents to tune into what these 'really are'. We can analyse the sytactic relations in their speech or the semantic relations of the words that they use. But what will these tell us? To understand the relation of the actions and vocalizations of the infant to the actions and decisions of the parents, we have to understand what sense they make of its cries, and what this sense suggests as courses of action. These interpretations are not fixed or static; their actions, interpretations and reactions are not timeless. The parents may have thought long and hard about whether to leave the baby to cry, whether or not to breast feed. In other words I am arguing that to understand the relation of the baby's cries to what they say and do, we have to understand how the cries are variously interpreted as, for example, 'hungry', 'dirty' etc. If 'hungry', then we have to know how that relates to their decisions concerning feeding and to know these we have to understand how their decisions relate to what is said and written on feeding and their decision in relation to this. Thus to understand their actions and their 'discourse' we *do* have to look at action, at gesture, at sound, at word; but we cannot stop here, for we must also include current thinking and writing, fashions etc. about feeding, mothering and so on. There is a historical and social dimension which we must include to understand their discourse. It is the positioning of their discourse in relation to a number of other discourses and practices which enables us to make sense of its functioning in the process of signification. These discourses and practices are not the context but actually have a constitutive effect. This approach is most obvious in the work of Foucault (1972, 1977), but it is usually applied to the understanding of discourse in texts and not the relation of speech to text suggested here.

An examination of some discursive contexts

Let us return to Donaldson's primitive matrix; I am suggesting that it is not so much the case that early reasoning consists of skills or qualities which develop in the mind, though they are tied to the context, but rather that children acquire and create different discursive formats simply by taking part in everyday practices. Children's acquisition of certain discursive formats is extremely rapid: certainly by the age of three they are able to switch in and out of discursive positions, taking up for example positions in play which they can never have taken in real life. Children's acquisition of discourse formats actually involves them in being able to take up various *positions* within that discourse.

How do children learn to switch in and out of discourses? In order to examine this question I shall refer to a corpus of data collected in a nursery class in East London. The children in this study were aged between three and five years. Now, the children are only subjected to realizations of discourse rules: nobody actually tells them explicitly what to do, so we cannot say that their knowledge of discourses is conscious. In play and learning situations neither the children nor the teacher explicitly tell each other what discourse they are operating in and yet the children manage a vast selection of discursive relations.

In the first example, two girls are playing in the Wendy House. In this case the social practices associated with the Wendy House already signify in such a way that the children are likely to engage in domestic play. However the form of the game and the roles of the participants has to be negotiated. It is never *explicitly* negotiated, but takes place in terms of childrens' assertion not only of a particular discourse but also of a particular position within that discourse. It is impossible in a transcript to convey the full force of the interchange, since the children's intonation as well as their choice of words is important in conveying their discursive position.

The opening sequence is as follows:

Nancy: Hello Diane. Let's watch telly.
Diane: I'm just tidying baby's bed up. You sit on that wooden chair. Here y'are . . . Alright I'm working I can't watch telly.
Nancy: Mum can I watch telly mum?

In the first line Nancy attempts to set up a television-watching game in which both participants have equal power to determine the flow of the discourse. The way that she achieves this is interesting. She refers to 'watching television' and yet there is nowhere an actual television set, a toy one or even a picture of one. What she does is to use 'television watching' as a way of alluding to a topic and to therefore a particular kind of play which articulates a particular discourse. She calls Diane by her name and sets up what is to be imagined – watching the television – but implies the participants are to play themselves. But Diane rejects this – not entirely, nor explicitly. She achieves the rejection by positioning herself still within the 'television-watching' discourse, but

inserts herself in a position of control, rather than the equality
envisaged by Nancy, by asserting herself in the role of 'mother' and by
implication therefore addressing Nancy as a child. Nancy picks this up
immediately and accepts it by referring to Diane as 'Mum'. None of the
negotiation is explicit: it is all carried by the form and role structure of
the discourse which the children adopt. And the key into the choice of
discourse would appear to be in the opening suggestion of 'watching
television'. I shall refer to this as the opening *metaphor*, because it has
the effect of 'calling up' for the participants the relevant discourse. It
provides a discourse for reading the actions and objects of the participants and it occurs and appears to function in this way in all of the play
sequences I have observed as well as sequences involving the teacher
and children, as we shall see later.

(In this sequence the objects and participants can then all be located
in ways consonant with the discourse – e.g. the doll becomes *baby* and
so forth.) Taking a rather different example, this time of children
engaged in what would be described in nursery discourses as 'object
play', I want to show that although features of the objects themselves
are crucial, what is important is that these objects can never be understood except in terms of a specific discourse, such that the objects are
'read' metaphorically to produce the actual linear sequencing of the
game. In the following sequence Jason, a four-year-old, is playing with
pieces of Lego. Let us see how he constructs the framework to operate
the game.

J:	This big crane look . . . Trying to make a long b. . . . sit down eh? Wanna sit down? No? That's what we got the seats for.	
T:	. . . . work for yourself won't you. It's like a fireman's ladder.	5
J:	Yeah. We has to put these on the top don't we 'cos if they . . .	
T:	Why do you have to put those on?	
J:	But so the fireman can climb up . . .	
T:	Is that the fire engine? You might need something else on here to balance so it doesn't fall over.	10
J:	No, no no I've got one.	
T:	No not wheels. If you put something heavy up there it'll stop it from falling over. Want to join it on. No wait a minute, oh go on then.	15
J:	This is 'ow we do it . . . another wheel another one.	
T:	Wait a minute, take it off and let's see. Take those off. Now find one of the other pieces that you can put in the middle there. That's it. See if you can get, will that go in there well maybe in this one one round here. Right now see if this one will go on the top.	20

J: Now I can carry on doing the ladders but there's not
many.

P2: Would you like your car fixed yeah ( ) yeah

J: No I'm making a big car.   25

P2: Big car yeah.

J: No, no.

P2: Mine is another car.

J: Yeah.

P2: Big car.   30

J: Yeah big car.

P2: Elephant yeah? Elephant car yeah? yeah elephant car?

J: No elephant car. Look we can put ladders on. Look we
can put ladders on it. Hey look wehey look an elephant
car (*Jason adds a trunk-like piece to the lego*) Elephant   35
car, elephant car.

P2: Yeah a big car

J: A big car the elephant car. The elephant car nearly fell
over.

P2: ( )   40

J: Elephant car, an elephant car eh, ooh that's save us.

P2: Mine was a good idea . . . . over here.

J: Look quick it's come off. . You pull it over. Don't pull it
over this side. No, it won't Another one fixed. Oh no.
Now make a fire Now this is a fire engine a car. This . . .   45
this, this is a crane.

P2: Yeah, yeah, it's a big car

J: No no no. Just want one more brick, put no.

P2: Indian car yeah? racing car yeah?

J: Indian car.   50

P2: Racing car yeah.

J: No no. I'm not making a racing car . . . I know

P2: My car is an Indian car your car is an Indian car . . . . is a
Cortina my car is a Cortina is a racing car.

J: I've seen, I've seen racing cars before I 'ave on telly. No,   55
try and make . . . no.

(*Jason begins by taking two pieces and joining them together.*)

At line 1 he begins the exchange with an opening metaphor, calling his
construction 'a big crane'. But, at this point the teacher intervenes with
the 'fireman's ladder' metaphor. Clearly in both of these metaphors,
each of which opens up a different potential discourse, the object's
shape itself is a crucial link in the potential chains of meaning. The
object has the potential to be understood in terms of a range of possible
metaphors (as in fact happens) but it is not possible that it could be
understood in a way which is external to any discourse whatsoever. In
this instance the fireman's ladder metaphor is developed to incorporate

more features of the discourse, namely a fireman (9) and a fire engine (10) with reference to a construction which is added onto the end of the object by Jason. At this point in the exchange, Jason is joined (24) by another pupil (P2). Now P2 introduces a new discourse by referring to the object as 'car' (24). Jason, apparently happy to change tack and begin a new discourse, retorts by calling it a 'big car' (25). P2 then produces, in relation to 'big', the formulation 'elephant car'. This leads Jason to extend the metaphor further by referring to an aspect of elephants other than their size, in this case the 'trunk'. At line (34), as Jason says: 'wehey, look an elephant car', he adds a trunk-like piece to the construction. Later, Jason revives both fire engine and crane metaphors (45,46). At line 50, P2 makes an unsuccessful attempt to control the flow of the game by changing the discourse. This attempt is rejected by Jason (52). As the sequence progresses, several other changes occur.

In the foregoing sequence it does not seem to be the case that the children are acting upon the objects in such a way that the language they are using should be seen as a secondary process, relegated to a level of representation that is grafted on *after* concepts are formed. It seems more plausible to infer that it is the relation of signified to signifier which is determinant in structuring the course of their play.

In the analysis of both of the above examples of play, I have argued that the children construct *metaphors* out of signified/signifier relations to 'read' the objects and that these are crucial in understanding the way that a particular discourse is 'called up'.

Let us examine further my use of the term 'metaphor'. Jakobson characterized language in terms of two basic axes of *selection* and *combination*. He referred to the process of combination, contextualization and contiguity as *metonymy* and those of selection, substitution and similarity as *metaphor*. Classically, metaphor has been treated in relation to *semantic* theories; and we can see that metaphor, whether it is understood as a phenomenon internal or external to the linguistic system, might well be central to an understanding of context. Perhaps the best known treatment of semantic relations in terms of child language research is Eve Clark's (1973) Semantic Feature Hypothesis, derived and developed from Bierwisch's (1970) Semantic Field Theory. This approach treats semantic relations in terms of a branching tree structure of related words, possessing from root to branch more and more 'features' added on to a basic stock. The roots of this model are seen to exist in basic human attributes, and pose again for us the problem of origins residing in the presocial cognitive subject.

There has been an increase in interest recently in the problem of metaphor, posed also in a variety of other ways. Gardner *et al.* (1978) pose the problem of children's acquisition of metaphor in terms of figurative language, and oppose it to rational forms of thought. Ortony (1979) edited a book called *Metaphor and thought* which also examines the relationship of metaphor to scientific thought and covers two opposing approaches to the study of metaphor: 'metaphor as an essential characteristic of the creativity of language; and metaphor as deviant and parasitic upon normal usage' (2).

Although the approaches discussed by Gardner *et al.* and in Ortony's book reveal considerable variation, they all pose as central the relation of language, context and the emergence of rational and scientific thought.

For the French psychoanalyst Jacques Lacan (1968), the problem of metaphor is also central. He has attempted to combine a Freudian with a semiotic analysis in which he poses the problem of 'the unconscious structured like a language' (Thom 1981). For Lacan, metaphor is what provides a key to understanding the construction of subjectivity. Metaphors stand in relation to and replace each other over time in the history of the life of an individual. To understand that history, and the process by which the unconscious is constructed, Lacan makes reference to the positioning of subjects within discourses.[1] In all of these approaches, the central question of the crucial importance of metaphors to children's understanding and the supposed absence of metaphor in mathematical discourse appears, though in different guises.

Potentially, an understanding of the importance of metaphor might provide a way to the relation of language to reason and to emotion. But this is speculative at this point. The importance of the use of the term 'metaphor' in the examples of data is that the choice of metaphors by the children provides a way of understanding their insertion into a particular discourse, and emphasizes the importance of the incorporation of the axis of *selection* into our understanding of child discourse, as opposed to the combination approach of most linguists (cf. Ervin-Tripp and Mitchell-Kiernan 1977).

The metonymic axis

We have seen how, in the play of young children, metaphors provide an opening into the use of a particular discourse, relating to particular practices. Once having established themselves as operating within particular discursive boundaries, children can both take up a variety of positions within a discourse and recognize what is both internal and external to the discourse. It is my hypothesis that young children can reason when a task is, to use Margaret Donaldson's term, 'embedded', because they can examine what is permissible within the particular practice which is called up by the metaphoric significance of that task. I am proposing that 'context-dependent' reasoning involves conscious reflection on the operation of a particular practice in terms of its articulation in discourse. I shall go on to examine some examples of this in more detail later in the paper, but first I want to speculate about the way in which formal reasoning differs from this.

[1] I have discussed this is more detail, particularly in relation to the learning of mathematics, in Walkerdine and Corran 1979 and 1981.

Formal reasoning also involves conscious reflection by the subject on a set of rules, but in this case the rules in question are the internal relations of combination of the metonymic axis. In practical reasoning we determine the truth or validity of a statement in terms of its correspondence to the rules of a practice, whereas in formal reasoning truth is determined in terms of the internal relations of the statement itself. To reflect on the internal relations alone we have to ignore the metaphoric content of a statement which might distract from the focus on the logical relations entailed in the statement, namely by directing attention to the practice to which the statement refers. Olson (1977) has argued convincingly that the process of reflection on the internal relations of a statement is facilitated by the technology of writing, and particularly the work of religious reformers, such as Luther, who asserted that the meaning of the Scriptures did not have to be explained by the interpretation of priests, but that the meaning was to be found within the text itself. Thus to find the 'truth' of the Scriptures one had only to examine the internal relations of the text. This process of looking for the meaning inside rather than outside the text is facilitated by writing, which allows us more easily to step back from the text in order to examine its internal relations.

I would argue further that the basis of formal reasoning need not be sought as an essential quality inside the mind, the result of the internalization of structures of action. Rather, we can see that the linguistic system itself provides the tools necessary to formal reasoning. The task then becomes one of explaining how children learn to reflect consciously on their practices and, later, on the internal relations of the statements themselves. Here again, we need not have recourse to explanations which focus solely on the properties of the mind. Olson's work indicates that it is the actual technology, the incorporation of individuals into particular practices in which spoken signs are translated into writing, which actually helps people to distance themselves from the production of the signs and to 'notice' their internal relations. Olson is not the only psychologist to relate reasoning in terms of the production of signs in their development in relation to technologies; Vygotsky (1979) and later Luria (1973), also emphasized the importance of this relation.

Learning to reason

There are now many studies which reveal that young children can reason when the logical relations of the task are 'embedded' in a meaningful context. I have argued earlier that what children are doing in these circumstances is reflecting upon the rules and relations of social practices which are represented as discursive rules in language. To support this claim I shall examine several of the studies referred to by Margaret Donaldson.

In McGarrigle and Donaldson's (1974) experimental study of conservation of number, they compared children's responses to a classic conservation problem with a version of the task in which the transformation of the array was effected by a naughty teddy bear who 'spoiled the game'. McGarrigle and Donaldson showed that young children perform better in the 'teddy bear' condition. Donaldson's argument implies that the children in each case are operating on the same logical relations, which are in one case supported by contextual relations. Let us, however, for a moment examine the tasks in more detail. I shall concentrate on the question, 'Are they the same?'

Clearly the metonymic relations are the same when the question is asked in each condition. However, the discursive conditions are quite different. In the teddy bear task the question is made to relate to the teddy's 'spoiling the game', thus calling up the discursive relations of a familiar practice involving playing games. In the standard task there is no explicit metaphoric relation to anything else; school practices may be implied for some children, but children as young as this have only a limited familiarity with such practices. The conditions for making inferences in relation to the boundaries of practices represented in discourse already exist as possibilities within language, in terms of the linguistic devices for linking statements in various ways. They are the conjunctors 'and', 'but', 'if', 'because' and so on.

Let us examine another of McGarrigle and Donaldson's tasks, it is a version of the classical Piagetian class-inclusion task, in this case:

Are there more black cows or more cows?

The experimenters found that young children's performance improved considerably when they changed the format to:

Are there more black cows or more sleeping cows?

Why should this be? The author's explanation was that the insertion of the word 'sleeping' placed greater emphasis on the total class. I would argue that the reason for this is that the addition of the terms 'sleeping' allows a sign to be created at the intersection of the material objects, 'cows', and the adjective, 'sleeping' – that is, it sets up a discursive frame in which to read the objects ('the cows are lying down'). The first task on the other hand relies far less on the metaphoric and far more on the metonymic axis for its comprehension, making the tasks discursively dissimilar.

Consider some examples of spontaneous 'embedded' reasoning on the part of young children, quoted by Donaldson (1978, 55):

One child, after seeing a picture of a house with no food in it, said: 'She must have eaten all her food on the other day.'

(*Premises:* (1) houses normally have food in them; (2) this house has no food.
Conclusion: the food must have been all eaten up).

'But how can it be [that they are getting married]? You have to have a man too.' (The book contains an illustration of a wedding in which the man looks rather like a woman. The child thinks it is a picture of two women.)
Premise: (1) you need a man for a wedding; (2) there is no man in the picture.
Conclusion: It can't be a wedding.

The first thing to note is that it is Margaret Donaldson who has converted the comments by the children into premises: the children's utterances do *not* take that discursive form. And, since it may well be the case that learning to reason involves learning to use particular discursive forms, then it could be a mistake to imply that somewhere *underneath* the discourse children are really reasoning. Not only do the children in these instances *not need* to reason formally – it *would not help* them. Their comments are based on their understanding of the everyday social practices, and in any case are based upon a limited data base. There is a difference between drawing inferences on the basis of knowledge of a practice and formal reasoning, and it is incorrect to assert that there is some hidden and essential way in which they are both really the same thing. Let us take the following invented example:
A child is on a train going from London to Edinburgh, which has just drawn in to Gretna Green station. He has been told that the train has just crossed the border into Scotland, and he remarks: 'This can't be Scotland, because there's nobody wearing a kilt.' In this statement the child is conforming discursively to some of the criteria of formal reasoning in that the conjunction, *because* is used. However, the major difference is that formal reasoning requires the determination of truth in terms of the internal relations of the statement, while in this case truth is determined by the fact that the child simply does not know certain facts about the construction of national boundaries. It would certainly be incorrect to infer from this that the child cannot reason, but it is just as mistaken to draw the conclusion that the child has mastered essential 'reasoning skills'. My point is that formal reasoning is an act performed upon language; it is a peculiar one which is not in any sense of the term 'natural', and we do not have to seek explanations in terms of the structures of the child's mind.
Let us take another example; consider the following:

All reds are blues
All blues are greens
Therefore all reds are greens

On first sight this appears to be nonsense and yet it is logically and internally correct. Indeed, it is the inclusion of *colours* which allows us to examine the task in relation to our colour knowledge and ignore the internal relations of the statements.

This helps us to clarify certain questions about the difference between formal and informal reasoning. In formal terms, the inference in the last statement is correct. Yet of course we know that this is 'not true'. But this is the point − there are different ways of discovering 'truth', and the point about formal reasoning is that the premises in no way need to conform to the 'truth' of our understanding of the world. Formal reasoning draws its validity from, and depends entirely upon, reflection on the metonymic axis − on the relations between signs and not on their metaphoric content: in other words, the 'meaning is in the text' (Olson 1977). In fact the metaphoric content of reasoning tasks serves only to confuse, in the sense that it is likely to send the subject off into the realms of the practice which the metaphor calls up, rather than allow concentration on the internal relations of the problem. Indeed, the importance of mathematical discourses is that they minimize the presence of metaphor so that internal reasoning is facilitated: they deliberately take out the content. But can human beings as easily take out the content when they approach formal tasks? We have seen that metaphor actually provides a crucial service in children's operation in the day-to-day world of social practice. Thus in approaching formal reasoning they actually have to suppress their metaphoric axis. Importantly, children do make sense of nonsense tasks by inserting them into the framework of a particular practice. Martin Hughes and Robert Grieve (1980) described how they asked children questions of the form:

Is yellow bigger than green?

The children always made sense of the task, for example, by making reference to examples of objects in the room, reporting that the answer was 'yes' because the yellow book was bigger than the green pencil.

That children will search for a discourse in which to situate a task is amply supported by the fact that children will and do interpret developmental tests, such as conservation tests, by picking up a feature of the task and making it the object of a familiar discourse, although the experimenter usually is unaware of this. On one occasion a colleague gave a conservation-of-number task to a girl and told her that they were going to do a trick. Afterwards the girl whispered to me that she had not been fooled and had watched the experimenter's hands the whole time.[2] Consider also the following examples from a top infant (6- to 7-year-olds) classroom of an interaction between children who are idly waiting in a queue to see the teacher:

---

[2] For examples of this in relation to school tasks see Walkerdine and Sinha 1981.

P1:   First one to say green is the winner.
P2:   Green.
P1:   I've already said it!

There is no indication of previous conversations about colours, and yet the children are able to produce and make sense of an apparently non-sensical task by incorporating it into a game. The children are already recognizing the substitutability of metaphors within particular metonymic strings which go to make up discursive formats.

I am arguing then that children have to learn particular discursive forms incorporating particular turns of phrase, which they acquire very early, but later they have to learn to examine these discursive statements in terms of their linguistic relations alone. They tend to learn to do this by recognizing that certain (usually school) practices require that statements be treated in particular ways. This can be aided by transforming the statements into written texts, which performs a distancing function, allowing the learners to focus on the internal construction of the statements. Although I have approached this as a developmental question, there is no evidence to suggest that it actually has anything to do with children *per se*. I have argued that the techniques of formal reasoning depend upon exposure to certain practices and to reflection on the metonymic axis; this is neither natural nor an everyday phenomenon, in the sense that formal reasoning is not required to fulfil the exigencies of everyday life. Thus it is not surprising that many psychologists report similar findings to those of children with illiterate or unschooled adults. There is no basis for inferring that the results of reasoning tasks show that such people are childlike or have undeveloped minds.

To reason according to the internal metonymic relations of a statement is not easy, and although adults like to think of themselves as 'rational', most everyday decisions are not taken formally. That this is so becomes clear when we are confronted with statements which are at odds with the conditions of a particular practice. Margaret Donaldson (1978, 79) quotes one such example from the work of Mary Henle: here is the task:

> A group of women were discussing their household problems. 'It's so important to talk about things that are in our minds. We spend so much time in the kitchen that, of course, household problems are in our minds. So it is important to talk about them.'
> Does this follow?
> One subject answered: 'No, just because one spends so much time in the kitchen it does not necessarily follow that household problems are "in our minds".' But this answer is not a judgement on whether the conclusion ('So it is important to talk about them') is necessarily true if the premises are true. It is a rejection of one of the premises.

The problem seems difficult, and it is little helped by the fact that it is written down here. It is at odds with a familiar practice which makes it difficult to accept the premises and words on their 'internal' truth value. (Cole and Schribner (1974) report a similar refusal to accept the premises of formal tasks on the part of the Kpelle farmers of Liberia. For example, in response to a syllogism beginning 'Fluomo and Yacpalo are drinking cane juice', respondents would typically refuse the task on the grounds that they did not know the participants, or they did not drink, or whatever.)

However, the question of the metaphoric content of the premises is an important one. Even statements in science contain metaphoric content. When the premises or metaphors appear to be uncontentious we believe ourselves to be reasoning according to the internal relations. In scientific discourse, for example, we believe that the 'truth' gained is done so in a way external to ideological content. Yet the metaphoric content ensures that this is not so. Is it possible even here to separate one kind of truth from another? Hirst and Woolley (in press), discussing non-Western cultures and their relation to rationality, assert:

> *Post eventum* we may be less than happy with the 'criteria of effectiveness' of Western science and technology. To judge a civilization 'superior' by its own standards of technique is to ignore the objectives those techniques can be asked to serve. In a world busily consuming its nonrenewable forms of stored energy, probably dependent for the continued maintenance of its current scientific and technical order on the hazards of nuclear power, and possessing the *means* to create conditions of life in which the survivors would envy the Azande, we raise the question of relative 'rationality' of forms of belief at our peril.

Practices for reasoning

In this section I shall show how certain practices in early education lead the way to formal reasoning. First of all, it will be no surprise to anyone who has worked in early education that the prevailing concern is with *doing*. Children learn how to *do* things, and reference is constantly made to what is to be done and how it is to be done. Children are led into new discourses by learning the rules of educational practices, and because of the focus in early education on learning through doing the focus is on what has to be done and what it is permissible to do. Hence the question of power and authority is very important here. The boundary between what is allowed in the classroom and what is permitted in the discourse is extremely blurred. This is important because it allows us to see how children are weaned from the authority of the teacher to the authority of the text itself (cf. Olson 1980).

In data collected in three infant schools in London, focusing on children doing mathematics, the examples of children talking about what to do and about the rules of the procedures in which they are involved are ubiquitous in our corpus : examples appear on almost every page of the transcript. Here are just two examples of exchanges from two different schools.

In the first example, a group of top infant (6- to 7-year-old) children are doing work on place value. In the teacher's instructions to the children, instructions about the rules of place value are delivered in the same form as instructions which are simply points of style:

> *T:*   What I want you to do is to take the matchsticks that are on the table over there. Be very careful with them because they're not ordinary matchsticks, they're some that Miss – bought and I want you to take ten and with the elastic bands that I've put there make them into little bundles for me. Be very careful that there are ten.''

Now, this is the teacher's introduction to the topic. In a way typical of the classrooms we have observed she does not explain the propositional content of the topic but focuses on what has to be done.

A few lines later we can see that the children are already focusing on what is and what is not allowed:

> *M:*   There, that's me first one. I done me first one. Good. Two-four-six-eight-ten. Doesn't matter what you do, how many you do.

The teacher makes several references to the work as a game, which sets the children up to read it in terms of that discourse and hence as something which is rule-governed. In all the sequences it is very difficult for the children to tell the difference between operational rules and the rules of the discourse because they are all presented in the same mode. The children ask such things as whether to write in pencil, which way round to have the paper, whether to write the date and if they have to leave spaces between numbers. They often work out what to do in terms of references to what has already been done, for example, 'It's like the ones we did yesterday', as in the following example in which one of the researchers comes to ask the children what they are doing:

> *GC:*   What are you doing?
> *M:*   We're doing the same as yesterday, you know.
> *To:*   Two, that's not right, OK I'll put two on.
> *K:*   You're not doing all of them are you?
> *To:*   There, twenty-three.
> *M:*   All of them, all of them. Close your eyes.
> *K:*   Yeah, but you've already done all of them once.
> *M:*   Yeah, but we can do them twice.

K: You can't.
M: You can.
K: You can't.
M: You can.
K: You can't. Right, I'm going to ask Miss.
M: Come on. C'mon let's go and ask.

I suggest then that the transfer to formal reasoning is helped by the fact that children are introduced to discourses in terms of what they have to do and what is and is not permitted. It is in this way that they learn to approach texts in a particular way, recognising that certain features have to be attended to while other features can be ignored. In the following sequence the teacher is explaining to a group of children how to proceed in a task that she has given them. It is a subtraction exercise in the form of a ten-pin bowling game.

T: First of all, put your name on the top. . . . leave your boards on the chairs, I think your pencils will slot through the little holes on the clip so they're not rolling about. . . .
Tra: You can put yours through here can't you? No it won't go.
T: Can you carry on for a few minutes now? Who's going to have the first go? Who's got the ball?
Tra: I got it.
T: Look, Hilary's waiting to give her the ball. Right off you go and when you have had a go, go and. . . .
Tra: I had two.
T: Right, now write the sum down on your score sheet.
Tra: Oh yeah, I gotta write my sum what I had haven't I? Oh dear, oh I done it wrong. Ten, ten take away two leaves . . . eight.

Interestingly, while there is considerable attention paid to the rules of the practice, there is very little evidence of teachers encouraging children to approach problems using the discursive patterns of reasoning either in relation to the limits of practices or in relation to statements themselves. I would submit that the reason for this is to be found in the approach in primary schools, which accounts for the development of reasoning in terms of the internalization of action and not in discourse. In fact when children try to speculate about the relations about numbers they are often discouraged and led back to experience.

From practice to discourse, from context to text

There is one particular technique which is practised by the teachers observed in the London schools. In each case the teachers describe their technique as giving the children experience of objects in order to teach them a particular mathematical concept. However, what the teachers do is to get the children to perform a series of translation exercises so that a statement embedded in a particular practice is transformed into written numerals where the meaning is internal to the text. I shall examine one instance of this strategy: it comes from a lesson in which a nursery school teacher is introducing a small group of children to a task which she describes as the union of sets. (Another example may be found in Walkerdine and Corran 1979.)

The teacher begins:

T: . . . . and I know Debbie did so we're just going to go over what you did at home and what you started before. How many's there?
Ch: Two
T: How many's there? There? How many's there? Two and put them altogether. How many have we got already?

She puts the blocks in two piles on the table, and as she says 'put them all together' she moves them together with her hands. This her first relation of signified (moving the blocks) and signifier (saying the words). The task is practised a second time and then the teacher makes an interesting move in discourse:

T: Good boy, let's count them altogether. One-two-three-four-five-six-seven. So Nicola had four, Debbie had three, so three and four make . . . (*she puts the blocks together*)
Ch: Seven.

She repeats the same exercise of putting the blocks together, but this time the phrase that she uses refers to the blocks *implicitly* but makes no reference in language to them, so that she introduces the children in this way to the 'disembedded' form of the statement: 'three and four make . . . '. (Hughes (1980) has observed that young children can in fact respond to statements in this form *only* when the referents remain implicit, and fail to comply when the statement is produced without previous referents, either material or imaginary.) Hughes's finding lends support to the assertion that children have to be led to the discursive forms of mathematical statements via a process which retains the same metonymic form but gradually strips away the metaphors. The teacher's next move is to take the children from utterance to the first stage of written representation.

T: Seven when they're together and we wrote it down. Debbie did this —
        (*She produces a diagram*)
        — do you remember those funny pictures? and we had four

up here and a three down there and these mean you've got four and they all go along there and we've got three and they all go along there so we put them altogether and count them and how many have we got? Seven. We've still got seven let's do another one. Right see if Nicola can do this one for me just like I did them. Put them altogether, see how many you've got in each one and put them altogether.

N: Seven

The teacher has drawn three large circles on a sheet of paper and joined the top two circles with the bottom circle by a line. This time, as she makes the statement of the same discursive form as the last, she moves the blocks down the lines into the bottom circle. This task is practised several times and the children are encouraged as the movements are made to repeat the discursive form: ' − and − makes −'.

Each time the word 'makes' is articulated the teacher actually does make the two piles into one. Thus again new metaphoric relations of signified and signifier are produced while maintaining the same metonymic form. The next stage is to make the relationship between the metonymic form in speech and in a written (in this case drawn) representation.

T: Good girl. Now we've got some on cards like this . . . and to make it a little bit easier we're going to trace over so it won't take us a long time. Right, Nicole, can you get me the pencils from over there? Three we want, three nice pencils. Right now, Debbie, are you watching? Thank you. Now that's what you're going to have and you've got to trace over first of all everything that's on there. Right? Then you go round the squares and count them as you go. One-two-three and one and then you've got to draw what you've got there. So we've got to draw three and we've got to draw − are you watching me 'cos you won't know what to do − so I'll put those three in there instead of moving them 'cos we can't pick them up, so I've drawn them in and I've drawn that one in, and three and one make?

N: Four.

Here the children's task is to trace the circles, lines and blocks which have now been drawn on paper. The drawings act as iconic metaphors for the blocks, again by producing a new relation of signified to signifier. The relation of representation between the drawings and the blocks is made quite explicit by the teacher:

I've drawn that one in and one and three make?
And again later:

If we had then on there like this we could pick them up couldn't we and move them, but we haven't, so you've got to draw how many you've got in the circle.

The making metaphor is still related to physical action even when the drawings are used, as the teacher still moves her fingers down the line as she says 'makes'. Soon one of the children uses this herself. The same child describes her work in terms of 'carrying' even though there are no physical objects involved:

Ch: 'I carried them up and then I drawed them.'

(Of course the 'carrying' metaphor is not a stranger to the discourse of mathematical education, as in 'carrying tens' etc. in place value work.)
    The teacher then encourages the children to write the numeral 4 next to their drawing of four blocks. Again we can interpret this in terms of the construction of a relationship of signified (drawing) to the signifier (numeral). The teacher then performs the next translation exercise converting the metonymic form from iconic to symbolic representation of numerals.

T: And we draw those two and those three and altogether they made? What you said before. One, two . . .
D: Three, four, five.
T: Right can you draw a five? Do a five there. Now in our books just one stage further. . . . Now then in our books. That's how a five goes. Do me a five there. Now then Nicole do you remember you did this at home?
N: Yes.
T: Now this is exactly the same except I've written in the numbers and what you do. Let's do one together first. How many have I written there?
S: Two.
T: And how many have I written there?
Ch: Two.
T: So then you think, oh I need two – (*She gets two blocks*) – and I need another two because it says two and then you do exactly the same you move them altogether and count them up. . . .
N: It says four.
T: . . .'. but you don't draw them you write the number. Right, let's do another one. How many does that say?

Indeed at this point at least one of the children becomes very excited and urges the teacher to 'do another'. I can think of no other plausible explanation for her excitement than that she is pleased by the relation of numeral to drawing. To her the move from utterance to text seems complete. Interestingly, later, when one child appears to be having difficulty, the teacher takes the child back to the explicit use of metaphor and in this case substitutes a metaphor which locates the task more firmly in terms of an everyday practice: she refers to the circles as 'houses' and to the blocks as 'people'.

> *T:* Got to go down, these lines. Right that's my house and that's your house. Right and that's you and your sister. Right and that's me and my brother and my sister. . . .
>
> *N:* Seven, one, two, three, four. . .
>
> *T:* Right and we're all going to visit somebody and that's their house, so I've got there with my brother and my cat and you've got there with your sister. So (. . .) and two of you and we've all gone in the same house and they're altogether and how many's in that house altogether now?
>
> *D:* Five.

In this case the task is not in any sense made more 'concrete' or related more closely to action: it is the posing of the task in the terms of a familiar practice which allows it to enter into a system of meaning which is crucial.

Some problem aspects of metaphor

I have argued earlier that children learn to operate within a variety of practices through the medium of discourse. When they come to school they are already adept at this, as we have seen.

In the early mathematics curriculum children are regularly provided with tasks in the form of the practices with which the children are familiar. For example, a subtraction task can be carried out as a 'shopping game' in which the children have to buy articles written on playing cards and subtract the amount from 10p. It is generally felt that such problems must be helpful to children because they 'embed' new tasks in familiar contexts. . . . However, it is my argument that the kind of analysis of discourse that I am advocating pinpoints the fact that children's understanding of situations in terms of discourse and in terms of their relation to the rules of the discourse in which they believe themselves to be operating means that we can show *specific* and *precise* effects of the children's understanding. The argument which sees context as external to skills still makes the assumption that in an 'underlying' way there is similarity of psychological tasks.

When Michael Cole and his colleagues (1979) explored the emergence of reasoning skills in home-like contexts, they reported that they rarely witnessed an example of what we could see as a laboratory type of psychological task.

The most striking feature of these club sessions was the extreme rarity of identifiable cognitive tasks. If the classroom could be characterized as an environment where cognitive tasks were identifiable with intervals of 'doing nothing' interspersed, the club sessions could be characterized as an environment of chaotic activity with identifiable tasks interspersed at rare intervals. It is certainly *not* the case that the children were sitting quietly, lost in thought. They were active, argumentative and constantly busy. But classification, inference and other tasks we had hoped to discover weren't easily detectable, even after several repeated viewings of our videotaped record. We found ourselves in the somewhat absurd situation where *activities* that clearly required the cognitive processes we were interested in studying *must* have been operating, the recipes got read, the cakes baked and the animals trained, but we could not identify how these goals were accomplished in a way that was directly related to those intellectual tasks that are the backbone of process-oriented cognitive psychology. (Cole *et al*. 1979, 11)

In our work (Corran and Walkerdine 1980) we found that preschool children often engage in tasks in which numbers are mentioned. However, these tasks fall into two distinct types: there are *instrumental* tasks in which the goal is the accomplishment of something in relation to a practice. A mother might say to a child when she is making a cake, 'bring me two eggs'. On the other hand, there are tasks whose only purpose is *pedagogic*: the children may be asked to count their coat buttons or the stairs as they climb them and there is no practical purpose for their so doing. These two types of task are quite distinct and do not overlap. So, firstly we can infer that children *do* have experience of *explicitly* pedagogic tasks and so are used to operating according to a discourse in which the object of the task is merely the production of the required demand. However, these are distinct formats which are discursively quite different from those of the practical tasks.

In the presentation of mathematical tasks 'embedded' in practical tasks we then have a discursive overlap. Here the tasks appear to be instrumental and yet the *purpose* is pedagogic. The children in the school example do not really go shopping and, in fact, the rules of the game are such that they have to subtract an amount from 10p each time they pick a card, rather than, as in a real shopping task, having less and less money left each time. Now, most of the children who undertake this particular task explicitly recognize that it is not 'real' shopping.

'It's Hilary's go now. It's good innit. What you buying?'
'She's buying a basket 2p. Isn't it cheap! My mum's shopping bag was £6.'
. . .
'2p's not rich. It's not enough to buy bubble gums and a bazooka.'

One boy, Gordon, really does think he is to treat this as a real shopping task and consequently makes errors in his sums because he operates as though he has less and less money each turn and ends up with no money left: several times he mentions that he can't go on playing because he hasn't enough money and finally the teacher intervenes:

Tr: He's got a dolly.
T: Well buy it for me Gordon, I should love a doll
G: I've just got 1p.
L: No you haven't you got all them.
G: That's over there I spent that
T: Oh, I see what you're doing. No, it's alright, you . . . each time, you get another ten pence to go shopping with.

In this instance we can see that context is not simply an effect, nor always helpful, but is a question of different and distinct domains of discourse with varying rules of operation.

Let us examine one more instance of school mathematics in which a mismatch between the discourse of the teacher and the discourse within which the children believe her to be operating. The children are in a nursery (3 to 5 years old) class and the teacher is teaching one-to-one mapping of number; to do this she has drawn on paper two columns of circles each containing a number of dots, from one to five:

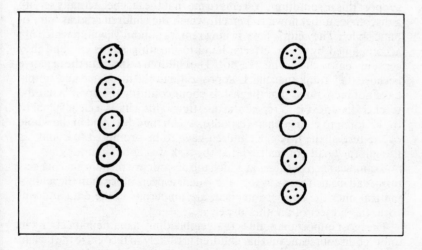

The task for the children is to join up with the pencil line the circles containing the same number of dots. This task acts as a preliminary to another task, which is one I want to examine in detail. After the children have done the mapping exercise the teacher presents a fresh piece of paper as follows:

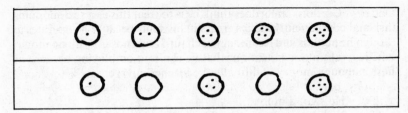

The sequence of dots goes from one to five, left to right. In the top row all dots are there, but in the bottom row some circles contain no dots. The teacher's aim is to get the children to specify the missing numbers. This is how she introduces the task:

> 'Now whoever drew these kept on yawning and every time she yawned she missed some out. So, we've got that one . . . Have we got the two?'

Now, the response of the children is to chorus 'No-oo!' in a manner which is best described as a pantomime style. The teacher then asks: 'Have we got the three?' to which the children respond in precisely the same manner as in the previous example: 'No-oo!' In this case there *are* three dots, so why do they make this mistake? It certainly cannot be the case that the children cannot count or that they do not recognize three dots. There is ample evidence elsewhere in the classroom data to support this assumption. It seems to me that the teacher actually sets up a discourse, unbeknown to herself, which the children read as 'pantomime style'. They enjoy her opening remarks about yawning which are accompanied by sound effects, hand-to-mouth gestures etc. and they certainly enjoy chorusing 'No-oo!' The children respond in the negative because they think that this is appropriate to the discourse and simply have not recognized that the task is about counting the dots. What the teacher does next is to repeat the question. This acts as a clear signal to the children to change their response, which they do.[3] And in the whole of the rest of the task the children have to be prompted to count, as though they had not realized that the task was about counting.

Examples such as these, in which the discourse which the teacher sets up is read in such a way as to make salient aspects other than the mathematical ones the teacher intended, are numerous in the data and will form the subject of another paper.

The most important point is that 'embedding' a mathematical task in another discourse means that children are likely to recognize the task in terms of that discourse. If they recognize that it is 'really' a mathematical task it is because they have learned that the 'embedded' discourse

---

[3] Cf. the discussion about asking the same questions twice in conservation tasks is relevant here.

features of the task are irrelevant to the solution of the problem. Since this has to be learned and is not a 'cognitive skill', it is not surprising that young children often mistake the mathematical tasks for 'real' practical tasks. So, we need to be aware that the discursive relations called up by the metaphor not only map on to *some* of the mathematical relations, but introduce *other* relations which may well be at variance with the mathematical relations.

These examples reveal some of the difficulties in an explanation which sees children as possessing underlying cognitive skills which have to be 'disembedded' from the context. The fact that the children are engaged in operating within a variety of discourses and learning that certain pedagogic discourses require information to be treated in particular ways clearly provides a more fruitful line of analysis.

Conclusion

Throughout this chapter I have developed the theme that in order to account for the development of abstract thinking, it is more fruitful to seek explanations in terms of language and signification than to have recourse to psychological essentialism. Even explanations, such as Piaget's, which envisage the production of mental structures in terms of their interaction of the human being and the physical environment, account neither for the linguistic nor for the social nature of our understanding of ourselves and our world. Children do not have raw experiences of concrete objects: meaning is created at the intersection of the material and the discursive, the fusing of signified and signifier to produce a sign. These meanings are located in, and understood in terms of, actual social practices, represented in speech as discourse. It is by analysing the form and content of discourse, the processes of selection and combination, of metaphor and metonymy, that we can account for the origins and processes of reasoning. Young children are able to shift in and out of discourses from an extremely young age and I have examined some of the ways in which they adopt different discursive positions. I have argued that young children can reason in familiar contexts not because they possess reasoning 'skills' which are contextually bound, but because the metaphoric context of the task allows them to examine the task within the boundaries of a particular practice. Formal reasoning, on the other hand, requires reflection on the internal metonymic relations of the statement itself, whether or not it is 'truthful' in terms of what makes sense with in a particular practice. This is not a natural phenomenon: it has to be learned, and I have looked at some of the ways in which young children are helped towards formal reasoning in school − in particular, how teachers manage in very subtle ways to move the children from utterance to text by a process in which the metonymic form of the statement remains the same while the relations on the metaphoric axis are successfully transformed, until the children are left with a written metonymic statement, in which the same metaphors exist only by implication. It is this process which is crucial to the production of abstract thinking.

We can, however, end the chapter with a salutary reminder that even in the 'disembedded' realm of numbers the metaphors we use for the purpose of classification can have lasting effects. A six-year-old in a mathematics lesson, when asked what she was doing, replied: 'You have to colour all the evil numbers in. First you have to write it up to a hundred and then you colour all the evil numbers in.'

Her task was to do a 100 square and to colour in the *even* numbers! In another infant classroom during a discussion of odd and even numbers, the teacher found that the children cheered every time an even number was mentioned and booed the odd numbers. Such was their introduction to the universe of rational discourse.

References

Adlam, D., Henriques, J., Rose, N., Salfield, A., Venn, C., and Walkerdine, V. 1977: Psychology, ideology and the human subject. *Ideology and Consciousness* 1.

Bierwirsch, M. 1970: Semantics. In J. Lyons (ed.), *New horizons in linguistics*. Harmondsworth: Penguin.

Bruner, J. 1975: From communication to language: a psychological perspective. *Cognition* **3(3)**.

Clark, E.V. 1973: What's in a word? On the child's acquisition of semantics in his first language. In T.E. Moore (ed.), *Cognitive development and the acquisition of language*. New York and London: Academic Press.

Cole, M., Hood, L. and McDermott, R. 1979: *Ecological niche picking*. Rockefeller University Monograph.

Cole, M. and Schribner, S. 1974: *Culture and thought*. New York: Wiley.

Corran, G. and Walkerdine, V. 1980: Making it count: children's acquisition of natural numbers in speech. Paper presented at British Psychological Society Education Section Conference, Lancaster.

Donaldson, M. 1978: *Children's minds*. London: Fontana.

Ervin-Tripp, S. and Mitchell-Kernan, C. 1977: *Child discourse*. New York: Academic Press.

Foucault, M. 1972: *The archaeology of knowledge*. London: Tavistock.

—1977: *Discipline and punish*. London: Allen Lane.

Gardner, H., Winner, E., Bechhofer, R. and Wolf, D. 1978: Figurative language. In K. Nelson (ed.), *Children's language*, vol. 1. Gardner Press.

Hirst, P.Q. and Woolley, P. in press: *Social relations and human attributes*. London: Tavistock.

Hughes, M. and Grieve, R. 1980: On asking children bizarre questions. *First Language* 1.

Lacan, J. 1968: *Ecrits*. London: Tavistock.

Luria, A.R. 1973: *The working brain*. Harmondsworth: Penguin.

McGarrigle, J. and Donaldson, M. 1974: Conservation accidents. *Cognition* 3, 341–50.

Nelson, K. 1980: Paper presented at the British Psychological Society Developmental Section Conference, Edinburgh.

Olson, D. 1977: From utterance to text: the bias of language in speech and writing. *Harvard Educational Review* 47, 257–81.

——1980: On the language and authority of textbooks. *J. Communication* 47.

Ortony, A. (ed.) 1979: *Metaphor and thought*. Cambridge: CUP.

de Saussure, F. 1974 edn.: *A course in general linguistics*. London: Fontana.

Thom, M. 1981: The unconscious structured like a language. In C. McCabe (ed.), *The talking cure: essays in psychoanalysis and language*. London: Macmillan.

Vygotsky, L.S. 1979: *Mind in society*. Cambridge, Mass.: Harvard University Press.

Walkerdine, V. and Corran, G. 1979: Cognitive development: a mathematical experience? Paper presented at British Psychological Society Developmental Section Conference, Southampton.

—— 1981: Experience and discourse in mathematics learning: some examples from classroom practice. Paper presented at conference on Piaget and the Helping Professions, Los Angeles.

Walkerdine, V. and Sinha, C. 1978: The internal triangle: language, reasoning and the social context. In I. Markova (ed.), *The social context of language*. New York and Chichester: Wiley.

—— 1981: Developing linguistic strategies in young school children. In Wells 1981.

Wells, G. (ed.) 1981: *Learning through interaction*. Cambridge: CUP.

7

Classroom constructs: an interpretive approach to young children's language

Michael Beveridge and Chris Brierley

Children in nursery schools are unlikely to view their classroom activities in the same way as their teachers. A child building with Lego is not concerned whether his hand eye coordination is being improved; a group of children holding a party in the Wendy House are not concerned that their social skills and understanding of the concepts of sharing and cooperation are being fostered; when the teacher reads a story to the whole class, no child is wondering about the extent to which concentration and memory are being exercised.

What then is the classroom as experienced by children? And what meaning do they attach to the various activities? In this chapter we are concerned with the ways in which children in nursery school think about the classroom situations and activities to which they are exposed. We are interested in what goes through a young child's mind when he chooses, for example, to make plasticine figures. And when he rejects the facilities provided for him what makes them unsuitable? Overall, what do children make of it all?

Our approach to this problem was to spend a period of three months with 30 children in their classroom, observing them and asking them about what they said and did. Towards the end of this period of participant observation, when we had a clearer idea of what was important to them in their classroom activities, the children were asked about pictures of classroom events. Our data base thus consisted of a series of children's spontaneous utterances and behaviours, plus recording of some interviews. The difficult methodological problem is not collecting such data but making some sense of it, on the assumption that it did make some overall sense to the children. After some time in the classroom we felt there were interesting patterns in the children's views of their environment and that it was worthwhile trying to capture these patterns. Our attempt to do so, offered in this chapter, uses the framework devised by Kelly (1955) in his elaboration of Personal Construct Theory. We would like to stress that, while we feel that the resulting analysis does capture an important part of what was happening, the rules for inferring constructs from our data cannot be made completely explicit. We have however given a large number of examples which we hope will give the reader some insights into how we derive the system which is presented. But before turning to the data we will explicate briefly what Kelly meant by the concepts we have borrowed.

Kelly's approach is unusual in that he set out a formal theory, not designed to account for any sub-area of psychology nor to 'disprove' other psychological theories, but intended as merely an alternative way of looking at the same phenomena. Kelly claims that 'A person's construct system is composed of a finite number of dichotomous constructs' (1955, 22). This might seem to mean that events are construed as either x or y, but Kelly goes on to point out that this is not necessarily so, and his use of 'dichotomous' does not imply exclusion but is a scalar concept. An event may be construed as more or less congruent with either pole of the construct, according to its usefulness in 'anticipating the greater possibility for the elaboration of his system'.

Kelly points out that 'A construct is convenient for the anticipation of a finite range of events only' (68). Each construct is especially applicable to one aspect of experience – its focus of convenience. It is also applicable, though less so, to other aspects which compose its range of convenience. Outside of the range of convenience lie whole areas to which the construct cannot be applied. Constructs vary in their range of convenience from narrow (sheep/goat) to broad (good/bad). In the light of experience, a person may elaborate his construct system in several ways, developing new constructs, widening their range of convenience and articulating the relationships between them.

A person uses his constructs, Kelly notes, in three different modes. The first of these, the preemptive mode, involves construing an object as x and only x. In this mode, a child might see a cupboard in the Wendy House as only a cupboard, preventing him from conceding that it can be a barrier, a car, a seat, a stage or anything else, according to his purposes. The preemptive mode, when applied to objects, blocks the imagination, but when it is applied to persons it is not only limiting but dangerous. Thus to see a child as nothing but a child, obviating the possibility that he can be a friend, colleague, rival etc., has serious consequences.

Not quite so extreme is the constellatory mode. In this, a person sees something as 'x and therefore y and z'. For teachers the mode is extremely tempting: to see a child as 'untidy' can often lead to assumptions regarding his scholastic incompetence, manners and overall potential; similarly, the constellation of constructs focusing on 'broken home' or 'lower-class' must have had disastrous effects on the life-chances of innumerable children. And, in the educational context, children as a whole often come out in a poor position: 'child' often implies incompetence, irrationality and the absence of a need to be taken seriously.

The last mode, the propositional, recognizes that our hypotheses about the world are not intrinsically or necessarily true, and should always be open to a form of falsification; not because they are not 'true' in any absolute sense, but because they are not as useful as an alternative construction. There are therefore, in Kelly's terms, no *a priori's*:

> Kelly is asserting that we cannot contact an interpretation-free reality directly. We can only make assumptions about what reality is and then proceed to find out how useful or useless these assumptions are. (Bannister and Fransella 1971, 19)

Two more bipolar dimensions are essential to Kelly's explanation of how a 'person's processes are channelized'. Our construction systems are developed by what he terms 'dilation', in which an apparently unassimilable experience is made congruent with our constructs by a reorganization of superordinate constructs, so that the range of convenience of a lower-order construct can be extended to include the experience. At the opposite pole, constriction is the process by which the range of convenience of a construct is narrowed in order to eliminate apparent contradictions, by keeping subsystems separate.

The second pair of terms, forming a single dimension (tight/loose) refers to the processes by which the interrelationship of constructs is made explicit or allowed to be open to reorganization. These two poles are not conceived by Kelly as either good or bad *per se*, but as necessary stages in the process of elaboration. Thus, for instance:

> A person may dilate successfully and become a larger personality or extend out into chaos; while another person may constrict and thereby make more tidy and controllable his world, or move inexorably towards the ultimate constriction of suicide. (Bannister and Fransella 1971, 33)

Kelly was not critical of either tightness or looseness in themselves, but of the use of one to the exclusion of the other. Both are necessary stages in development: beginning from a tight construct system, there is a need to loosen it up, to dilate and thus open up new potential; but this must be followed by a tightening, in which new connections are made secure; the process can then begin again. This notion of a cycle of development in construing is central to our discussion of the way in which children see the classroom.

The elaboration of a person's construct system is, according to Kelly, an ongoing process, 'the thing itself', and what needs to be explained is the particular direction in which elaboration is executed. By 'elaboration' Kelly does not mean loosening or dilation alone, but the whole cycle of movement from tight to loose and back again. It is necessary then to specify under what conditions movement will be in a particular direction.

The extreme relativism of construct theory means that any application is tentative and exploratory, so that no clear directives as to its use can be given. This does not mean that the theory itself is in any way vague. As Peck and Whitlow (1975, 53) point out: 'Personal construct theory constitutes a brave and imaginative attempt to create a comprehensive cognitive theory of personality.'

Kelly is not however, beyond reproach, though some of the criticisms levelled against him involve an oversimplification of his position – for example, Bruner's point:

> I rather suspect that when some people get angry or inspired or in love, they couldn't care less about their system-as-a-whole. One gets the impression that the author is, in his personality theory, over-reacting against a generation of irrationalism. (Bruner *et al*. 1956, 356)

However, Kelly did not see men as wholly rational; indeed, he emphasized the irrationality of many of our actions, and his specific concern was with those whose behaviour was apparently irrational. His seeming neglect of affect is merely superficial, and is part of his refusal to separate affective and cognitive aspects of the person. Nor is it true that he neglected, as Peck and Whitlow (1975, 54) claim, unconscious processes and learning.

Some criticisms, however, seem to be justified. Some of Kelly's concepts are circular. Thus permeability/impermeability is used to explain the fact that some constructs are easily elaborated while others resist elaboration, but it is simply another way of stating the same thing: we can only infer permeability/impermeability from the extent to which constructs are elaborated. The only way in which Kelly might resolve this problem would be to develop his thesis around the concept of context, drawing out the ways in which certain situations inherently encourage the use of preemptive modes of thinking, or of loose constructs etc. As Maddi (1968, 115) says, 'What Kelly fails to give is an explanation of why people will continue along a particular line. He simply does not deal with the question.'

This is related to Kelly's failure to extend his work beyond the individual, to specify his relationship to society. What is missing from Kelly's work is an account of the origins of constructs, or their association with persons situated in certain social positions. This point is made by Maddi (1968, 116): 'Nowhere in Kelly's writing is there a list or typology of likely constructs. Kelly could . . . provide such specification on the content of personality by describing the kind of constructs one can expect to find in persons with particular histories of environmental interaction.' The study to be described here takes up this point, and is specifically concerned to provide the beginnings of such an inventory for three-year-old children in the nursery class. But before discussing our work we should indicate some of the ways children have been studied using Kelly's framework.

Children and personal construct theory

In some ways, Kelly's account of the development of the person has common points with that of Piaget. From the earliest stage, he points out, infants see the world in terms of constructs. At first these are pre-verbal, and physicalistic, and the only way to observe their use is via behaviour. As the child grows older his construct system is constantly elaborated, perception being in terms of complex constructs of increasing abstraction; but this is not seen as the result of development in the Piagetian sense, rather as a result of direct serial confrontation with experience. Whereas Piaget's view rested on the assumption of the accessibility of absolute truth, as represented by formal logic, Kelly's assumptions deny this accessibility:

> Reality can never be known in any final, absolute way, but only through our constructions which, as a result of the varying valida-tional outcomes of the behavioural experiments we make, are subject to continual revision. (Salmon 1976, 214)

While at first the child's constructs are preverbal, in time he learns to articulate them (though there is always a nonverbal component in con-struing, which accounts for the fact that the greater part of our reality-construction is 'unconscious', and thus contradictions may persist, the construer never becoming aware of them).

Ravenette (1975) developed techniques for investigating the con-structs of children, but in his empirical work he used provided elements and provided constructs, rather than eliciting them from the child, and he confined his investigation to areas which were directly relevant to the child's clinical problem. Nevertheless, Ravenette proceeds to document the contrasts between children and adults, and concludes that the clearest differences are that whereas adults anticipate change on the basis of reasonably stable expectations, this is not true of children, but that the foundation of the construct system is laid down in childhood.

Ravenette's account is fairly convincing, but his work does little more than confirm what we would expect from a Piagetian perspective. However, with respect to our own study Ravenette makes an important methodological point:

> Repertory grids provide flexible means whereby children can be invited to communicate various aspects of the ways in which they affect, and are affected by, their world of people. *They are suitable· for children from about the age of eight years and upwards.* (82)

Applebee's (1975, 1976) work places the emphasis on the cultural dimension of constructs, and he was especially concerned with consensus in construing. Such consensus, he pointed out, 'in patterns of construing is the basis of a shared or common cultural experience, providing a general framework within which each individual develops his own unique construction of the world' (1975, 473). His findings can be summed up as demonstrating an increasing amount of consensus with age, between six and thirteen, so that children were generally brought into line with a 'group norm' in their constructs.

The mean variability between children of any age group in their constructions of an event decreased slightly with age on each test, and the standard deviation from the mean decreases significantly, indicating a tightening-up of consensus. Throughout there is a decrease in both mean and standard deviation in the tendency to construe events according to extremes on a bipolar construct, and to bias the rating to one pole only. This indicates that both individuals and the group as a whole are achieving what appears to be a more 'balanced' view of the world, and that there is increasing consensus on what constitutes that balance. Again, while the number of constructs used by any individual increases significantly, there is a tendency for individuals to resemble each other to an increasing degree in their breadth of construing. Finally, the ability to verbalize both poles of the construct apparently increases with age, and it is conceivable that this verbalization in itself provides the basis for the increasing consensus.

However, despite these changes with age, Applebee concludes that the apparent differences within the lowest age-group were not so great as might have appeared, and that the changes involved did not mean a dramatic reorganization had taken place.

The simplest summary of Applebee's results is the percentage or possible interclass correlations which were significant at each age, which increased from 38.3 to 48.9 between the ages of six and nine on the oral grid, and from 48.4 to 82.6 from nine to thirteen on the written grid.

Brierley (1967) took a similar approach to that of Applebee, comparing the construct systems of children of three different ages, insofar as they related to children's perceptions of persons. Her work was not so much concerned with the structure of the system as such, but with the content of the particular subsystem here involved. She found that there is a change from the perception of persons in terms of kinship and social role at seven to a concentration on appearance and overt behaviour at ten, to an assessment of underlying 'personality factors' at thirteen. This change was accompanied by a decrease in the use of common constructs from the age of seven to thirteen, and an increase in the use of 'rare' (i.e. applied only once) constructs between the ages of ten and thirteen (rare constructs apparently not being used at all at seven).

Brierley's interpretation of these results is as a move from the parent-orientation of the seven-year-old to the more independent and introspective outlook of the thirteen-year-old, with more emphasis on reflection and less on doing. This is interesting, as it constitutes an attempt by the child to move from a purely descriptive mode to an explanatory mode, and thus an attempt to get at formal or underlying relationships rather than superficial appearances. Brierley's work goes some way to demonstrating the shaping influence of the child's place in the social structure on his developing construct system, and to show how, in terms of that position, the child's construct system is perfectly adequate.

Philida Salmon (1969, 1976) has also carried out some tentative explorations in this area, but her work was also based on provided constructs rather than elicited constructs, plus the results of a rather problematic questionnaire to determine parental attitudes. Her investigation was concerned with the extent to which children who have been either accepted or rejected by their parents, and subject to parental control or neglect, conform either to the adult culture or to that of their peers.

Her conclusions, she claims, go some way towards demonstrating that children who have been rejected do not conform to either their peers' use of constructs or the culture of their parents. Those who were accepted by their parents exhibited no significant relationship between the degree to which they had been controlled or neglected and conformity to adults or peers. While her study might have told us something about the propensity to conform of children in differential social relationships with their parents, the inconclusiveness of her results, and the variable with which she was concerned, tell us nothing about the structure of the content of children's construct systems, except insofar as they conform to those of adults; and in any case a developmental overview is absent.

Finally, the work of Honess (1976) is concerned with a particular subsystem, again that of person perception, and his work is an attempt to investigate, using a construct theory perspective, the phenomenon of 'cognitive complexity' with regard to this subsystem. This term was devised by Bieri (1955) to characterize the variations in individual construction processes, insofar as they can be summarized by reference to the extent to which one construct implies another. The less the degree of identity between constructs, he claimed, the less the degree of cognitive complexity. This line of theorization has been developed by, for example, Carr (1970) and Scott (1962), who have gone some way towards clarifying what constitutes the concept of cognitive complexity, and they have developed techniques for the investigation of the phenomenon. No-one, however, had applied the technique or the concept to the development of children, and Honess set out to remedy this. He points out that it is generally assumed that high cognitive complexity implies high developmental status, and he classes together the theories of Kelly, Piaget and others (Honess 1976, 23):

The unifying theme of these theories is that cognitive development is characterized by increasing differentiation and specification of a person's relatively-global concepts coupled with increasing hierarchic integration of concepts.

To count as cognitively complex, it is not sufficient that the construct system contain a large number of elements, or that one construct does not imply all the others in its subsystem, but elements must be 'integrated hierarchically by relatively extensive bonds of relationship'. Methods of characterizing complexity in this extended sense have been devised by Crockett (1965) and by Smith and Leach (1972), but Honess's conclusion is that, of all the conceptions of cognitive complexity which have so far been put forward, none actually characterizes the phenomenon. And so far as children are concerned, none is applicable anyway, either because of the difficulties involved in eliciting constructs and the doubtful status of the constructs once elicited, or because provided constructs do not get at the child's view at all.

We now turn to the interpretation of the data gathered during our period of participant observation in the nursery classroom. As indicated earlier, we have borrowed some of Kelly's concepts in organizing the children's remarks about their world. Despite the 'soft' nature of the interpretive process, we do feel that something of the real differences between children has been captured in our analysis. It is part of the theory behind participant observation studies that knowledge gained by being in the situation allows a more valid interpretation of the events which occur. We do not wish to hide behind such a self-justifying view, but we would encourage the reader to try a similar exercise in order to experience the way contextual information can give the transcribed remarks the force we found.

Content of the children's system

1 My world/Not my world

Perhaps the predominant construct which the child brings to the classroom situation involves the distinction between what 'belongs' in his world and those things or actions which cannot be comfortably accepted. We have called this dimension the 'My world/Not my world' construct, and it will be referred to as My/Not my.

The construct is well illustrated by Erika's running commentary as she played on the outdoor apparatus.

> (*As the paddling pool is brought out*) . . . I've got a paddling pool . . . I've got pictures on mine . . . I've got a red dress . . . (*on seeing someone skipping*) I've got a skipping rope . . . (*climbing on to slide*) I've not got a slide.

While this instance is unusual in the clarity with which it illustrates the use of My/Not my, this mode was used by the majority of children in most situations. In its usual form, the My/Not my discrimination relates to the familiarity of objects or situations with unfamiliar situations being either totally excluded from the children's thoughts or, when they force themselves into consciousness, causing distress. Instances of this abound:

> (*David W, who never plays with plasticine or paints, is gazing around the classroom.*)
> *CB:* Will you make me something out of plasticine, please?
> *DW:* (*No answer*)
> *CB:* Would you like to make me something out of clay, or would you rather paint a picture?
> *DW:* I'm making a gun with Lego.
> *CB:* Wouldn't you like to paint a picture or make me something out of clay?
> *DW:* (*No answer. Walks to Lego table and picks up bricks*)

In this instance, the request that he should make a choice between two activities with which he was not familiar was aimed at finding his preference, with the hope of eliciting the constructs on which his preference was based. David answered the request in his own terms, however, by effectively classing together the two activities with which he had been presented as not his type of activities. He introduced his own activity, which could be discriminated from the other two in terms of his familiarity with it; inferred in this case from the frequency of his participation in each activity. Another example is:

> (*Samantha is playing with plasticine, making long, thin shapes.*)
> *CB:* Do you think you could make a circle out of clay?
> *SS:* Yes. (*She makes one, joining up the ends of her elongated rolls.*)
> *CB:* That's lovely. Can you make any other shapes?
> *SS:* (*Uses another roll to make a rough quadrilateral.*) A Square.
> *CB:* Can you make me a triangle?
> *SS:* (*She makes another square.*) A square.
> *CB:* Now you've got two squares. Can you make me a triangle?
> *SS:* Can I do a painting?
> (*Samantha appeared to be totally ignoring the request, and CB thought this indicated that she was unfamiliar with the word 'triangle'.*)
> *CB:* We'll go over there in a minute. Can you say what this is?
> (*making plasticine triangle*)
> *SS:* Triangle.

CB: Can you make me one?
SS: Can I do a painting now? *(Gets up.)*

Here, Samantha's actions indicate, in effect, that while she understands 'triangle', the activity of reproducing one is not a 'My' activity. Again.

(Discussion of some pictures of another nursery group playing in the classroom, with Elizabeth)
CB: Can you see what these children are doing?
EH: He's building . . . and that's a house . . . and there's Mrs Perch.
CB: What would you make if you had those bricks?
EH: She's got a dress like mine.
CB: Yes, she has, hasn't she? When I took this picture, she'd built a house. Can you build houses out of Lego?
EH: I build a house with plasticine.
CB: Could you make another out of bricks?
EH: What's he doing?

Exchanges such as these seem to indicate failure to establish a reciprocity of perspectives. What was happening, apparently, was that Elizabeth was responding as if questions were requests for her to give a running commentary on her train of thought. She rarely played with Lego, and as a result does not easily apply the 'My' role to that situation. She is recasting the questions so as to allow her to perceive the photographs in terms of 'My', referring to 'my dress' and 'my plasticine house'. When she realizes that this is not acceptable she rules the photographs out and proceeds to move on to the next one. Similar incidents to these occurred so frequently as to demonstrate the strength of the 'My/Not my' construct as a first step in organizing experience.

As suggested earlier, the 'My/Not my' construct is often active when children became anxious as a result of the unfamiliarity of a situation. Thus Joanne burst into tears when a male teacher, visiting from another class, began to play his guitar when she had been expecting a story. Her reaction was seemingly brought on by the fact that she had been absent on the only other occasion when a guitar had been used, so that the situation could not be anticipated and controlled. Unlike the previous situations cited, however, this incident was not amenable to redefinition in terms which Joanne did understand, and she was unable to avoid it, being confined in the quiet room. This was accentuated by the ease with which the other children were able to construe the situation, so that here the inapplicability of the 'My' pole of the construct set her apart from her peers.

This pole seems to be the principal means by which the children establish stability in situations. Whenever insecurity, for whatever reason, threatens, solace is found in familiarity. Again Joanne (who often appeared insecure) provided an instance of this in that, on an extremely hot day, she refused to take off her cardigan, even when engaged in energetic exercise on the outdoor apparatus. Eventually she was persuaded to take it off, but even then she refused to be parted from it, carrying it wherever she went. Similarly, Emma carried a book which she had brought from home wherever she went, and became very anxious when she thought she had mislaid it.

In many instances, children brought toys from home. Of course, this can be understood in a variety of ways – they may have been brought to show off, to provide variety, to capture the teacher's attention – but above all, merely the presence of the toy appeared to provide reassurance. Thus it is true to say not only that the classroom and objects in it are construed in terms of 'My/Not my' but also that objects themselves serve to define and anchor the self. This is evident in the following exchange with Peter.

PB: This is my birthday present and I brought it to school. I'd better not let anyone see it. *(A car)*
CB: Why's that?
PB: Because it's mine.
CB: Don't you like other people seeing your things?
PB: No, because it's mine.

By guarding the car, he seemed to be engaged in an enterprise of self-protection, and the object gave him a sense of identity. In the anonymous situation of the classroom (at least when compared to the home) objects which can unambiguously be defined as 'My' give a certain amount of security.

2 Supervised/Unsupervised

There is a clear discrimination by the children in terms of the apparently 'objective' fact that some activities are supervised while others are not. Thus David W engaged only in activities which were unsupervised, and never willingly joined in activities he saw construed as 'supervised'. Other children (e.g. Sara M) obviously preferred supervised activities, and when left without supervision some of them became anxious. This is not simply the result of whether the children concerned liked to have clear directions; for instance, Sara, once given the attention of the teacher or nurse, and directed to an activity, could get on without further instructions, so long as the adult remained present. It seemed almost as if the presence of an adult, and initial instructions as to what she should do, were necessary for her to be 'switched on'. After this, she could proceed competently.

In other cases, children were quite able to choose their own activities, but directions from an adult were necessary for the activity to become focused. Thus Sara B and Michelle never needed guidance in their choice of activity but, once started, they did not seem to know how to proceed without further instructions. Sara, having taken off her coat, marched straight to the straw-construction table and picked up a handful of straws, then stared at the table in front of her, making no effort to get started:

> *CB:* Are you going to make me something?
> *SB:* Yes. *(She clips two straws together.)*
> *CB:* What's it going to be?
> *SB:* What should I make?
> *CB:* Let's put some more straws in and see what it is.
> *(She clips some more straws on.)*
> *CB:* What's it look like?
> *SB:* *(No answer)*
> *CB:* Can you turn it into an umbrella?
> *(She sets to work immediately, taking away some straws and adding others, until the umbrella is made.)*
> *SB:* There.

All that Sara seemed to need was supervision of aims, apart from her own intention of making *something*. Michelle was somewhat different in that while, like Sara, she was decisive in choosing her activities, she also had clear intentions as to end-product. In her case, supervision was necessary only regarding means:

> *MC:* Me make box.
> *CB:* All right then. Where will this go? *(I give her a straw. She picks up some and pushes them all into my hand.)*
> *MC:* You make it.
> *CB:* I'll help you. Look, put them together like this. Where will the next one go?
> *(She looks at the two sides of a square I have made and picks up another straw which she clips in to make another side to the square.)*
> *CB:* What next?
> *(She completes the square then pushes a handful of straws at me.)*
> *MC:* You.
> *(I put the next straw into position, changing a 2-D construction into a 3-D one.)*
> *CB:* Can you put the next one in?
> *(She goes on to complete a cube, but often gives me a straw and repeats 'You do it'.)*

In Michelle's case, she did not need supervising either in her choice of activity or in her aims, but only as an aid in bringing the activity towards the desired conclusion.

In other cases, direction was needed in choice of activity, aim and means. Martyn was leaning against a radiator:

> *CB:* Have you nothing to do, Martyn?
> *MS:* No.
> *CB:* You like playing in water, don't you?
> *MS:* Yes.
> *CB:* Shall we go over to the water tray?
> *(He takes my hand and we cross to the tray. He stands looking at it.)*
> *CB:* Can you fill this up? (I give him a pan.)
> *(He picks up the pan, but doesn't know what to do next, then tries scooping it on the bottom.)*
> *CB:* Can you fill it up with a cup?
> *(He picks up a plastic cup, looks at the pan, then begins to fill it, becoming absorbed in the activity.)*

While some children need supervision with regard to choice, ends and means, others reject supervision of any kind. David W is the clearest example of this, and he avoided any activity which was supervised (especially games, and some 'art' activities such as stencilling). Attempts to give him direction in any other activity were similarly resisted:

> *(David is swooping down on the Lego table, knocking bricks around and damaging other children's constructions.)*
> *CB:*   What are you doing, David?
> *DW:*   *(No answer, but continues swooping)*
> *CB:*   David, come and make me a gun.
> *(He comes, still knocking the occasional brick as he passes, then picks up some bricks.)*
> *CB:*   Do you know how to make a gun?
> *DW:*   I can make a gun.
> *(He puts together a few bricks, then throws them, with other loose ones, across the table.)*

This was not an isolated instance of David's resistance to supervision, but was fairly typical. Not once during work did he succumb to pressures to comply with instructions from the teacher or the nurse, unless the instructions were wholly compatible with the intentions he already had. On one such occasion, he broke off from chasing David G and Matthew C when the teacher told him to do so, only to go to the Wendy House and disrupt activities there. David's resistance was not, in itself, a rejection of the classroom situation, as he clearly enjoyed school, and was full of enthusiasm for activities in which he could take control.

David's resistance to supervision was most apparent in organized games. At the opposite extreme was Emma who gravitated to any game which was in progress and who, in a highly-structured situation, was at ease.

> *EB:* Can we have a game? *(standing near the cupboard in which games are stored)*
> *CB:* What kind of game?
> *EB:* Farms. *(On the previous day, she had played a matching game involving a picture of a farmyard.)*
> *CB:* Wouldn't you rather paint?
> *EB:* I want to play farms.
> *CB:* Who else can play?
> *EB:* Nicola and Ericka. Kate can play.
> *CB:* Can you play it together while I get on with writing?
> *EB:* You tell us what to do. *(They all knew how to play.)*
> *(We set up the game and I show them the first card, then I leave them to get on. Emma continually comes for direct supervision.)*

What Emma wanted was not simply to take part in the game, but for her activities to be closely supervised throughout. For Emma, Supervised/Unsupervised was a significant dimension; and characterizing it as a construct allows us to link Emma with David, who is sensitive to the distinction but reacts to being supervised in the opposite manner to Emma.

For some children however the distinction was not relevant: Andrew, for example, enjoyed supervised games and was willing to accept directions in his own activities, but could work competently on his own. His choice of activities was not apparently guided by reference to this construct.

The contrast between David and Martyn comes out in their discussion of photographs. Comparing two pictures David preferred the one of a solitary, unsupervised child reading, despite the fact that he himself could not read, nor even looked at the books in the quiet room.

> *CB:* What do you like about this one? *(solitary child)*
> *DW:* He's reading.
> *CB:* And what about this? *(child with teacher)*
> *DW:* Mrs Hollingworth's reading.
> *CB:* Isn't the girl reading?
> *DW:* But Mrs Hollingworth's reading.

The example illustrates David's resistance to seeing activities in which an adult was involved as cooperative; he seemed to have a strong preference to view such activities as dominated by the adult.

When Martyn compared the same pictures, he preferred the cooperative one, again despite the fact that he himself did not read:

CB: Why do you like that one?
MS: Mrs Hollingworth.
CB: What about Mrs Hollingworth?
MS: Reading.
CB: Isn't the boy reading?
MS: Pictures.

Perhaps because of his own inability to read, Martyn sees the activity as not only assisted by the presence of an adult, but actually made possible thereby. The contrast between Martyn and David is not simply of differential orientation to supervised behaviour, but also of different functions being attached to adults.

3 Doing/Listening

By and large, activities which are easily placed on the 'Doing' pole are preferred to more passive situations. Thus Matthew C's comments on the photograph of story-time:

MC: They're listening.
CB: Do you like Mrs. Hollingworth telling stories?
MC: No. I just listen *(which was not, in fact, the case, as he disrupted passive sessions)*.

David G is perhaps the best example of the way in which this construct is used:

CB: Would you rather play in the water or listen to the story? *(showing him photographs of these activities)*
DG: Play in water.
CB: Don't you like stories?
DG: Yes.
CB: But you'd rather play in water?
DG: Yes.
CB: Why don't you like listening to stories as much?
DG: You just have to sit there. There's nothing to do.

His dislike of passivity was evident at story-time, when – unlike David W, who confined his disruption to 'meddling' with other children, thus ignoring the story situation entirely – David G tried hard to become involved, pushing himself to the front, standing up, calling out comments. For him, apparently, the situation was one which required him actively to participate rather than sit back passively, and he attempted to assimilate the situation accordingly. The teacher, on the other hand, demanded accommodation, and this incompatibility resulted in David G's being frequently rebuked.

Sara M, on the other hand, never made any attempt to participate in story-time but passively attended to the teacher's words. On the other hand, in situations where participation was demanded, she was at a loss until clearly directed. As noted, when she was required to choose amongst various activities, she became anxious. She apparently preferred 'Listening' to 'Doing'.

> *CB: (showing photographs of various activities)* Do you like story-
> time?
> *SM:* Yes. I like stories.
> *CB:* You like making things too, don't you?
> *SM:* I like Lego. I like clay.
> *CB:* Which do you like best?
> *SM:* Quiet room *(i.e. story-time)*.
> *CB:* Why is that better?
> *SM:* Stories.
> *CB:* What about the stories?
> *SM:* I can listen.

Generally speaking, listening implied 'just listening' with a negative connotation, while 'doing' or 'making' were positively evaluated. In one case (Peter) the discrimination did not necessarily imply an evaluation, and 'Doing' could be either chosen or rejected:

> *CB:* Shall we go on the go-kart?
> *PB:* No. I have to push with my feet.
> . . .
> *CB:* Are you going on the swing, Peter?
> *PB:* Yes, I can push.

The pushing was seen negatively in the first instance, and positively in the second, so Peter was clearly using another distinction in addition to 'Doing'.

It appeared that all of the children are *able* to discriminate according to the Doing/Listening distinction, and its variants, but some children do not do so automatically; they only apply the construct when requested to do so. For these children, the discrimination is not in itself significant and is close to what Kelly calls a propositional construct, carrying a low number of necessary implications.

4 Together/Alone

In the classroom there is a continuum, from activities which require joint effort (as exemplified by the see-saw) or competition (as in supervised games) to those which can only be done alone (e.g. riding a tricycle). The children differ considerably in their choice of activities along this continuum, from Cara (who almost always plays alone) to

Katie and Stephanie (who almost always do things together). Lee seemed to see most activities as solitary, choosing those which were inherently so (construction, looking at books, kicking a ball against the fence) and even reconstructing apparently cooperative activities as solitary, balancing the see-saw himself, playing in the Wendy House along with a group but talking to himself and getting on with his own activity while the rest of the group played together. In comparing photographs, the following exchange occurred.

> *CB:* Which of these do you like? *(a girl on a tricycle, a boy in a go-kart being pushed by a companion)*
> *LJ:* This. *(the tricycle)*
> *CB:* What do you like about it?
> *LJ:* She can go round there.
> *CB:* *(indicating the go-kart)* Can he not go where he wants?
> *LJ:* No. He's pushing him.

What Lee apparently valued was control over his own actions. This did not mean that he resisted supervision, as he made clear in his discussion of other photographs:

> *CB:* Which is best?
> *LJ:* This. *(Mrs Perch with a group of children, drawing)*
> *CB:* Why is that best?
> *LJ:* That's a house and that's. . . . (unintelligible)
> *CB:* You like to draw things?
> *LJ:* Yes. I draw a house.
> *CB:* What don't you like about this one? *(Mrs Hollingworth playing dominoes with a group of children)*
> *LJ:* You have to put them down.
> *CB:* You mean you can't choose?
> *LJ:* Mrs Hollingworth tells you which one.
> *CB:* Doesn't Mrs Perch tell you what to draw?
> *LJ:* She helps.

So supervision was constructed as either helpful or constraining, but not necessarily either (as David W or Sara M would have seen it), and those supervised activities in which he could call on the teacher's help were valued, while those into which he had to fit his own activities were not. His preference was systematically for activities which he could identify as falling on the pole of 'Alone'.

Other children were prone to choose activities which fell for them on the 'Together' pole of the construct. Thus Katie always chose coopera-tive pursuits when possible, as in the yard she would choose either the see-saw or the go-kart if those were available, and in using this equip-ment she would enlist the assistance of Rosalind or Stephanie. When asked what she liked about these activities, her answers were clear:

CB: Why do you like the see-saw better than the scooter?
KJ: I can play with Rosalind.
CB: Don't you like to do things on your own?
KJ: Rosalind's my friend. We play together.

In Katie's case, 'Together' applied not only to activities which were necessarily cooperative, but to some which were only incidentally so. Thus she also liked building with Lego, and using a tricycle, as in the case of the former she and Rosalind could both build (not necessarily cooperative but in parallel) while the tricycle enabled them to push one another. Even an apparently solitary activity such as painting was thus construed, as with one painting and two pots of paint they could both stand at the easel.

In some cases, children did not make a choice according to whether activities were 'Together' or 'Alone', though they could distinguish between the two. Thus Sara B spoke of various activities:

SB: I like painting 'cos I can do it my own self. I can paint mummy
. . . . I can build Lego. Me and Samantha builded a house. We play house in Wendy House.

While she could distinguish between these activities according to this construct, it did not in itself define her preferences.

David W used the construct to direct his choice of activity, with 'Together' activities being engaged in and 'Alone' activities being avoided entirely. However, his understanding of 'Together' did not involve cooperation, and he avoided cooperative games or pursuits in which a joint end-product would result. By 'Together' David seemed to mean situations which were potentially antagonistic.

DW: *(of Wendy House)* I can smash him and *(unintelligible, grabs David G and shakes him)*
CB: Can you not play without smashing him?
DW: No.

The same process was apparent when he referred to water-play:

CB: Do you like playing in water?
DW: Yes . . . . *(incomprehensible)* . . . . splash, splash . . . . squirt and tickle them *(accompanied by a fanatic waving of arms)*

While avoiding solitary play, David engaged in situations involving other children as communal only if he could relate to them in terms of his aggression. Though he spoke of 'playing together' on more than one occasion, his behaviour suggested that his use of the term was decidedly idiosyncratic, and this should serve as a warning to those who would equate a construct with the words used to express it, and who see constructs as easily derivable in grid tests.

5 Home/School

This construct is in some cases closely related to My/Not my, in that elements subsumed under the 'My' pole are often those with which the child is familiar from home, while elements construed as 'school' are not so familiar. Thus activities in the classroom which are also engaged in at home are often preferred:

> *(Sara is building with Lego)*
> *CB:* You like playing with Lego, don't you?
> *SM:* Yes. I've got Lego at home.
> *CB:* Why do you like it so much?
> *SM:* Daddy makes things.
> *CB:* Do you make things together?
> *SM:* Susan makes things.
> *CB:* Do you help?
> *SM:* No.

Here, the activity is not seen in terms of inherent satisfactions, but only insofar as it connotes the associations with home and her family. This is not so much a construction in terms of My/Not my, as she is not directly involved at home in the situations of which Lego reminds her; rather does it evoke the affective component of the home situation. Thus situations which are reminiscent of home give the child a sense of security, while those which are particular to the classroom evoke different feelings. Sara is perhaps the clearest instance of this, in that she did not often play games at home but, unusually, read with her father. Thus, in an entirely open situation where she could choose amongst several activities, she was perceptibly anxious, standing in one spot, shuffling her feet with her hands clenched to her chin, staring at the floor until she was directed to any activity by the teacher or the nurse. The situation in which she was most secure was that of reading to the teacher, and she would gladly spend the best part of the morning sitting by the teacher with her book. This is in sharp contrast to most of the other children who preferred free activities, perhaps because these corresponded most closely to the home situation as far as they were concerned. This is a vivid example of the necessity of finding the meanings that children attach to classroom situations, rather than merely assuming that they are able adequately to construe and participate in any activity which is provided for them.

The My/Not my and Home/School constructs were not isomorphic on all occasions, the latter apparently being subordinate to the 'My' pole of the former in some situations. Thus, having categorized an activity as 'My', the next step was to construe it under either the 'Home' or 'School' pole. When looking at photographs of children playing in the classroom, Katie (almost alone among the children in her ability to make sense of direct questions) replied in terms of the Home/School discrimination:

> CB: What's different in this picture?
> KJ: They're drawing. I draw at home and Elizabeth *(her sister)* draws things.
> CB: And what about this one?
> KJ: I don't go on a see-saw at home. I draw at home.
> CB: But you go on the see-saw at school?
> KJ: I like the see-saw.

Here, Katie is not discriminating in terms of My/Not my, as both activities can be subsumed under the 'My' pole, and the crucial difference between activities is whether she does them at home or not.

Here there is no simple determinism, as there seemed to be in the My/Not my construct. Whereas 'Not my' was often used in the exclusion of situations from the field of attention, in most cases both poles of Home/School were used in constructing situations attended to by the child: making a further discrimination necessary for him to orientate himself to it. In some cases, the allotting of a situation to the 'Home' pole, as in Sara's case, encouraged a positive affective orientation, and in the assignment of a situation to the 'School' pole a negative response of strong anxiety was generated. Thus she could not be persuaded to use the swing or slide as 'I don't go on swings when I'm with my daddy' and 'Jane's got a slide but I don't go on it'.

In some cases, the affective connotations of the poles were reversed. Thus Emma was always keen to paint despite the fact that she had never painted at home, and she never played with the dolls' house 'because I've got one'.

In other cases, the Home/School construct was not seen as relevant. Peter pointed out that he played with water and built with Lego at home, though in the classroom he never participated in the former activity but often used Lego. Matthew C claimed that he had never played in a sandpit at home, nor had he used Meccano, though in school he ignored the former and indulged in the latter.

Perhaps the most obvious way to explain these data would be in terms of personality. Following the equation, extroverts would prefer activities which they did not indulge in at home, while introverts would prefer activities they could associate with home. This would be much too easy an answer, in that some thoroughly outgoing personalities such as Matthew C ignored most of the 'school' activities while some shy, retiring girls preferred these. What seems to be happening is that, in using the Home/School construct, the children do not abstract this axis but apply it together with a number of other constructs with which it is intimately interlocked, and discriminations must be explained by reference to these relationships. This prevents an easy equation of Home/School with differential propensity to enagage in activities, and there is no simple one-to-one correspondence.

6 Can/Can't

In a school situation, this construct is central in the teacher's assessment of children, as it is in the children's constructions of one another and of themselves. In some situations, for some children, the notion of competence was dominant in their construing activities. Thus Paul Anthony would not paint because 'I can't paint' though he would use bricks, and when asked why replied 'I can make a car', and he used the slide because 'I can do it'. On the other hand, present incompetence did not always imply inherent inability:

> (Samantha and I are in the yard)
> *SS:* I can't bounce. *(rolling football)*
> *CB:* Let me show you. *(I demonstrate, then hand her the ball. She tries to bounce it, then hands it back.)*
> *SS:* Show me.
> *CB:* Like this. *(I demonstrate)*
> *(Samantha then sets about perfecting her technique).*

Similarly, Joanne did not construe situations which fell on the Can't pole as needing to be avoided. While she admits that she can't swim, she says she enjoys swimming, and her incompetence in using plasticine (which she recognizes in her 'Oh, I can't do it') doesn't prevent her from attempting to fashion recognizable pieces.

What seems to be involved here is two possible uses of the construct. On the one hand, 'Can't is seen as not only implying incompetence, but also a self-imposed ban on engaging in that activity, analogous to the 'Can't' of 'I can't run into the road'; on the other hand, 'Can't' can imply challenge and possibility, and situations construed on this pole are not avoided but met.

In situations where 'Can't' is such a powerful construction, as in school, it would be interesting to follow through the differential implications for several children, and to see how their imputation of meaning to the construct correlated with performance. If performance is indeed associated with differential usage of the construct, it is conceivable that, by encouraging reflection on and extension of the Can/Can't construct, performance might be altered. This might be especially so in cases such as Steven, who appears to refuse to admit to 'Can't' because of the implications of this for him.

All of the constructs discussed so far were either frequently used by the children or at least accessible to them, even if not much used. Others, however, are idiosyncratic, and there is a gradual shading through constructs used by only some children to those specific to a single child.

Of those which are common to some, the distinction between making and playing has some importance. Some activities (Wendy House, climbing frame, train set) are play activities, allowing the children to fantasize freely, and there is only the momentary involvement. Others (painting, plasticine, Lego) have an end product which can be displayed. Some children (Sara M for example) choose only the latter, insisting that there is something to show for their work:

> *CB:* You like plasticine, don't you?
> *SM:* Yes.
> *CB:* What do you like, is it how it feels?
> *SM:* I like making animals.
> *CB:* Do you like playing in sand?
> *SM:* You can't make something.
> *CB:* You like the dolls' house, don't you?
> *SM:* I like dolls.
> *CB:* What is it you like about them?
> *SM:* You can move them . . . dress them.

The dolls' house is ambiguous here; while everything is prefabricated, there is an end product insofar as the dolls themselves can be transformed and the scene arranged. Other children (e.g. Cara) who used the making/playing construct did not place the dolls' house on the 'making' pole:

> *CB:* Are you going to make me an animal? *(with plasticine)*
> *SM:* A hedgehog. *(She begins to mould plasticine.)*
> *CB:* Every time I look, you seem to be at the plasticine table. *(She smiles.)* Are there no other things you like doing?
> *SM:* Painting.
> *CB:* I've never seen you playing with the dolls' house.
> *SM:* You can't make things.

The discrimination was taken further by some children who distinguished between activities with an end-product which was permanent, and those for which it was only temporary. One of these was Sarah B:

> *CB:* You've done an awful lot of painting this morning.
> *SB:* I can show them my mummy.
> *CB:* You like plasticine too, don't you?
> *SB:* Yes, but you have to squash them.

CB: What about Lego?
SB: I made a garage and Mrs Perch broke it.

This might account for the enthusiasm with which the children approached baking. When making buns, 20 or more children would sit around a table, awaiting their turn in giving the mixture a stir. Clearly, the part which any child took in the process was very small, but they were nevertheless prepared to wait for several minutes for their turn. Matthew C (usually very impatient) said about this:

CB: You have to wait an awful long time.
MC: Yes.
CB: I didn't think you could sit still for so long.
MC: I want a stir.
CB: It'll be here in a minute.
MC: I can have some cakes of my own.

Here, we see the relationship of the Making/Playing construct to the My/Not my discrimination in that when an end product results, it is the child's own, something that he has produced himself and can take away with him. Thus, while it is no doubt true that development is equivalent to elaboration of the construct system (akin to Piaget's accomodation) we should never forget the equal importance of a sense of transforming the world according to our intentions, as exemplified in processes involving some kind of production (akin to Piaget's assimilation).

Strangely, some children are at the other extreme and avoid making things. David W is the best example, and he never completed anything which he had begun. As noted elsewhere, he chose those activities which gave him the opportunity to express his aggression. Only a few activities were entirely suitable, and all of these were 'Playing' rather than 'Making' situations. Thus the washroom became a park where a fight was taking place, or he used furniture in the quiet room to form a car which he could crash into other children in the quiet room, or the train set was used to crash into other toys or children; sand and water-play were activities which permitted him to attack other children, while Lego and plasticine were only useful insofar as he could use them as missiles. For him, the Playing/Doing distinction seemed to correspond to a Communal/Solitary and Active/Passive discrimination. His own construct system was certainly the tightest of all the children in the class, in that the number of implications of any construct was extremely high.

Not all children discriminated between playing and doing on such hard and fast lines. Michelle seemed able to use any activity, whether there was an end product or not, as a vehicle for her fantasies. Thus plasticine and Lego were useful only in that they gave her the raw materials to construct a scenario, and the end-products she produced were used symbolically to represent an element in her fantasies, rather than having any 'intrinsic' nature. A lump of plasticine could be a hedgehog at one moment as she trotted it across the table, and a space-ship the next as she zoomed it around her head.

This ability to transform any activity and use it as a vehicle for fantasy was apparent in almost all of the children. Activities with apparently set aims (e.g. painting and construction) were appropriated by the children and used to fulfil their own needs. It has been noted that some children discriminated activities according to the construct of Playing/Making, but in a real sense, for most children, any activity was 'Playing', and construing was close to pure assimilation, rather than accommodation to the apparently 'inherent' qualities of an object of activity. It has been noted by many writers that children of this age seem to be 'realists', and the world appears to them as a massive, opaque, solid entity. In their play, however, most of these children are idealists, in their belief that almost anything can serve almost any purpose, and reality can continually be transformed according to intentions. The realists, who see properties of objects and situations as untransform-able (as exemplified by David W) are in a minority. It is surely this plas-ticity which allows young children to learn so much so quickly, and which provides the basis for teaching.

The structure of children's systems

So far we have tried to indicate what seems to be the most significant constructs used by the children. In this section we will attempt to demonstrate the way in which these constructs are organized for indi-vidual children, giving some tentative insights into individual children's ways of organizing the classroom. There is not space here, however, to indicate the way in which all 30 children organized their experience, so we have focused on the systems of three children, selected both because a large data base was collected for each child and because of the inter-esting differences between them.

For each of these three children a grid (See Tables 7.1, 7.3 and 7.5) was constructed with activities as elements combined with the six con-structs elicited from the children as a whole. If, for example, in an utter-ance, a child used the construct Doing/Listening and applied it to an activity, an entry was made in the relevant space. If he construed the activity as 'Doing' a 1 was placed in the box, indicating reference to the first pole; if he construed it as 'Listening' a 2 was placed there. If he used the construct to refer to the activity on more than one occasion, difficulties arose. For instance, he might construe it as 'doing' on more than one occasion; this was resolved by making a single entry. Further difficulties arose when he construed an activity as 'Doing' on one occasion and as 'Listening' on another. In that case both poles were entered indicating the ambiguity.

Table 7.1 David's constructions of classroom activities

	Elements	Sand and water	Const-ruction	Outdoor apparatus	Wendy House	Painting	Singing	Supervised games	Story	Drawing	Books
C	My/Not my	1	1	1	2	2	2	2	2	2	2
O	Unsupervised/ Supervised	1	1	1	1	2	2	2	2	–	–
N	Doing/Listening	1	1	1	–	2	2	2	2	2	2
S	Together/Alone	1	1	1	–	2	–	2	2	2	2
T	Home/School	2	2	2	2	2	–	1	1	1	1
R	Can/Can't	1	1	–	–	2	–	2	1	1	2
U											
C											
T											
S											

Table 7.2 The tendency of constructs to correlate with other constructs and the index of constellatoriness of David's construct system

	My/Not my	Supervised/Unsupervised	Doing/Listening	Together/Alone	Home/School	Can/Can't	
My/Not my	(+10)	+7, −1 (6)	+9 (9)	+8, −1 (7)	3, −6 (3)	+6, −1 (5)	30/46 (65%)
Supervised/Unsupervised	+7, −1 (6)	(+8)	+7 (7)	+7 (7)	+2, −5 (3)	+4, −1 (3)	26/35 (74%)
Doing/Listening	(+9)	+7 (7)	+9	+8 (8)	+2, −6 (4)	+5, −2 (3)	31/39 (80%)
Together/Alone	+8, −1 (7)	+7 (7)	+8 (8)	(+9)	+2, −7 (5)	+5, −2 (3)	30/40 (75%)
Home/School	+3, −6 (3)	+2, −5 (3)	+2, −6 (4)	+2, −7 (5)	(+9)	+2, −5 (3)	18/40 (45%)
Can/Can't	+6, −1 (5)	+4, −1 (3)	+5, −2 (3)	+5, −2 (3)	+2, −5 (3)	(+7)	17/33 (51%)
							152/233 (66%)

Table 7.3 Steven's constructions of classroom activities

Elements	Sand and water	Construction	Outdoor apparatus	Wendy House	Painting	Singing	Supervised games	Story	Drawing	Books
My/Not my	1/2	1	1	1	1/2	2	1/2	1	1	1
Unsupervised/ Supervised	-	1/2	1	1	2	2	2	2	1	1/2
Doing/Listening	1	1	1	1	1	2	-	2	1	-
Together/Alone	2	2	1	1	1	-	1	-	2	1/2
Home/School	2	1	2	-	1	-	2	-	1	1
Can/Can't	-	1	-	-	1	-	1	-	1	1

Table 7.4 The tendency of constructs to correlate with other constructs and the index of constellatoriness of Steven's construct system

	My/ Not my	Unsupervised/ Supervised	Doing/ Listening	Together/ Alone	Home/ School	Can/ Can't	
My/ Not my	(+10)	+4, −1, ±4 (3)	+5, −1, ±3 (4)	+3, −2, ±4 (1)	+4, −1, ±3 (3)	+3, −0, ±2 (3)	14/40 (35%)
Unsupervised/ Supervised	+4, −1, ±4 (3)	(+9)	+5, −1, ±1 (4)	+2, −3, ±2 (1)	+2, −3, ±2 (1)	+1, −2, ±3 (1)	10/36 (28%)
Doing/ Listening	+5, −1, ±3 (4)	+5, −1, ±1 (4)	(+8)	+3, −3, ±1 (0)	+3, −2, ±0 (1)	+3, −0, ±0 (3)	12/31 (38%)
Together/ Alone	+3, −2, ±4 (1)	+2, −3, ±2 (1)	+3, −3, ±1 (0)	(+8)	+2, −4, ±1 (2)	+2, −2, ±1 (0)	4/35 (11%)
Home/ School	+4, −1, ±3 (3)	+2, −3, ±2 (1)	+3, −2, ±0 (1)	+2, −4, ±1 (2)	(+8)	+4, −1, ±0 (3)	10/32 (31%)
Can/ Can't	+3, −0, ±2 (3)	+1, −2, ±3 (1)	+3, −0, ±0 (3)	+2, −2, ±1 (0)	+4, −1, ±0 (3)	(+5)	10/29 (38%)
							60/203 (35%)

Table 7.5 Cheryl's constructions of classroom activities

Elements	Sand and water	Construction	Outdoor apparatus	Wendy House	Painting	Singing	Supervised games	Story	Drawing	Books
My/Not my	1	1	1	1	1	2	1	1	1	1
Unsupervised/ Supervised	1	1	1	1	1/2	2	2	2	1	1/2
Doing/ Listening	1	1	1	1	1	2	1	2	1	1
Together/ Alone	-	2	1	1	2	1	1	-	2	2
Home/School	2	1	2	2	2	-	1	1	1	1
Can/Can't	-	1	-	-	1	1	1	-	1	1

Table 7.6 The tendency of constructs to correlate with other constructs and the index of constellatoriness of Cheryl's construct system

	My/Not my	Unsupervised/Supervised	Doing/Listening	Together/Alone	'Home/School	Can/Can't	
My/Not my	(+10)	+6, −2, ±2 (4)	+8, −1, ±0 (7)	+3, −4, ±0 (1)	+5, −4, ±0 (1)	+5, −1, ±0 (4)	17/41 (41%)
Unsupervised/Supervised	+6, −2, ±2 (4)	(+10)	+7, −1, ±2 (6)	+2, −4, ±2 (2)	+2, −5, ±2 (3)	+2, −2, ±2 (0)	15/43 (35%)
Doing/Listening	+8, −1, ±0 (7)	+7, −1, ±2 (6)	(+10)	+3, −5, ±0 (2)	+4, −5, ±0 (1)	+5, −1, ±0 (4)	20/42 (48%)
Together/Alone	+3, −4, ±0 (1)	+2, −4, ±2 (2)	+3, −5, ±0 (2)	(+8)	+2, −5, ±0 (3)	+2, −4, ±0 (2)	10/36 (28%)
Home/School	+5, −4, ±0 (1)	+2, −5, ±2 (3)	+4, −5, ±0 (1)	+2, −5, ±0 (3)	(+9)	+4, −1, ±0 (3)	11/39 (29%)
Can/Can't	+5, −1, ±0 (4)	+2, −2, ±2 (0)	+5, −1, ±0 (4)	+2, −4, ±0 (2)	+4, −1, ±0 (3)	(+6)	13/29 (45%)
							86/230 (35%)

In this way three grids were constructed with a range of 48 to 53 spaces out of a possible 60 filled.

From each of these grids, an 'index of constellatoriness' was derived for each construct, 'constellatoriness' being taken to mean 'the relationship between a construct and others, such that a polar position on the given construct implies a polar position on the others.'

Thus, if a child construed five activities as 'Doing' and as 'Together' and five other activities as 'Listening' and 'Alone', this indicates a strong relationship between the two dimensions, and the index of constellatoriness is 10. Another child might construe six activities as 'Doing', of which three were construed as 'Together' and three as 'Alone'; and four activities as 'Listening', of which two were construed as 'Together' and two as 'Alone'. There is in this case a zero correlation, and the index is also 0. Between the two are tendencies of constellatoriness, in which other constructs are differentially implied. An actual example of the construction of an index is perhaps the simplest means of illustrating the process (see Table 7.2, 7.4 and 7.6).

David construed three activities as 'My', and in every case they were also construed as 'Unsupervised'. He construed seven activities as 'Not my'; of these, one was construed as 'Unsupervised', four as 'Supervised' and no entry is available for the other two. Here, there is a tendency for 'My' to be associated with 'Unsupervised' and for 'Not my' to be associated with 'Supervised', but the correlation is not perfect. In seven cases the correlation exists, and in one the correlation is reversed, so that the index of constellatoriness is $7 - 1 = 6$ (the activities for which no comment is available being ignored). This can be repeated for any pair of constructs, so that five scores for each construct (in a six-construct system) are derived. In Table 7.2, the scores for David's use of the 'My/Not my' construct are arrayed along the top line. When these are added together, they give a score of 30 (the numerator in the fraction to the right of the scores). On its own, this is insufficient, for it is apparent that the final score is at least partially dependent on the actual number of correlations which have been obtained. If all activities had been commented on using all constructs, the maximum score would have been 60 (with ten activities and six constructs), but if only half of the possible intersections of constructs and activities had been commented upon, the maximum score would be only 30. To resolve this, the actual number of possible correlations has been entered as a denominator in this case 46, giving a fraction of 30/46. This is then expressed as a percentage: 65 per cent. This score gives an indication of the way in which a child uses any construct in practice, and the extent to which one construct implies the others.

We now have scores indicating the extent to which two constructs are correlated (in this case 6, 9, 7, 3, 5) and the extent to which any construct implies all others together (65 per cent). Finally, a measure of the constellatoriness of the construct system as a whole was derived simply by adding all 30 of the separate scores obtained and dividing by the number of potential correlations; in this case 152/233 = 66 per cent.

These are the measures used in the following analysis, in which three children's construct systems are dealt with at length. The only difficulty which arose in computing scores derived from a child's construction of an activity ambiguously, using both poles of a construct at different times. In this case, the alternative constructions were allowed to cancel each other out.

Interpretation of David's grid

In interpreting David's grid, the most striking characteristic is the extreme tightness with which he uses his constructs.

My world/Not my world   In almost every case, 'My' activities were also 'Unsupervised', 'Doing' and 'Together', while any 'Not my' activity, was also deemed to be 'supervised', 'Listening' and 'Alone'. Only one exception to this rule exists, the Wendy House, which is not construed as 'My' despite its being seen as 'Unsupervised' and 'Together'. To seek the reason for this exception, we need to look beyond the six common constructs used by all children and find how David sees that activity. The answer seems to lie in David's belief that the Wendy House is only suitable for girls! Thus, despite its 'togetherness' and the lack of supervision, it is not seen as a worthy activity.

The relationship of 'My/Not my' to the other constructs is somewhat less obvious. While no 'My' activity is associated with 'Home', so that there appears to be mutual exclusion, the reverse is not the case and some 'Not my' activities are carried on at home. Similarly, David sees himself as competent at the 'My' activities, but he also sees himself as competent at two activities not construed as 'My'. The assignment of an activity to the 'Can' pole would seem to be a necessary but not a sufficient condition for David to construe it as 'My'.

Supervised/Unsupervised   Again, the implications of an activity's being 'Unsupervised' or 'Supervised' are strong. Any 'Unsupervised' activity, with the exclusion of the Wendy House, is also construed as 'My', while 'Supervised' activities are seen as 'Not my'. The relationship of Supervised/Unsupervised to Doing/Listening is even tighter, forming two disjoint sets, and the same is true of the relationship to Together/Alone.

The Home/School and Can/Can't constructs are not involved in a similar one-to-one correspondence. Any 'Unsupervised' activity is necessarily seen as particular to school, but the reverse does not hold, some 'Supervised' activities being seen as particular to school while some are associated with home. Similarly, while David sees himself as competent at 'Unsupervised' activities, he also sees himself as competent at some of the activities he construes as 'Supervised'.

Doing/Listening The relationship of this construct to My/Not my and Supervised/Unsupervised has already been noted and a similar relationship exists towards Together/Alone. Again, the relationship to the Home/School and Can/Can't constructs are more complex. While any activity seen as 'Doing' is construed as 'Can', and as 'School', activities seen as 'Listening' may be assigned to either the 'Can' or the 'Can't' pole, and either the 'Home' or the 'School' pole.

Together/Alone The 'Together' pole implies (with the exception of the Wendy House) that an activity be construed as 'My', and with no exceptions it must be 'Unsupervised' and 'Doing'. The reverse relationship exists in the case of the 'Alone' pole. 'Together' activities must also be seen as particular to school, and as those in which David is competent, though this is not sufficient, some 'Alone' activities being proper to 'Home' and some to 'School', some to the 'Can' pole and some to the 'Can't'.

Home/School Any activity which David sees as 'Home' is also assigned to the 'Not my' pole of the first construct, though the reverse is not true, other criteria being used before an activity is construed as 'My'. This relationship also holds for Unsupervised/Supervised, Doing/Listening and Together/Alone. There would seem to be no clear relationship with Can/Can't.

Can/Can't Any activity at which David sees himself as incompetent is assigned to the 'Not my' pole. Those at which he sees himself as competent may be assigned to the 'My' or the 'Not my' poles on other grounds. There are no unsupervised activities at which he sees himself as incompetent, though an activity at which he sees himself as competent may be either 'Supervised' or 'Unsupervised'. Similar relationships hold with 'Listening' and 'My own self'. There is no significant relationship with the Home/School construct.

To generalize, it can be seen that there are two constellations of activities, construed respectively as My, Unsupervised, Doing, Together, Can and Proper to school, on the one hand, and Not my, Supervised, Listening and Alone (with no necessary assignment to the Home or School and Can or Can't poles) on the other. With these constructs combined in the way, approximate to a single dimension, there is necessarily little ambiguity in David's world, and its massive facticity allows him little room for movement.

This is not to say that David has not developed structures which allow him to cope with classroom reality. While he is not, in Bieri's terms, cognitively complex, his construct system is certainly extremely well integrated, which is often seen by developmental psychologists as a goal at which development is aimed.

David's difficulty lies not in an absence of useful constructs (he uses all six and more besides) nor in a lack of integration but in the mode of construing which he uses in the classroom. His construction processes are, however, constellatory to an extreme degree, as is indicated by his score on the constellatoriness index of 66 per cent. It would seem to be difficult for David to construe in a propositional manner, and any construction necessarily implies a whole series of others.

Interpretation of Steven's grid

There is a strong contrast between Steven's grid and that of David. While David is unusual in the tightness of his construing, Steven is extremely loose. It certainly cannot be said that his system is over-integrated, the highest index of constellatoriness being 38 per cent, as compared to David's 80 per cent, while his lowest index is a mere 11 per cent compared to David's 45 per cent. Overall, Steven's index is 35 per cent, compared to David's 66 per cent.

My world/Not my world The My/Not my construct implies, only one other construct. 'My' activities may be either 'Supervised' or 'Unsupervised', 'Doing' or 'Listening', 'Together' or 'Alone', 'School' or 'Home'. The exception is that activities construed as 'My' must be those at which Steven sees himself as competent. No activities at which Steven sees himself as incompetent are construed as 'My'.

On the other hand, only one activity is consistently construed as 'Not my' and this also construed as 'Supervised' and 'Listening'. However this one case is not sufficient to conclude that 'Not my' must always be associated with these poles. The picture is complicated by Steven's ambiguity in construing, so that at one moment an activity may be construed as 'My', at another time as 'Not my'. This is the case in three out of ten activities.

Unsupervised/Supervised Apparently Steven's preference is for unsupervised activities, in that he classifies as 'Not my' some 'Supervised' activities, while all activities he construes as 'Unsupervised' are also seen as 'My'. Nevertheless, of activities he construed as 'My', there is a good balance of between 'Supervised' and 'Unsupervised' activities, and some activities are again ambiguous, being viewed as 'Supervised' in some contexts and 'Unsupervised' in others.

A similar picture emerges in the relationship between this construct and Doing/Listening. 'Doing' is usually associated with 'Unsupervised' though there is no necessity here, some 'Supervised' activities being construed as 'Doing'. On the other hand, only 'Supervised' activities are associated with 'Listening'. Thus, to be 'Unsupervised' there is a necessity that an activity be construed as 'Doing' though the reverse does not hold.

In the case of Home/School, all we learn is that Steven participates in a good number of activities at home, both on his own and supervised by or together with his parents. Again there is no clear relationship between this and Unsupervised/Supervised.

Lastly, we learn nothing of the relationship of Unsupervised/Supervised to Can/Can't because of the absence of comments on activities at which Steven sees himself as incompetent.

Doing/Listening Steven apparently has a strong preference for 'Doing' activities over those he sees as 'Listening'. It must not be overlooked, however, that while many more 'Doing' activities than 'Listening' activities are 'My', more are also 'Not my'. There appears to be no significant relationship between the two constructs. What is important here is the plethora of 'Doing' activities and the dearth of 'Listening' activities. Clearly, for Steven 'Doing' encompasses a greater number of activities than it does for David.

The second relationship between Doing/Listening and Unsupervised/Supervised corresponds to 'objective reality' more than it did for David. All 'Unsupervised' activities are also 'Doing', while 'Supervised' activities may be either 'Doing' or 'Listening'. All 'Listening' activities are 'Supervised' while 'Doing' activities may be either 'Supervised' or 'Unsupervised'.

The absence of possible correlations with 'Listening' activities means that no relationship with Together/Alone can be discerned, though the balance of 'Together' and 'Alone' activities seen as 'Doing' is significant. This is also the case with Home/School, and the single correlation of 'Listening' with 'Home' is sufficient to allow us to draw any conclusions. Even more, the final relationship with Can/Can't provides only three possible scores, all indicating that 'Doing' and 'Can' are constellatory, but the absence of further information does not permit us to say more.

Together/Alone The extreme looseness of Steven's construing again prevents us drawing definite conclusions from the data. 'Together' activities may be 'My' or 'Not my', 'Supervised' or 'Unsupervised' and 'Home' or 'School'. Similarly, activities construed as 'Alone' may be 'My' or 'Not my', 'Unsupervised' or 'Supervised' and 'Home' or 'School'. In the case of the other two relationships, with Doing/Listening and Can/Can't, nothing can be said apart from the fact that there is a good balance between 'Together' and 'Alone' in activities seen as 'Doing', and in which Steven sees himself as competent.

Home/School Again, the looseness of construing does not allow us to draw many conclusions. 'Home' activities may be 'My' or 'Not my', as 'Unsupervised' or 'Supervised', as 'Doing' or 'Listening', and as 'Together' or 'Alone'. 'School' activities may be 'My' or 'Not my', 'Supervised' or 'Unsupervised', and as 'Together' or 'Alone'.

No relationship with Can/Can't can be specified because of the absence of data. The only significant relationship is with Doing/Listening, where no 'School' activity is construed as 'Listening', all activities associated with the 'School' pole being 'Doing' activities. This is possibly merely a function of inadequate data, in that some activities (e.g. singing) on which Steven did not comment would probably have been allotted to the 'School' and 'Listening' poles.

Can/Can't The absence of data on Steven's construction of activities allotted to the 'Can't' pole allows no conclusions whatever to be drawn here. This absence of the necessary data seems to indicate that either Steven did not wish to admit that he saw himself as incompetent in any activity, though he did in fact do so, or alternatively that the 'Can't' pole of the construct was submerged, giving extreme bias in his constructions.

Steven is at the opposite extreme of integration to David: his construct system is extremely loose, no construct necessarily being associated with another. However, insofar as looseness of construing allows him to make propositional rather than constellatory constructions, Steven would appear to be in a better position to develop. It is worth noting that of all the children in the class, David and Steven were classed together as 'tearaways' by the teacher. Both were seen as boisterous, sometimes silly, aggressive, disobedient, extrovert, lively and mobile. The only way they differed was that David 'lacks concentration and has a speech problem' and Steven 'likes making things'.

Interpretation of Cheryl's grid

Cheryl differs in several ways from David and Steven in organization of her construct system. The teachers' impressions of her include the comment 'well adjusted', which the two boys are not thought to be. What, then, is distinctive about Cheryl? How is her construct system organized? And does its organization throw any light on her apparent 'adjustment'.

My/Not my Cheryl's openness and willingness to participate in all classroom activities, except singing, make it difficult to discover what criteria she uses in construing an activity as 'My'. By looking at her view of singing, however, we can see that, for an activity to be seen as 'Not my' it is likely to be 'Supervised', 'Listening' and 'Together'. However these three constructs come together in this way in only the one activity.

Unsupervised/Supervised The activities which Cheryl construes as 'Unsupervised' are also construed as 'My' and as 'Doing'. They may be either 'Together' or 'Alone' and 'Home' or 'School'. Nothing can be said about the relationship with Can/Can't. On the other pole, activities seen as 'Supervised' do not have any strong correlations with other constructs, but there is a tendency for them to be 'Home' rather than 'School' and a weak tendency for them to be 'Doing' rather than 'Listening'.

There seems to be quite a strong constellation here of 'Unsupervised', and 'Doing', associated with 'My', with a tendency to be construed as 'Alone'. A weaker constellation exists in which 'Supervised' is associated with 'Listening'. There is no strong determination here, as there was with David, whose index of constellatoriness for this construct was 74 per cent compared to Cheryl's 35 per cent. This is, however, slightly higher than Steven's 28 per cent.

Doing/Listening 'Doing' activities may be 'Unsupervised' or 'Supervised', as 'Together' or 'Alone', and as 'Home' or 'School'. They are apparently construed as 'Can', though so also are 'Listening' activities, (so no conclusions can be drawn here) and as 'My', though Cheryl's willingness to see most activities as 'My' makes any conclusions unwarranted. On the other hand, 'Listening' activities are apparently invariably also 'Supervised', 'Together' and 'Home'. The dearth of data on her use of 'Can't', 'Listening' and 'Not my' make it difficult to derive any hard and fast rules from her grid. Nevertheless, her index of constellatoriness for the Doing/Listening construct is sufficiently high (48 per cent, as against David's 80 per cent and Steven's 38 per cent) to give her a fairly stable view of the classroom without freezing it totally.

Together/Alone If an activity is construed as 'Together' then it is not necessarily construed as falling on any one pole of the other constructs. There is a slight tendency for it to be construed as 'Doing' and as 'School', rather than as 'Listening' and 'Home'.

On the other hand, activities assigned to the 'Alone' pole are invariably also 'My' and 'Doing', and tend to be seen as 'Unsupervised' and 'Home'. The measure of correlation is much higher for this pole of the construct, giving Cheryl a certain amount of stability in construing activities which she enters into alone, but giving a more open, flexible view of those activities which involve other children.

Home/School Again, the bias of the data means that we can say nothing about the relationship of Home/School to My/Not my and Can/Can't. There is an index of constellatoriness of only 29 per cent, indicating that Cheryl is able to construe activities in which she participates at school only, and those she takes part in at home, in an open fashion.

Can/Can't The absence of data on Cheryl's use of the 'Can't' pole makes it impossible to draw any conclusions here.

Cheryl's construct system clearly differs from that of David, in that it permits her to manoeuvre effectively in the classroom, because of the propositional nature of most of her constructs. Steven also appears to construe in a propositional way, but he does not have the stability of Cheryl which is apparently related to the middle range of constellatoriness of Doing/Listening and Can/Can't, two constructs which are central in her constructions.

For reasons about which we can only speculate, she sees herself as competent in most activities. Perhaps it is this view of self-competence, which she now takes for granted, when coupled with flexible construing, which differentiates her from Steven.

Conclusion

Teachers need to know 'where the kids are at'; and the many problems of 'objective' testing of three-year-olds leave the teacher with no means of assessing children but her own subjective impressions, often framed in a neo-Piagetian perspective which emphasizes the discontinuities of child and adult thought.

This research has endeavoured to explore the possibilities of adopting an approach designed for use with adults in order to get at the child's own version of the world in which he operates. Construct theory assumes nothing about the individual's thought processes, except that it is useful to see him as working with bipolar constructs, so that the most significant dimensions of his thinking can be isolated and their interrelationships exposed. When allied with a naturalistic observational approach, in which ecologically invalid experimental situations are avoided, the dangers both of supposedly 'objective' testing and of wholly impressionistic assessments might be reduced.

What then can we conclude about the three-year old's view of the classroom? First of all, it seems that, even at this age, there is something of a common culture, in which categories are embedded which help the child to structure his world. The six categories with which we have been concerned were used by all of the children, not just the three who have been considered in detail. The origin of these categories is not our concern here, but it seems plausible that they constitute a resource by which the children make sense of the classroom.

Secondly, the children do not merely conform to or deviate from this common culture, but use the categories it provides in their own idiosyncratic ways. A danger of relying on subjective impressions is that the child will be 'typed' according to the teacher's own categories rather than his own, and his essential qualities thereby missed. In this classroom the teacher classed David together with Steven, while according to our analysis they are very different. This appears to be a function of her category system, in that both were disruptive of classroom activities and deviated considerably from the 'ideal pupil', and so were equivalent in this respect. In a child-centred approach however, it is essential that we know not only *that* a child is deviant but *how* and if possible *why* he is so. In this case, we would suggest that needs of the two children are different. David needs to loosen up (dilate) considerably so that the extensive range of classroom activities which are at present effectively excluded from his own construction of the classroom can be accepted by him. On the other hand, Steven needs to tighten up, so that the inconsistent, shifting world he inhabits can assume some substance. Cheryl differs from both, in that she can adequately cognitively organize most aspects of the classroom but has enough flexibility to extend her range of activities into new areas.

Overall, we suggest that three-year-olds are active thinkers about their world. They make many propositions about the classroom, often of a highly complex kind. These propositions might be formalized into a rule system. For example, if an activity is 'Doing' and 'Unsupervised' it can be construed as 'My' provided that it is 'Together'. If it meets the first two criteria but is 'Alone', it can still be construed as 'My' if it is a 'Home' activity which can be assigned to the 'Can' pole.

Clearly, the children could not articulate these rules – nor for that matter could most adults explicate the process by which they reach decisions. This does not mean, however, that the process is not 'real'.

This throws light on the debate about the child's ability to decentre. Piaget points out that complex operations cannot be executed by children of this age, because of their inability to hold two or more dimensions of a problem in mind simultaneously. Thus reversibility cannot be understood because it requires the child to take into account both reciprocity and inversion. However, in this chapter we have suggested the possibility that, in their everyday behaviour in the classroom, the children were using a multiplicity of dimensions simultaneously in arriving at a view of reality. Children who reduce their constructions to a single dimension (e.g. David) are in a minority, and this reduction is indeed a problem to be overcome.

We have adopted the view that the essential point about children is not their 'child'-ness, any more than the essential point about women is their femininity. There are clearly differences between children and adults which need to be explicated, and there is a need for an examination of the development of the one into the other. This development, however, is not simply the filling-up of an empty vessel, but a process undertaken by the vessel himself in order to come to terms with the contradictions he confronts as he deals with the world. Here the Piagetian concepts of accommodation and assimilation are crucial, but in themselves inadequate, insofar as the notion of culture is neglected. The approach adopted in this chapter, using a combination of Personal Construct Theory and naturalistic observation can only give an account of how a child uses his battery of constructs at a given moment. When viewed as a *process* in which the origins of his constructs and the experiences which led to his adoption and reorganization of categories provided by his culture are examined, together with the relationship of his constructs to his position in relation to others, it might prove possible to explore the ways in which the child makes himself into the adult.

References

Applebee, A.N. 1975: Developmental changes in consensus of construing within a specified domain. *B.J. Psychol.* **66(4)**, 73–80.
— 1976: The development of children's responses to repertory grids. *B.J. Soc. and Clin. Psychol.* **15**, 101–2.
Bannister, D. and Fransella, F. 1971: *Inquiring man*. Harmondsworth: Penguin.
Bieri, J. 1955: Cognitive complexity – simplicity and predictive behaviour. *J. Abn. and Soc. Psychol.* **51**, 263–8.
Brierley, D.W. 1967: *The use of personality constructs by children of three different ages*. Unpublished Ph.D. thesis, University of London.
Bruner, J.S., Goodnow, J.J. and Austin, G. 1956: *A study of thinking*. New York: Wiley.
Carr, J.E. 1970: Differentiation similarity of patient and therapist and the outcome of psychotherapy. *J. Abn. Psychol.* **76**, 361–8.
Crockett, W.H. 1965: Cognitive complexity and impression formation. In B. Maher (ed.), *Progress in experimental personality research*. London: Academic Press.
Honess, T. 1976: Cognitive complexity and social prediction. *B.J. Soc. and Clin. Psychol.* **15**, 23–31.
Kelly, G.A. 1955: *The psychology of personal constructs*. New York: Norton.
Maddi, S.R. 1968: *Personality theories: a comparative analysis*. London: Homewood.
Peck, D. and Whitlow, D. 1975: *Approaches to personality theory*. London: Methuen.
Ravenette, A.T. 1975: Grid techniques for children. *J. Child Psychol. and Psychiat.* **16**, 79–83.
Salmon, P. 1969: Differential conforming and the development process. *B.J. Soc. and Clin. Psychol.* **8**, 22–31.
— 1976: Grid measures with child subjects. In P. Slater (ed.), *Exploration in intrapersonal space*. London: Wiley.
Scott, W.A. 1962: Cognitive complexity and cognitive flexibility, *Sociometry* **25**, 405–14.
Smith, S. and Leach, C. 1972: A hierarchical measure of cognitive complexity. *B.J. Psychol.* **63**, 561–8.

8

Talking to some purpose

Peter Lloyd

Language and cognition have been investigated in many ways but it can be argued that they are most intimately connected in tasks which require two children to communicate and cooperate in solving a problem. This technique has been used by a number of workers including Doise (1978), Flavell *et al.* (1979), Greenfield and Dent (1979), Miller and Brownell (1975) and Russell (1979).

Although the emphasis may vary, this research field is united in taking a social constructivist approach to intellectual development (see Russell, this volume) and in seeing awareness of one's own cognitive capacities as a significant factor in cognitive growth, (see especially Flavell *et al.* 1979, Markman, 1977, 1979). Another factor common to some, if not all, of these studies is a concern with the context in which cognition takes place, and, in particular, the move towards increasingly decontextualized modes of cognition, (see also Donaldson 1978, Walkerdine and Sinha 1978). Above all, communication itself is seen as the pivot on which these processes turn. Greenfield and Dent (1979, 34) put it as follows:

> Developmental study of this problem is important because determining something of the progressive growth of the ability to comprehend and communicate can help elucidate some central problems in the study of language and cognition. More specifically, it is possible to learn of the developmental interaction of the perceptual/cognitive system with the way in which language is used in context to communicate. A first step is to identify the relevant contextual variables and the cognitive abilities required to make use of linguistic and nonlinguistic elements in order to achieve effective communication.

The studies to be described in this chapter take the first step that is mentioned by Greenfield and Dent. It also happens coincidentally that the task chosen for investigation in this work and that of Greenfield and Dent is seriation.

In contrast to Greenfield and Dent's study, and most of the work cited, the present investigation was conducted with preschool children. If one is interested in the development of purposeful communication between peers, it seems necessary to examine the behaviour at or near its origins. The sparsity, if not lack, of studies of this sort with preschool children seems to be due to the baleful influence of Piaget's theory of egocentrism. Although Piaget's (1926) studies of communication were carried out many years ago, he seems never to have revised his view that preoperational children are severely handicapped in their ability to talk to one another. As late as 1969 he is found writing (with Inhelder):

> The fact is that the speech of subjects between four and six (observed in situations in which children work, play, and speak freely) is not intended to provide information, ask questions, etc. (that is, it is not socialized language), but consists rather of monologues or 'collective monologues' in the course of which everyone talks to himself without listening to the others (that is, egocentric language). (Piaget and Inhelder 1969, 120)

Piaget's influence in this area is undoubtedly on the wane (see for instance Shantz 1975, Donaldson 1978 and Light 1979), yet there are features of his method which are considered too valuable to discard, especially when compared to the standard referential communication paradigm pioneered by Glucksberg and Krauss (1967).

One of the merits of Piaget's original study, in which one child explained the workings of a household object such as a tap, is that an instruction or teaching function is built into the task. The task has, therefore, a purpose or goal. In this way it is superior to the Glucksberg and Krauss task − in which the listener is asked to identify one of a series of objects or pictures from a description provided by the speaker − where the motive is less apparent. Naturalistic studies (Shields 1978, Dore 1977, Cole *et al.* 1979) have shown that children do like telling each other about events that have happened, about how things work and about how to play games. Piaget's choice of somewhat obscure stories and mechanical functions has certainly much to do with the restricted abilities he found. But tasks do not have to be so far removed from the child's experience. Instead we can try to build on the sort of skills which we know that the child brings to his cooperative play (Garvey 1977).

The study to be presented here has borrowed from the approaches discussed in an attempt to include the naturalism that is the hallmark of Piagetian studies at their best, while retaining the degree of control necessary to examine the influence of subject and material variables. At the same time analysis has gone beyond frequency counts of simple behaviour measures to look at the pragmatics involved. The style and content of communication tells us much about the underlying cognitive abilities and limitations which govern performance.

The studies to be described, therefore, required one child to learn a task – putting blocks of varying size on a peg or in a line in order of size – and then to teach the task to another child who was not familiar with the 'game'. The method has the following features.

(1) The use of a set of discrete referents that were related but different. This allowed one to gauge the sensitivity of the participants to the referent non-referent array. In talking about one particular block did they take account of the perceived alternatives?

(2) Speaker and listener faced each other across a table in which they were talking about identical sets of material. The subjects could see one another but the material was hidden from the other by low screens. This procedure allowed one to see clearly the contributions of speaker and listener and the extent to which they took account of each other in their communications – for example, the listener indicating inadequacy of descriptions and the speaker modifying his message accordingly.

(3) The instructional context already referred to ensured that the goal of the exercises was explicit – to seriate a set of blocks or sticks. This, in turn, gave the participants clear motives: one child to teach another how to carry out a task he himself had acquired earlier; one to learn that task from his peer, well enough to be able to teach it himself.

Aims

An indication of the purpose of the study has already been given. What follows is a more explicit statement of the main aims.

(1) To test the still widely held view that preschool children are unable to engage purposively in an enterprise in which successful communication is critical to success.

(2) To examine the utility of the communication technique for the investigation of a concept like seriation, an operation which Piaget has shown is critically involved in the understanding of numbers. Further, it was hoped that the technique might have applications more widely in the field of cognitive development as described by Greenfield and Dent. Is it the case that children doing *and* talking about something tells us more about the nature of concept development than children who are only 'doing'?

(3) To ascertain if the process of learning from another child (or, indeed, teaching another child) is a significant educational experience. There are a number of possibilities. Children in both roles may gain an understanding of the task that is denied them in the usual educational context. Children in one of the roles may benefit but not the other. For example, the child teaching may gain insights into the problem he did not have before, while the learning child finds the experience of no value. It is also conceivable that the exercise is of value to neither participant though educational benefits need not be the only gain. The experience may be useful as a piece of social interaction and role-

taking, leading indirectly to important advances in communication skill.

Study I

Subjects

The sample of ten children — four boys, six girls, with an age range from 3;11 to 5;2 (mean age 4;6) — were split into five groups of two to provide the communication pairs.

Materials

These were two identical sets of six square blocks, with a uniform thickness of 1.8cm but increasing in length and breadth by equivalent amounts of 2 cm from the smallest, 3.4cm, up to 13.4cm. Each block had a centrally drilled hole of 1.2cm for stacking on a peg set vertically in a wooden base. To facilitate verbal description each block had a familiar object painted on it, each picture taking up an equivalent proportion (about 10 per cent) of the block. In order of ascendance the pictures were: *ball*, *flower*, *car*, *telephone*, *key*, *dog*. There were also two small screens, 16cm high and 60cm wide.

Procedure

Before the experiment all the subjects were individually shown the pictures to be used on the blocks to ensure they could identify them.

Preliminary session In a preliminary session one member of each of the five pairs was presented with a model of a completed seriation and asked to produce the same arrangement from an identical set. Care was taken that the adult did not provide a model in communication terms; apart from pointing out that sticks went in order from big to little, nothing was mentioned. In the familiarization session the children were required to learn ordering in only one direction, but in the communication session they seriated in the order learned and the reverse order. The preliminary session was concluded when one correct seriation, large to small, had been achieved.

Communication task In the communication session, the experienced subject (ES) was taken into the experimental room first and told that they were going to play the same game as before, but that this time he must tell a friend of his how to do it. As a reminder the blocks in the finished position were briefly shown to the child, and then taken off and scrambled on the table. The naive subject (NS) was then fetched and the following instructions were given.

'We are going to play with these blocks and this stick today. *(The blocks are lying in random order on the table.) ES has seen them before. We had a game with them before, and ES will tell you what to do. Can you see the pictures on them? Tell me what they are.' (The experimenter ascertains that NS knows the names. As NS identifies the blocks, E points out the same blocks in the other child's array.)* Small screens were then put in front of each child's materials so that they were not visible to the other subject.

(To NS): 'Now you've both got the same blocks, haven't you? Now will you listen carefully to ES, because he is going to tell you how to put your blocks on the stick.'

(To ES): 'Now will you tell NS what to do. Make the same thing you made before for me, so that you both have the same blocks on the stick.'

At the completion of a trial, usually when all blocks were on the peg but also if subjects indicated they had finished, the screens were removed so that a comparison of seriations could be made. The experimenter asked if the series were just the same and, if they were not, for the subjects to indicate the differences. ES invariably supplied this information.

When ES had successfully transmitted instructions about seriating in the order learned, the new subject took a turn as speaker and instructed the experienced subject. After this ES again assumed the role of speaker and was this time asked to build up the blocks in the reverse order, from little to big. If this was achieved successfully NS attempted the same task. A summary of the experimental design is given in Table 8.1. All sessions were videotaped.

Results and discussion

The sample used in these studies is specialized, in the sense that the children knew each other and the experimenter well. This is seen to be a strength of the work, however, since effective communication is less likely if the children are drawn in some random manner from the population. At the same time the sample is also small and the procedure is deliberately not rigorously defined. Accordingly, findings are presented in the form of broad, and sometimes tentative, inferences. These

Table 8.1 Experimental design of Study I in seriation

Part One Order Learned (Big ← Little)				Part Two Reverse Order (Little ← Big)			
Trial 1		Trial 2		Trial 3		Trial 4	
Speaker	Listener	Speaker	Listener	Speaker	Listener	Speaker	Listener
ES	NS	NS	ES	ES	NS	NS	ES

are based on an analysis of the complete behavioural records from videotape.

The first point to note is the general competence of the subjects. This was first apparent in the preliminary session when one member of each pair was given the opportunity to 'practise' the seriation task. Three out of the five carried out the operation successfully first time, and another subject achieved this on her second trial. Only one subject had serious difficulty, but she worked her way through by trial and error to a correct solution on her fourth attempt.

Table 8.2 summarizes performances in the communication session. The most noticeable statistic is that 15 seriations are completed in a total of 21 trials, that is 6 of the trials contain error. But, since some of these mistakes are corrected spontaneously by the speaker, a more realistic figure is 4 incorrect trials, a failure rate of only 19 per cent. These figures are based only on the spakers' performances, in other words the verbal report. But because both subjects play both roles, the experienced and naive subjects are represented. It is only experienced subjects, in fact, who make errors, but this is partly due to their playing a bigger part in the process.

So, it can be said that when they act as speakers, naive subjects perform creditably. Their rate of success is remarkable considering it is based on one exposure to the correct solution by way of verbal instructions from a peer. They have first created the correct assembly in response to their partner's description, and are subsequently able to reproduce this seriation accurately when asked to begin again with the blocks scrambled. It seems unlikely that this is a feat of rote learning. Some sort of cognitive rule must be hypothesised, though whether it is based on imagery, language or some other symbolic form is not clear.

In the more demanding reverse order seriation, where there was no direct experience on which to draw, subjects again performed very capably, there being no significant difference in terms of error rate. An estimation of the performances showed that there was initially some

Table 8.2 Number of successful and unsuccessful and unsuccessful seriations by speakers in communication situation (Study I)

Speaker	Order Learned Big ← Little		Reverse Order Little ← Big		
	Correct	Incorrect	Correct	Incorrect	Total
Experienced subject	5	4	4	2	15
Naive subject	4	0	2	0	6
Total	9	4	6	2	21

hesitation but that once the seriation was under way it proceeded without difficulty. A real understanding of the principle of serial order must be assumed if only in this limited context.

The speaker-listener relationship Miller and Brownell (1975) reported the effect of dominance on children's performance in joint solutions to conservation problems. They found that although conservers held sway over non-conservers in discussion, a control study showed that this was not a function of general dominance in argument. In this study it transpired that the experienced subject had leadership (if not greatness) thrust upon him. This was appropriate when ES was speaker and therefore instructor, but it was occasionally less satisfactory when ES was listener since it led to the speaker's teaching role being undermined. Here, briefly, are three examples of the sort of behaviour that was observed.

(1) The ES as listener assumes control, taking over the role of speaker even though NS is performing competently.

(2) ES ignores incorrect or inadequate information on the part of the speaker and operates independently, making no attempt to provide feedback for the speaker.

(3) In one pairing a strong element of competition entered the situation. The participants vied with one another to be first to announce the correct block. Communication did not cease; but, rather than being informative, it tended to be challenging, with the leadership of the dyad perhaps being at stake.

The dynamics of the communication situation

Constructing and interpreting messages The experiment provided some information about the young child's speech and thought processes during cognitive activity. It was noticeable that children did not usually communicate information until *they* were satisfied as to its correctness. In this task, when the speaker was uncertain about the block he had selected he would first assess the choice, check it against what had gone and what remained in the pool, and if he decided to discard it there would be no mention of it. Only the blocks that actually went on the stick were spoken about. This demonstrates a high degree of speech inhibition and, of course, greatly increases the communication effectiveness. It may be that a task such as this, which is stretching four-year-olds mentally, would as a consequence tend to eliminate unnecessary speech, because processing capacity is already being fully utilized.

This speech inhibition was also seen in error correcting situations with rather less beneficial results. When a subject put a block (or blocks) in the wrong order, and subsequently noticed it, he would either decide to remedy the fault immediately, or remark on it but nevertheless continue to the end giving an incorrect solution. It is the error correcting behaviour which is relevant at this point. What happens is that the speaker communicates what is a wrong block choice as it is put on the stick, then notices the error. At this point he will remedy the situation, often saying 'Oh or 'No' and effect a change — frequently a transposition — *but will not inform the listener of the change*. It is as if the extra concentration demanded to correct a fault precludes the ability to comment on the behaviour. Such behaviour is, of course, detrimental to the success of the communication operation. An example will illustrate the point.

The following extract gives the verbal record only, which largely represents the information available to the listener:

Speaker: *Telephone.*
Listener: *Telephone.*
Speaker: No. *Car*
Listener: *Car?*

When this is amplified by the rest of the behavioural record, the nature of the confusion becomes apparent.

Speaker: *Telephone* (puts it on the stick)
Listener: *Telephone* (puts it on the stick)
Speaker: (Picks up *flower*, puts it on top of the stick briefly, but quickly sees it is the wrong choice) No. (picks up the *car* and puts it on) *Car.*
Listener: *Car?* (Takes off *telephone* and picks up *car*).

Here we have examples of the two types of speech inhibition, one adaptive, the other maladaptive. The listener, not surprisingly, connects the speaker's 'No' with the previous instruction, 'telephone', and accordingly makes the adjustment on his stick. Confusion would also have arisen if the speaker had said '*flower*' when he handled that block, and the suppression of verbal comment about this is a positive aid to communication efficiency.

The effect of nonverbal cues Although it was stated that the verbal record is the main source of information to the participants, there are important additional aids. The speaker, for example, comes to expect the small cues which tell him that the listener has responded to his message. This is often a repetition of the message — a sort of acknowledgement — or merely the *sound* of the block going on the stick which many speakers wait for. Although they cannot see the block being put on the stick, they can tell by the listener's actions whether or not he is putting a block on the stick, and this is another cue they quickly come to use.

The material itself also provides clues. The experienced participant, particularly, can use these to good effect on occasions, compensating for confusions in the instructions provided by the speaker.

Taking account of the other Listeners are not always experienced, however, and the general pattern is that they take a passive role. The listener tends to act on the data given by the speaker as though it were sufficient to allow him to make a decision. In the present study a one-word message is sufficient to allow a choice to be made. Its efficiency is dependent on the speaker's understanding of ordering blocks according to size.

This study does suggest that speakers, especially experienced ones, do have some consideration for the listener. In this sense, awareness of the two-way interaction of the communication situation is present. This awareness showed itself in the form of questions ('Have you got the motorcar, Alan?') and repetitions.

An example of the latter follows:

S: And this time it's with (picks up *key*) the *key* (putting it on stick).
L: (No response — looks at E).
S: (realizing L has made no choice). It's the *key*.
L: (giggles — puts on *key*).

If the speaker had been behaving in an egocentric fashion he would not be concerned as to whether the listener had heard and carried out his instruction. Even less would he give an unsolicited repetition of the message. This lack of egocentrism may have something to do with the prior exposure to the materials for some subjects, giving them knowledge to which their partners did not have access. This may have motivated them in some sense to transmit this knowledge to their partner. To reiterate this point, the experienced subjects have two concrete reasons for feeling in an advantageous position *a propos* the naive children. They have played the game before and they *know* how to play it. Not only are they familiar with the materials but they are aware that they have properly constructed the 'castle'.

This real degree of confidence may be an important factor in good communication. Equally so might be the task itself. There may be something inherent in these materials which facilitated seriation, and this is what Piaget has argued. A further study with different materials would be required to ascertain this information.

Varieties of strategy As well as the materials themselves, the act of describing the behaviour necessary to carry out the task may also facilitate the process. Certainly Piagetian theory and Russian work (e.g. Luria 1959) suggests that speech needs to be describing an *active* process if it is to be successful. This is demonstrated in an incident occurring in the first trial of a female-male pair (Elizabeth/Gregory). The speaker (Elizabeth) begins to seriate but does not make use of the attached labels to transmit messages. Her first message is 'the big block' and she adds two further blocks without communication. The listener is not clear about his role and the experimenter suggests to the speaker that she tells Gregory what she has done. She finds this very difficult. The accurate reporting of an event that has already happened, even when the results are clearly available, does seem to present problems for young children. Part of the difficulty may be the need to use temporal phrases such as 'first', 'next' and 'then'. But it seems that the speaker needs to be describing the action as she is carrying it out to be effective.

Markman (1977) has suggested that the active mental monitoring of the component steps to a problem is an important feature of meta-cognition and a capacity not generally available to preschool children. Elizabeth's behaviour suggests that the monitoring has to be facilitated by explicit verbalization. This example also illustrates the problems the task would present when easily-recognized labels for the items are not present, a fact of which Piaget seems strangely unaware in his investigation of seriation in *The grasp of consciousness* (1977).

In contrast to Elizabeth there is the exceptional performance of another child, who starts to tell the listener what she should do without carrying out the actions herself. Since she has been exposed to the task and materials only once before, and then for a very brief period, it seems that knowledge of how to perform the task is present as a plan or scheme. Having carried out the task once previously in a sensori-motor fashion, the necessary information has been assimilated and a strategy formed. Presumably it is this on which the child draws to predict the operation verbally. She is helped by the materials before her, but these only represent the building blocks of the finished structure in a random order and do not, in themselves, indicate how this structure should be created. When it was explained that she may carry out the task manually, her performance (including the reverse order) was very competent, suggesting that the cognitive operation enabling seriation, at this level at least, is present.

Study II

The considerable success that was achieved in the first seriation experiment encouraged a further study with materials used in the standard Piagetian task (Piaget 1952), i.e. graded sticks. It would then be possible to see whether the results obtained in the first study were a function of the material. If it proved to be the case that material which could be said to achieve a 'good' form led to very much greater success in ordering objects, then it would suggest that material properties and perceptual factors in general have an even stronger influence at this stage of development than perhaps Piaget has emphasized. The configurations made by the completed series are shown in Figure 8.1. The outline made by (1) seems, intuitively, to be more 'powerful', but why this should be is open to debate. Whether it is a matter of gestalt laws of perception or simply a question of greater familiarity with one form rather than another, or again a question of experience in actively constructing such shapes, will to some extent depend on one's theoretical preferences.

Method

Subjects The sample consisted of ten children, four boys, six girls, seven of whom had taken part in Experiment I (see comment below). The age range was from 3;10 to 5;2, giving a mean of 4;5. The sample was divided into five pairs for the communication sessions.

Materials These consisted of two identical sets of six sticks, 2.4cm square and varying in height by equivalent amounts of 1.5cm from the smallest, 7.5cm, up to the largest, 15cm, the intervals used in Elkind (1964). Each stick had a familiar object painted on it for identification purposes. These were, in order of ascendence: *chair, cup, fish, house, train, cat.*

Procedure The procedure was identical to that followed in the first seriation experiment, with a preliminary session for half the subjects followed by communication sessions in which both experienced and naive subjects took the roles of speaker and listener. Seriations were carried out in the order learned and afterwards in the reverse order.

Results and discussion

Table 8.3 shows the number of correct and incorrect seriations achieved by all children as a function of their previous experience. Clearly,

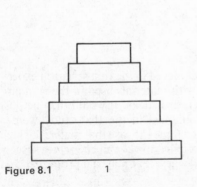 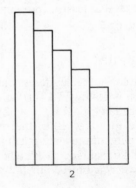

Figure 8.1　　1　　　　　　　　　　　2

Table 8.3 Number of correct and incorrect solutions in seriation task (Study II)

	Correct	Incorrect	Total
Experienced Subject	19(79%)	5(21%)	24*
Naive Subject	9(36%)	16(64%)	25

*One short as NS did not complete a trial

experienced subjects are much more successful than naive ones, obtaining a correct proportion of 79 per cent. In contrast naive subjects get the majority of their solutions incorrect, having a success rate of only 36 per cent. But these figures tell us nothing about the effect which one child is having on the other, nor the effect of the speaker/listener variable. Do ES errors all happen when NS is speaker, for instance? Is NS successful on his own account or only when acting as listener? If the latter, then does this support the notion that young children can be successful teachers?

Table 8.4 shows that, of the five errors, two occur when they are speakers and three when they are listeners. Thus incorrect ES solutions are not entirely the fault of naive partners. Nevertheless, it bears repeating that the number of errors made by experienced subjects is very small. As for NSs, their successes occur most often when they are listeners. Table 8.4 shows that there is only *one* correct NS solution as speaker, whereas 8 correct solutions out of 16 result when NS is listener.

This result shows more clearly in Table 8.5, where the 50 per cent success rate suggests that ESs are surprisingly successful as instructors considering the complexity of the task involved. Table 8.5 also shows that the lesson is not learnt well enough for naive subjects, in their turn, to become successful instructors. As speakers naive subjects appear to be totally ineffectual, achieving no mutually correct solutions.

Table 8.4 Number of correct and incorrect descriptions or solutions in the seriation task

Descriptions/Solutions	Order Learned			Reverse Order		
	Correct	Incorrect	T	Correct	Incorrect	T
Experienced Speakers	8	2	10	6	0	6
Naive Listeners	5	5	10	3	3	6
Naive Speakers	1	7	8		1	1
Experienced Listeners	5	2	7*		1	1

*One short since NS not able to complete descriptions and so EL does not complete trial.

Table 8.5 Percentage of trials ending in correct solutions for both subjects, as a function of prior exposure to the task. (All figures refer to subjects as speakers.)

Order learned		Reverse order	
Experienced Subject	Naive Subject	Experienced Subject	Naive Subject
5/10	0/8	3/6	0/11

The data also show (Table 8.4) how consistently correct the experienced subjects were when carrying out seriation in the reverse order. One further point to note from this table is the sparcity of data in the bottom right quadrant. This is because the experiment was carried out in one session and most of the subjects were thought to be either too tired or too disinclined to complete a trial as naive speaker.

Task demands

Before considering the factors which give rise to communication failure, it is worth looking first more closely at the task involved. There are some important differences between Studies I and II which are illustrated by the opening dialogue of one of the communication sessions. This highlights a major problem for subjects in this second study.

> *Alan (speaker):* 'Put them . . . stand them up like . . . the big one . . . then a we . . . little bit right up to the big one's shoulder . . . and I think . . . next one is it? Yes. Now measure that . . . then that one, the *fish*.'

Faced with a number of sticks and a verbal message like that above, anyone would be hard pressed to produce something constructive. Because Alan's nonverbal behaviour is omitted, the record is almost bare of information content – and yet that is the record on which the listener must rely, since she cannot observe the manipulation of the material. The excerpt above takes place over a period of 30 seconds, and in that time Alan erects four sticks. Only when he comes to the fourth, however, does he give a meaningful message – *fish* – and this is said largely to himself.

A description of Alan's motor behaviour would put some flesh on the bones of the verbal record. It would then reveal his words for what they were – an aid to himself. For Alan was just talking to himself as he engaged in a problem which demanded a large degree of concentration. His words are not instructions directed to an attentive listener. This seems to be a key concept in understanding the performances in this experiment. Although Alan was sufficiently familiar with the communication situation to know what his role was in it, it appeared that the task was such as to cause him to forget or ignore the duties of that role. Seriation in this form, apparently, is not the simple exercise it was in the earlier experiment. The preview session showed that the majority of the subjects handled the task competently. But they needed to bring to it a measure of attention unnecessary in the blocks-on-rod task. Because of this, the additional burden of communicating the actions to a dependent listener becomes a problem. It overtaxes the system; and, as a result it is either left out or its effectiveness is seriously weakened.

Causes of communication breakdown

At this point a brief diagnosis of communication break-down can be provided. Sufficient records are available to allow some conclusions to be drawn as to the factors which signal breakdown (see Table 8.6).

In quantitive terms, of the 18 trials which fail to lead to seriation by *both* subjects, in only five could the experienced speaker be said to be a major cause of failure, and three of these five occasions are perpetrated by one subject (Sally) who indicated she had not grasped the seriation concept.

The picture emerges that, given an accomplished listener, four of the experienced subjects would always communicate successfully — i.e. communication failure is seldom due to shortcomings on the part of the experienced speaker. As a listener the experienced subject can be helpful, but there are instances where his superior knowledge adversely affects the naive speaker. For example, under the heading 'inappropriate verbal comment' in Table 8.6, it is remarks by the experienced listener such as 'I've done it already', 'I'm doing it right', and laughter at the naive speaker's errors which largely contribute to communicative breakdown.

Table 8.6 Causes of communication breakdown and their frequency in unsuccessful trials as a function of role and previous experience of task

	Speaker			Listener		
	Exp.	Naive			Exp.	Naive
Stops verbal communication (absorbed in task)	0	2	Not attending, distracted		1	3
Selection errors	2	4	Inappropriate verbal comment		1	1
Inadequate communication	1	0	Independent		0	3
Total	3	6	functioning		2	7

Other limiting factors contributed by both naive and experienced subjects include task errors, that is, mistakes in seriating and failures of attention. The latter is betrayed by comments like 'I can build a castle', 'You can't see where you're going with your peak [cap] down there', 'Smell my perfume', 'I can do it louder than her' and task-irrelevant activity of which knocking over the sticks was a much favoured instance.

It is self-evident that if a speaker does not provide the necessary information then a naive listener is not going to be able to achieve the desired goal. But even if the speaker does carry out his part of the contract efficiently, success is not guaranteed. The operation can break down because of some inadequacy on the part of the listener. Although his role is passive − he has simply to do what he is told − it is this very passivity that is his undoing. A child is most successful in a cognitive task when he is actively involved. When the task appears to offer no scope for action, the child may very well initiate some himself. For example, in a dyad where Lee is the speaker and Paul the listener, a successful outcome would result if Paul simply complied with the speaker's instructions. But he seems to feel a need to make a contribution. In the first trial he says 'I haven't got my *fish* up' just before Lee instructs him to place the *fish* in line. Preoccupation with his own concerns causes him to miss this message and an incorrect solution results. In trial two he tries to go his own way when in response to the message '*train*', he says 'Well I'm going to put the *cup* up'. Both Alan (see p. 20) as speaker, and Paul as listener, illustrates how the communication set-up can break down if the subject fails to take account of his partner.

Egocentrism as a cause of communication failure The Piagetian explanation for communication failure in the areas that have been mentioned would be egocentrism. There would seem to be two points to consider. First, is egocentrism a useful term to use? Should we not try to be more exact in explaining behaviour that is said to fall into this category? Secondly, however defined, is egocentrism always the explanation for such behaviour? In the area of behaviour under consideration, is a 'failure to consider the other's point of view' a satisfactory explanation for breakdown in communication in young children? There are, for instance, sound reasons for thinking that in some cases breakdowns are due to a lack of comprehension on the part of the participants. In other cases, a failure to involve the child seems to be a contributory factor (see Lloyd and Beveridge 1981, Light 1979). The Piagetian notion of centration certainly plays a part in this process, but it is perhaps better regarded as one aspect of attention and one of a number of attentional factors that ought to be defined as precisely as possible.

We need to know if the cues in a particular situation are perceived as identical by speaker and listener, experienced and naive subject. This is highly unlikely. To give one example, even when speaker and listener are equally familiar with the material, the speaker is put in a special position by being instructed to choose an object and communicate his choice to the listener. As soon as he has selected an item, the speaker's task is facilitated by having the number of competing cues diminished. He can then describe that object without relating it to any other members of the array. If the description is full enough it will be adequate. The listener, however, is subject to all the cues, and his choice, though supposed to be a function of the message he receives from the speaker, may equally be dependent on the salience which the objects have for him. Even if he does systematically narrow down his focus using the verbal messages sent to him, his interpretation of the message is liable to distortion either because of linguistic incompetence, that is being unable to relate word to referent, or through the compelling influence of perceptual cues, outweighing the power of the speaker's communication (see Donaldson and Lloyd 1974). What this amounts to is that he is told to select one item but chooses another because its size, colour, texture or whatever captures his attention.

It would seem, therefore, that the relative failure of the naive subject and the subject as listener might be explained by attentional factors, comprehension difficulties and lack of active involvement. According to Piaget, egocentrism is a pervasive feature of the behaviour of pre-operational children. 'It is only when the child reaches the stage of concrete operations (7 to 8 years) . . . he acquires skill in interindividual relations in a cooperative framework. Further, the acquisition of social cooperation and the structuring of cognitive operations can be seen as two aspects of the same developmental process' (Fraisse and Piaget 1963).

When the performance of the children in the communication task is examined in the light of this statement, many examples counter to Piaget's hypothesis appear. Perhaps the most overwhelming evidence is that four of the five experienced children in this study successfully communicated the method of completing the seriation task such that the outcome was a mutually correct solution. So it is maintained that the degree of cooperation required and achieved for success, in what must be considered a fairly complex task, does much to weaken the Piagetian argument concerning egocentrism.

In conclusion consider the behaviour of Lee as speaker, describing seriation in the reverse order (chair, cup, fish, house, train, cat) to Paul after a number of trials in the other direction, big-little. Paul is rather slow at assembling the sticks, and after announcing the third stick and observing a fair amount of activity on Paul's part, Lee says, 'He's getting mixed up 'cos I put the *cat* first before, eh?' This seems to show not only a remarkably mature assessment of the seriation problem, but also behaviour far from egocentric. Lee has recognized that the change in order could lead to difficulties for the other child and as such has demonstrated a degree of perception much more sophisticated than the theory of egocentrism would predict. Later in the trial the dialogue is as follows:-

Lee: Now the *train* (stands it in line)
Paul: (Puts the *train* in line)
Lee: Have you got the *train* up?
Paul: I've put it up.

Once again Lee is showing a concern for the other child, a degree of cooperation not generally thought to be within the compass of egocentric children.

Evaluation of aims

To what extent have these studies achieved the aims expounded earlier? The main objective was to determine if preschool children were able to combine productively in a task requiring purposive communication. The results provide unqualified rejection of the view that egocentrism severely hinders communication at this age. In the first study the overall failure rate was only 19 per cent though it increased to 42 per cent in the more demanding sticks task. This points up the more productive way of seeing children's communicative capacity, namely as a function of specific task demands.

The second aim concerned the suitability of the communication paradigm for investigating conceptual development. The signs are promising. The work showed, for instance, that ordering skills are much more severely tested when a child has to specify the location of an item as well as determine its position in an ordered sequence. I have argued elsewhere, (Lloyd and Beveridge 1981) that children will adapt to the level of utility appropriate to the situation. In his recent study of seriation, Piaget (1977) maintains that an understanding of this operation is only present when a child can explicitly state a rule in the form: 'Start with the smallest one and then add successively those that remain.' In these studies (and those of Greenfield and Dent) young children can get their peers to order in terms of size with descriptions like 'put the red one on, then the blue, then the green', etc. This is not to say that one instruction does not represent a sounder grasp of the concept than the other, but that level of understanding, along with materials and goals, must be sensitive to the needs and experience of the participants. A more extended justification of this approach to cognitive development can be found in Lloyd and Beveridge 1981 and also Russell (this volume).

What, finally, is the educational significance of this work? While in principle it is possible to discuss this question, in practice it is made difficult by the fact that the children involved were not yet part of the formal education system. Nevertheless, there are some general points to be made. Children appeared to take their teaching duties seriously, showing concern for the inadequacies of their 'pupils' and using a systematic step-by-step method of instruction. A number of examples have been given to support this claim. Experienced subjects were able to teach the first task sufficiently well for the pupils to become successful teachers in their turn. As soon as the task became more complex we saw a deterioration in the performance of the naive children. This was not because the instructors made any less effort but rather that carrying out the necessary discriminations and providing information about where to locate items proved too large a cognitive load.

As to whether the experienced or naive subjects gained more from the exercise, the objective evidence is equivocal. Inspection of the protocols reinforced the belief that the children given prior experience responded very positively to the teaching role. Steinberg and Cazden (1979) have argued that such experiences raise the self-esteem of the child, an observation these studies support. It is less clear what benefits the tutee derives, though he clearly acquires the ability to carry out the first task.

Without further and better controlled studies it is not possible to make any strong claims. But there is reason to believe that children teaching children can represent an important contribution in schools, a contribution that undoubtedly is apparent to some teachers. Children may use unorthodox methods in instructing their peers but they may have one great advantage over adults as teachers. They eschew the formalism that pedagogues tend to adopt by operating in what Donaldson (1978) has called the embedded mode of thinking. Providing that that mode is not totally idiosyncratic it may be more effective in gaining and sustaining the interest of a peer, despite many obvious imperfections. At the same time the teacher may gain new perspectives on familiar problems and a greater awareness of children's capacities and limitations. At the very least this technique deserves further systematic study.

References

Cole, M., Hood, L. and McDermott, I. 1979: Ecological niche picking. Rockefeller University Monograph.

Doise, W. 1978: *Groups and individuals*. Cambridge: Cambridge University Press.

Donaldson, M. 1978: *Children's minds*. Glasgow: Fontana.

Donaldson, M. and Lloyd, P. 1974: Sentences and situations: children's judgements of match and mismatch. In F. Bresson (ed.), *Problèmes actuels en psycholinguistique*. Paris: Centre National de la Recherche Scientifique.

Dore, J. 1977: 'Oh Them Sheriff': a pragmatic analysis of children's responses to questions. In S. Ervin-Tripp and C. Mitchell-Kernan (eds.), *Child discourse*. New York: Academic Press.

Elkind, D. 1964: Discrimination, seriation and numeration of size and dimensional differences in young children: Piagetian replication study VI. *J. Genetic Psychology* **104**, 275–96.

Flavell, J.H. Speer, J.R., Green, F.L. and August, D.L. (in press): The development of comprehension monitoring and knowledge about communication. *Society for Research into Child Development Monograph*.

Fraisse, P. and Piaget, J. (eds.) 1963: *Experimental psychology: its scope and method*. London: Routledge & Kegan Paul.

Garvey, C. 1977: *Play*. Glasgow: Fontana.

Greenfield, P. and Dent, K. 1979: A developmental study of the communication of meaning: the role of uncertainty and information. In P. French (ed.), *The development of meaning*. Japan: Bunka Hyoron Publishing Co.

Glucksberg, S. and Krauss, R. 1967: What do people say after they have learned how to talk? Studies of the development of referential communication. *Merrill-Palmer Quarterly* **13**.

Light, P. 1979: *The development of social sensitivity*. Cambridge: Cambridge University Press.

Lloyd, P. and Beveridge, M. 1981: *Information and meaning in child communication*. London: Academic Press.

Luria, A. 1959: The directive function of speech in development and dissolution. *Word* **15**, 341–52.

Markman, E.M. 1977: Realizing that you don't understand: a preliminary investigation. *Child Development* **48**, 986–92.

—— 1979: Realizing that you don't understand: elementary school children's awareness of inconsistencies. *Child Development* **50**, 643–55.

Miller, S.A. and Brownell, C.A. 1975: Peers, persuasion and Piaget: Dyadic interaction between conservers and non-conservers. *Child Development* **46**, 992–7.

Piaget, J. 1926: *The language and thought of the child*. London: Routledge & Kegan Paul.

—— 1952: *The child's concept of number*. London: Routledge & Kegan Paul.

—— 1977: *The grasp of consciousness*. London: Routledge & Kegan Paul.

Piaget, J. and Inhelder, B. 1969: *The psychology of the child*. London: Routledge & Kegan Paul.

Russell, J. 1979: Children discussing the right answer: social influence under the microscope. Paper given at British Psychological Society Developmental Section Annual Conference, Southampton, September.

Shantz, C. 1975: The development of social cognition. In E. Hetherington (ed.), *Review of child development research*, vol. 5. University of Chicago Press.

Shields, M. 1978: The child as psychologist: construing the social world. In A. Lock (ed.), *Action, gesture and symbol: the emergence of language.* London: Academic Press.

Steinberg, C. and Cazden, C. 1979: Children as teachers — of peers and ourselves. *Theory into Practice* **28(4)** (October), 258–66.

Walkerdine, V. and Sinha, C. 1978: The internal triangle: language, reasoning and the social context. In I. Markova (ed.), *The social context of language.* Chichester: Wiley.

9

Substitutes for speech?
Nonvocal approaches to communication

P.H. Light, R.E. Remington and D. Porter

A child may fail to produce, or to respond to, the spoken word for any one of a number of reasons. For example, he may be physically unable to perceive speech, or to produce it; he may be unable to establish the associations involved; or he may be unable to enter into those kinds of social acts within which words have their place. In this chapter we shall be concerned with the small number of children who fail to acquire any significant productive or receptive speech despite having no obvious sensory or motor handicaps. We shall discuss some of the characteristics of such children and then selectively review studies which have reported attempts to teach them to communicate using speech, manual sign or visual symbol based systems. Finally we will present some results we have obtained using a symbol-based communication system. These illustrate some of the complexities involved even in teaching children the associations required for the simplest forms of communication.

Language intervention: an overview

Nonspeaking children

One of the striking things about speech (by which term we refer both to production and to comprehension) is that so many children master it. All but the most severe degrees of mental retardation or environmental deprivation appear to be compatible with the acquisition of functional speech. Obvious exceptions involve major problems of input (as in profound deafness) or of output (as in some cases of cerebral palsy). We are concerned here with the less obvious exceptions, which may be found under three main diagnostic headings: infantile autism, developmental dysphasia (or aphasia), and mental retardation. The last is included because, as Mittler (1970) observes, even when a child is quite obviously of subnormal intelligence it is not uncommon for him to show a language deficit far greater than would be expected on grounds of low intelligence alone. Under all three headings, the severity of the speech deficit is variable, with a complete absence of productive and

216

receptive speech being more the exception than the rule.

Although these diagnostic distinctions achieve some separation, there is still a good deal of overlap between the various groups. For example, Bartak *et al.* (1975) found a more severe and extensive language impairment in children diagnosed as autistic than in those diagnosed as receptive dysphasics, but also pointed to similarities between the two conditions. There was a history of speech delay in the families of both groups, and Folstein and Rutter's (1978) twin study indicated that autism is genetically linked to other disorders involving the acquisition of speech. Moreover, work using language samples instead of tests (Baker *et al.* 1976) found little difference in language use between autistics and dysphasics. Boucher (1976) has suggested that it might be sensible to think of some autistic children as suffering concomitant dysphasia, and the same might be said of some mentally retarded children. Moreover, autistic children who fail to acquire speech almost always show severe mental retardation (Lotter 1967, Rutter 1978).

A considerable body of experimental research using matched group designs has been dedicated to identifying specific cognitive and perceptual deficits associated with autism, dysphasia and retardation. Some of these studies will be referred to in this chapter, but a number of general issues which limit their value for our present purposes may be noted here.

Firstly, researchers have typically attempted to select as subjects children suffering one and only one type of handicap. Thus for example Boucher (1976), reviewing studies of the language disabilities of autistic children, deliberately limits herself to cases where autism is not associated with retardation. Since we have no reason to suppose that the characteristics of autism are simply additive to those of retardation, we can draw no confident conclusions about the mute, retarded autistic child.

Secondly, the basis of matching between different groups of handicapped children, or between groups of handicapped and normal children, is problematic. A mental age criterion has frequently been used. Ryan (1971) has pointed out the suspect assumptions on which this practice is based, and has shown how it can lead to the spurious attribution of specific deficits to the handicapped groups.

Thirdly, there are difficulties in interpreting the causal relationships involved. Take for example the finding (O'Connor and Hermelin 1973, 1978) that, in contrast to normal children, autistic and mentally-retarded children with low verbal skills appear to use visuospatial rather than auditory-temporal codes in a letter-recall task. Such a difference in cognitive processing could presumably be a cause, or equally a consequence, of the children's limited facility with speech.

Communication training studies

Although no sharp distinction can be drawn, an alternative to the traditional experimental approach in this area is provided by studies involving teaching rather than testing. Studies of this kind typically dispense altogether with comparison groups, attempting instead to develop a high degree of behavioural control in order to establish the capacities and limitations of the children. The question becomes not 'What can the children do?' but 'What can we teach them to do?' In some cases, studies of this kind have arisen in the course of remedial treatment with individual children or groups of children. In other cases they have been undertaken as research projects, without immediate remedial goals. The resulting literature is very mixed, and weaknesses both in methodology and in reporting have been commented upon (Yule *et al.* 1975).

Interest in the teaching of speech using operant conditioning methods was stimulated by the work of Lovaas and colleagues (e.g. Lovaas *et al.* 1966). Reviews of this research have been provided by Guess *et al.* (1974) and by Goetz *et al.* (1979). The first step in training programmes usually involves the establishment of vocal imitation, and this is often a very difficult task, especially with initially mute autistic children. Massive amounts of training appear to be needed merely to teach the child to articulate the first word, and then many more trials are needed before he can use it functionally. Goetz *et al.* (1979, 325) assess the current position as follows:

> Initial optimism about the prospect of teaching functional speech and language to nonverbal children has been tempered by several realizations. Many students acquire speech skills after thousands of learning trials over a period of years, others fail to ever acquire speech imitation skills necessary for subsequent speech training.

The training techniques employed have sometimes been successful with children who at the outset have some productive or echolalic speech, but the procedures have proved ineffective (or at least inordinately time-consuming) with children who at the outset were mute or who showed no capacity for vocal imitation (Lovaas 1967, Oxman *et al.* 1978). For these more severely handicapped children, therefore, consideration has begun to be given to alternatives to auditory-vocal speech.

Experimental studies of perceptual deficits are of interest in this connection, subject to the general reservations noted earlier. Since speech is so obviously dependent upon auditory processes, any suggestion of a modality-specific deficit is important. Autistic children have been reported as showing greater deficits on auditorily-presented than on visually-presented tasks (e.g. Tubbs 1966, Davis 1970), though

Hermelin (1976) suggests that this may reflect a difference between temporal and spatial processing rather than between sensory modalities as such. Since the referents of speech are so frequently visual, auditory-visual associations must play an important role in acquiring speech. Difficulties in forming cross-modal associations have been noted in autistic children (Bryson 1970, Hermelin 1978). Morton-Evans and Hensley (1978) found that both autistic and receptive dysphasic children were poorer than mental-age matched normal children on an auditory-visual paired associate learning task, but not on a similar task involving visual-visual associations.

Such studies suggest that nonspeaking children may sometimes show deficits in those general perceptual and cognitive processes which, *inter alia*, subserve speech. It has been suggested, however, that as well as depending on such general processes, the acquisition of speech may depend upon certain species-specific biological adaptations to this task. For example, Eimas (1974) reports studies which suggest that perception of speech differs from perception of nonspeech auditory stimuli from as early as one month of age. Condon and Sander (1974) have reported that even neonates show a delicate and precise synchrony of body movements with speech, greater than that shown with non-speech sounds. Such findings prompt consideration of the possibility that a failure to learn to speak may reflect a failure of the neural mechanisms which subserve these specific adaptations. Hughes (1975) has argued essentially this case in relation to aphasic children, and Cromer (1976) reviews evidence that such children are unable to process normal speech because they cannot sort out the temporal order of the phonemes. Experimental work by Tallal and Piercey (1973) suggest that aphasic children cannot handle rapid auditory processing, and that this deficit is modality-specific. Condon (1975) reports that autistic children do not show normal synchrony of body movements with speech sounds.

These findings, together no doubt with the success of Gardner and Gardner's (1969) attempt to train a chimpanzee to use American Sign Language, have stimulated training studies employing manual signing as an alternative to speech. The obvious attraction of this approach is that it largely avoids the need for both auditory processing and for cross-modal associations. Moreover, since it is possible to 'mould' the child's hands during training, dependence on imitation is reduced.

Reviews of projects employing manual signing with autistic, retarded and aphasic subjects are provided by Kiernan (1977) and Bonvillian and Nelson (1978). The literature relating to the mentally-handicapped deaf child is fairly comprehensive, but that relating to the non-deaf mentally handicapped is very sketchy (Kiernan 1977). A number of studies have been undertaken with autistic children. These are mostly small-scale, often being case studies initiated as a direct response to failure of speech training (Bonvillian and Nelson 1978). While there are no systematic comparisons of the efficacy of speech versus sign training, the indications seem to be that manual signs may be taught much more readily, and that all subjects, including mute children, acquire some signs. However, most studies in this area have been poorly reported. Descriptions of subjects are limited, and often omit all details of initial verbal abilities. Results are usually expressed in terms of number of signs learned, but criteria for scoring are usually vague and there is typically no comment on the quality of signs. The use of signs in combination is rarely mentioned.

These factors make it difficult to judge quite what has been learned, and how. For example, Bonvillian and Nelson comment that, because in so many of these projects little information is given on pretraining receptive language abilities, it is possible that success is based upon supplementing an already established skill in comprehension of speech with productive capacity in sign. This is especially true since speech and manual sign have virtually always been used simultaneously in these studies.

Many of the signs taught are clearly iconic, in that the hand movement in some way resembles the referent. For example, actions such as 'eat' may be signed by performing an abbreviated imitation of the act, while objects such as 'house' may be signed by drawing an outline in the air. It is possible, therefore, that the apparent advantage of signing over speech relates to its greater iconicity. Konstantareas *et al.* (1978) report a study conducted with five retarded autistic children in which they compared the learning of iconic and noniconic signs. Iconic signs were learned much more rapidly, leading the authors to conclude that, unlike deaf adults (see Bellugi *et al.* 1975), these children were relying on the iconic nature of signs when such clues to meaning were available. Although signs learned in this way may come to serve useful communicative purposes, it is clear that in such a case the sign does not stand in the same relationship to its referent as it does in speech, where the relationship is typically arbitrary and conventional.

Insofar as its medium is visual and the responses involved are amenable to physical 'moulding', manual signing may circumvent some of the difficulties which nonverbal children encounter with speech. However, other difficulties remain. Manual signs are fairly complex action patterns, and signs replace one another in temporal succession. Although signs are less evanescent than spoken words, the temporal features of manual signing impose demands on memory both in reception and in production. The temporal relationship between signs may not be important at the single-sign level, but becomes so as sign combinations are elaborated. A more radical departure from spoken language, involving spatial rather than temporal succession as in a written language, could circumvent these difficulties.

Written language is normally secondary to spoken language in developmental terms, and is also secondary in the sense of being a relatively recent cultural invention. Written and spoken forms of language characteristically serve rather different functions (Olson 1975), but it is obviously possible for a written system to serve some of the functions of speech.

Although the learning of written language is normally approached with an already-established knowledge of spoken language, some studies suggest that children with little or no speech can occasionally make surprising progress with reading and writing (e.g. Hewett 1964, Cobrinik 1974, La Vigna 1977). This phenomenon has been termed 'hyperlexia'. A number of case studies have been reported in which such observed abilities have been exploited as a basis for direct communication. For example, Ratusnik and Ratusnik (1974) used plastic letters with which the child 'wrote' on a communication board, while Marshall and Hargrenes (1972) used word cards, which the child carried around with him. Other studies, rather than starting from an observed 'hyperlexia', have attempted to train children in the use of a few written words. De Villiers and Naughton (1974) and La Vigna (1977) successfully taught several autistic children to respond appropriately to a small number of word cards, while McLean and McLean (1974) adopted similar procedures but used plywood shapes distinguished by colour and shape in place of word cards.

A major stimulus to this work came from Premack's (1970, 1976) investigation of the linguistic abilities of the chimpanzee, which also provided the foundation for a number of other more extensive and systematic studies with nonspeaking children.[1] Premack's system was analogous to a written language, but used coloured shaped pieces of plastic which we shall refer to as symbols. The chimpanzee's task was to produce or to comprehend spatial sequences of such symbols arranged on a board. Premack's concern was not so much to teach the chimp to use a large number of symbols, but rather to establish what the chimp's responses implied as regards language. In this way he laid the groundwork for a more analytic approach to training studies with children.

From the point of view of work with nonspeaking children, Premack's approach has a number of attractive features. Like manual signing it employs the visual modality, but the resemblance does not extend much beyond this. Since Premack's sequences are spatially rather than temporally arranged, the 'reader' can repeatedly scan the message, reducing demands on short-term memory. In contrast with speech and

---

[1] Another symbol system, known as Blissymbolics, has developed rather separately over the last decade (Archer 1977). The symbols are semi-pictographic and can be presented on cards, plaques or boards. The system has been developed principally for physically handicapped children who may be unable to produce speech but are able to make pointing responses. The highly iconic nature of the symbols, and the fact that in normal use the child points to the symbols in turn rather than assembling them spatially, set this approach apart from that discussed here.

manual signing, the production of a message does not involve the subject in creating the individual symbols. He has only to select them from those available in front of him, so that recognition rather than recall from long term memory is involved. The need for imitative responding is minimal, since production is simply a matter of picking up symbols and placing them on the board. Such responses are easily prompted.

Equally significant is the fact that Premack's system lends itself to very precise teaching methods. Because the teacher can regulate the availability of symbols, he can control the difficulty of the task at each stage. Responses are unambiguously right or wrong, so the recording and reinforcement of behaviour are greatly facilitated. These features are particularly attractive to the researcher interested in precise mapping of what the child can or cannot be taught – indeed the system owes more to these requirements than it does to the child's need for functional communication.

Premack and Premack (1974) used their system with one mute autistic child, but they do not give a detailed account of the project. Glass *et al*. (1973) and Gardener *et al*. (1976) have applied Premack's methods with considerable success with adult aphasic patients. Hughes (1975) used similar methods with four developmental aphasics. These children had nonverbal IQs in the normal range but very limited comprehension and expression in speech. All children could use at least three spoken words and had some facility in manual signing, mostly at the single-sign level. Neither speech nor sign was used to support training, which followed Premack's procedures closely. In general the children readily learned the functions taught ('word,' 'sentence', 'class concept', 'question', 'negation'), though not all children learned all functions to the criterion used.

Carrier (1974, 1979) has applied a modification of the same system with effectively mute mentally-retarded children. He has reported results from 60 such subjects who made some progress under his training scheme, but details of degree of retardation and speech comprehension are not given (Carrier 1974). An unspecified number of other subjects failed in the programme, apparently as a result of attentional or motivational problems. The first stage of the programme involved the child learning ten 'nouns' by matching pictures of objects with 'geometric' (noniconic) symbols. The second stage marks Carrier's approach off from Premack's. Instead of building up gradually more elaborate sequences, he introduced the child directly to an eight-symbol sequence modelled on English grammar (article + noun + verb auxiliary + verb + verb ending + preposition + article + noun). Subjects were required to learn this sequence by rote, using colour and number cues to insert symbols into particular slots on a specially constructed board. This rote-learned sequence subsequently acted as a frame within which the child was taught to differentiate the meaning of each of the constituents of his response. While Carrier has claimed considerable success, at least for the early stages of his programme, his rationale for the use of the rote-learned frame, in terms of the child never being reinforced for a partial response, hardly seems adequate. From a practical point of view such a procedure, apart from its intrinsic rigidity, requires the child to make a very large number of essentially meaningless responses. From a research point of view, the colour and number coding of the different 'parts of speech' restricts the arbitrariness of allocation of symbols to referents and makes the interpretation of the child's behaviour difficult.

A procedure rather closer to Premack's has been adopted with mentally-retarded children by Hodges and Deich (1978, 1979) and Deich and Hodges (1977). They report on a pilot study involving eight mute severely-retarded children, and on a larger ongoing study involving 22 'low functioning' children with IQs below 30, together with six children of rather higher IQ. This larger study encompassed a wide range of initial language skills, from mute and incomprehending at one extreme to a 'language age' of five years at the other. Little detail, especially on initial comprehension of speech, is available. Speech was used in support of symbol use throughout training.

In Deich and Hodges' scheme children were initially taught to label objects which were themselves reinforcers (apple, cracker etc.). Then names for teacher and child were taught. The attempt to teach the verbs *give* and *take* met with great difficulties, and after further training of nouns the verbs *eat* and *insert* were introduced. Four-word sentences of the type 'child insert cracker box' were employed to teach the verbs. Two of the children in the pilot programme learned only a few concrete nouns, while the other six reached at least the verb stage. In the larger study outcome has been very variable, with the higher-functioning group predictably progressing much faster than the others. The mean number of symbols learned in the low-functioning group after four months was seven, mostly concrete nouns.

A number of minor problems cloud the interpretation of these studies. For example, it is not always clear that the children were given choices between fully interchangeable symbols (cf. the verbs *eat* and *insert*). Also, like Carrier's, Deich and Hodges' symbols were colour-coded for part of speech, and some were also iconic. Kuntz *et al.* (1978) have shown that, as with manual signs, iconic plastic symbols facilitate initial learning, but they also showed that subsequent transfer to (non-iconic) printed words was easier for those whose initial training had been with abstract symbols.

In summary, there seem to be good grounds, both theoretical and empirical, for giving serious consideration to alternatives to speech for certain types of severely-handicapped children. Studies with manual signing have generally produced positive results, but limitations of design and recording in such studies make it difficult to tell quite what has been learned in most instances. Other studies have employed endur-ing symbols (written words, iconic or noniconic symbols) in place of manual signs. Such studies have tended towards greater precision (Kiernan 1977), perhaps because this approach lends itself better to experimental control and to the recording of responses. At least at the basic level of associating particular symbols with particular objects, results have been good, leading Deich and Hodges to conclude: 'Even the very low functioning developmentally disabled child can master the labelling functions of the Premack system' (1977, 184).

However, even at this 'concrete noun' level there are problems of interpretation of the available studies. Where the objects are referred to verbally in training and little or no information on children's speech comprehension is given, as in Deich and Hodges' studies, it is hard to know quite which associations are being formed. The lack of attention to generalization of learned symbols to novel objects makes it hard to know quite what is being 'labelled', and indeed further analysis of symbol usage would seem to be indicated before one can properly speak of 'labelling' at all. We are currently engaged in research which addresses some of these questions, and we shall present some preliminary findings in the following section.

Symbol utilization: a training-study

We have been conducting a series of small scale experiments using an enduring symbol system with autistic and other severely mentally retarded children, our intention being to take a rather closer look at training procedures and the resultant learning than has been usual in this field. We have selected some of the teaching and testing procedures used to establish and analyse nominal and adjectival symbol use in order to illustrate our approach.[2]

The children

We have chosen three children for discussion. They include our most successful in training (Mick) and our least successful (Jack), and have been chosen because the data which they have provided best illustrate those aspects of training and testing on which we wish to focus here. All three children are 14 years of age.

Jack and Catherine, the third child, both carry a diagnosis of infantile autism and attend a special school run under the auspices of the Hampshire Society for Autistic Children. Both clearly satisfy the diag-nostic criteria outlined by Rutter (1978) in terms of early onset,

[2] We should like to thank the Social Sciences Research Council for their financial support, and the head teachers and staff of Hope Lodge School, Southampton and Coldeast Hospital School, Fareham for their cooperation.

impaired social development, sterotyped behaviours and limited language development. Mick has been resident in a subnormality hospital since the age of five and attends a hospital school. There is a family background of retardation and Mick is diagnosed as severely mentally retarded. Merrill-Palmer Scales (excluding explicitly verbal items) indicate an IQ in the region of 30 for both Mick and Jack, but in the region of 50 for Catherine.

Jack has absolutely no productive speech, while Mick's is limited to 'yes' and 'no'. Catherine has some speech, but it is difficult to elicit and very poorly articulated. Reynell Developmental Language Scales were used in assessment. 'Comprehension ages' were 1;6 (Jack), 2;6 (Mick) and 2;9 months (Catherine). Only Catherine obtained an 'expressive speech age', which was 1;11. Additional *ad hoc* comprehension tests indicated that Mick and Catherine (unlike Jack) understood a range of spoken nouns, and Catherine also understood colour adjectives. Neither responded appropriately to the verbs used, or to shape adjectives.

General procedures

Teaching was done in the children's own school, but outside the classroom setting. It consisted in individual sessions, between 10 and 40 minutes in length, which were daily insofar as practical constraints allowed. During the sessions teacher and child sat on opposite sides of a table, across which a metal board was mounted vertically. A video camera was used to record the sessions for scoring purposes.

The symbols used were cut from perspex of various colours and were backed with magnetic tape so that they would adhere to the board. Each was a unique shape (although not a unique colour), and meanings were assigned to particular symbols on a completely arbitrary basis. Thus the relationship between sign and referent was merely conventional.

Although training procedures varied considerably in detail, depending upon the particular function concerned and the child who was being taught, there were a number of constant features. Initial training always involved production rather than comprehension of a symbol or symbol string – the child was taught to place the symbol(s) on the board in response to some action or object produced by the teacher. Initial symbol placement was trained using prompting and positive reinforcement. Both gestural and physical prompts were used. The reinforcement varied from child to child, as will be discussed in relation to our examples. Training sequences were designed so that the child was reinforced for correct responses at the outset without the possibility of error, choice between symbols only being introduced gradually. We considered a function trained only when the child could respond discriminatively to at least two examples of it. Therefore a minimal teaching procedure consisted of 'no-choice' trials in which two symbols in the same functional class were trained consecutively followed by choice trials in which the child was required to use both symbols to a specified criterion.

Training 'nouns'

Initial training involved associating particular symbols with particular concrete objects. For convenience of exposition, we shall refer to this as 'noun' training. The nouns selected were 'cup', 'ball', 'doll', 'box', 'apple' and 'dish'. During training the objects were never referred to in speech, since we were interested in object-symbol and noι word-symbol associations.

The training sequence can be summarized as follows. The child was given a single symbol (S_1) and the teacher presented a particular object (O_1), the child being prompted if necessary to place the symbol on the board. Two identical 'no-choice' trials followed. On the following trial the child was given S_1 together with an unknown symbol, and had to select S_1. Failing this, the sequence was repeated. Otherwise the child moved on to an identical sequence with a new symbol (S_2) and a new object (O_2). Once S_2 had been correctly selected from a choice between it and an unknown symbol, the two symbols S_1 and S_2 were given to the child, who had first to select S_2 in response to O_2, and then to select S_1 in response to O_1. Next the third symbol was introduced in a similar way, and then a sequence of six choices between pairs of symbols followed. Errors in any of the choice trials resulted in the child's being taken back to 'no-choice' trials on the required object-symbol pair before encountering further choices. Successful completion of the sequence led on to nine trials in which the child had all three symbols available and the three objects were each presented three times in a random sequence. If completely successful on this the child moved on to a second group of three nouns, which were taught in the same way. Finally, the child was given test trials with all six trained symbols available.

Two of the children, Mick and Catherine, were quick to learn. Mick met the criterion (100 per cent) on the first three nouns after two sessions (approximately 50 choice trials) and on the second three nouns after one further session (approximately 25 choice trials). Catherine's learning was even more rapid, and she required only one session for each trio of nouns. Mick was reinforced socially, by praise and hugs. With Catherine, social reinforcement was supplemented with chocolate.

Various food reinforcers were also used with Jack, but by contrast with the others his performance on choice trials never exceeded chance. The videotapes of the early sessions showed him responding without even looking at the symbols. This we overcame by covering the symbols, causing him to look in order to uncover them. His continued poor performance led us to examine the reinforcement contingencies more closely. Since he was being reinforced on a high percentage of all trials (the 'no-choice' trials), there was little additional payoff for his learning the associations. However, alterations in the contingencies had no effect, and nor did the introduction of a light and buzzer to 'mark' correct choices. He adopted a number of systematic response strategies (spatial biases, win-stay: lose-shift sequences) but showed no evidence of learning the associations. After a total of 200 choice trials involving trained symbols over 11 sessions, we gave up and tried another tack. Premack (1970) and Deich and Hodges (1977) had both used symbols which actually stood for food reinforcers (banana, cracker etc.), a device which allows the reinforcer to become an integral part of the exchange. We devoted 12 sessions to trying to teach Jack to use two new symbols standing for biscuit and raisin. However, his performance was still no better than chance.

It occurred to us belatedly that this failure might not have anything to do with the arbitrary relationship of symbol to object. We decided to try Jack on the much simpler task of matching identical objects together. The teacher held up an object (a small toy) as before, but now Jack's task was to indicate which of the toys in front of him matched that offered. Since the toys were highly varied, the child can hardly have been incapable of discriminating them. However, his performance on this task was almost as poor as that on the object-symbol task had been. Of 74 choices between two alternatives he chose correctly only 43 times, and this despite systematic reinforcement of correct responses.

What do these results tell us about the effects of our noun-training procedures? Successful outcome of such training arguably depends upon learning at two levels. Firstly, the child must learn the general features of the situation — the 'rules of the game'. He must understand that the objects placed before him are members of either a symbol or a referent class, that different actions are appropriate to these two classes, and that each transaction involves a one-to-one relationship between symbol and referent (Premack 1976). Secondly, he must learn the particular correspondences obtaining between the symbols and the referent objects.

The results we have presented can be interpreted in this light. Mick took twice as long to learn the first set of nouns as he took to learn the second, presumably because learning the first set entailed learning the general features of the task. Catherine also learned the second set slightly faster. Jack learned to trade symbols for referents in the appropriate manner, but either failed to grasp that a one-to-one relationship between symbols and referents was involved, or failed to learn the particular correspondences. In the light of our subsequent failure with the object-symbol task, the former seems the more likely. However, it may be significant that the object-object matching task was introduced only after Jack had had prolonged experience of failure in the object-symbol task. It is therefore possible that his poor object-object matching was a result of experience in a situation in which variations in his behaviour had failed to produce significant variations in outcome (cf. Seligman 1975, Koegel and Egel 1979).

These considerations suggest that testing, and if necessary training, on simpler matching tasks should precede attempts to train object-symbol matching. They also underline the importance of the noun-training procedure – it provides both a set and a precondition for further training procedures, and an initial experience of failure may actively interfere with subsequent learning.

Following noun-training, we explored the teaching of verbs, but we shall not discuss this in detail here. Mick successfully learned to use symbols standing for the actions point to, invert and insert, and we went on to teach him two further symbols which functioned as 'proper nouns' standing for Mick and Teacher.

Thus when we approached the teaching of 'adjectives', as described in the next section, Mick could produce and understand simple three symbol strings of the form agent-action-object, while Catherine was still operating at the single-symbol level.

Training 'adjectives'

Our first objective was to teach the children to mark three colours. As before symbols were assigned arbitrarily, the outcome of which was that the symbols representing the colours red, yellow and blue were, respectively, white, green and orange pieces of perspex. Training procedures were formally identical for the two children though they differed on points of detail. We first trained a symbol for a plastic Lego brick in the way that we had trained other nouns. We then selected two differently coloured bricks and required the child to place the colour symbol appropriate to the presented brick, beginning with 'no-choice' trials in which the child only had one symbol available, and moving to choices between two symbols. For Catherine this involved learning to place the appropriate colour symbol to the left of the symbol for brick which was already on the board, while Mick was taught to place the colour symbol within the sentence frame: *Teacher point to* (colour) *brick*.

Mick learned the first two symbols rapidly, and the third was introduced via a further series of 'no choice' trials. He met the criterion (90 per cent) for choices between the three colour symbols after a total of three sessions. We went on to teach him shape adjectives in a similar way, first teaching him a symbol for *piece of wood* and then teaching *square*, *triangular* and *circular* in relation to large neutrally-coloured wooden shapes. After a series of colour and shape generalization tests, to be described in detail later, we employed an analogous procedure to teach him to mark both colour and shape attributes simultaneously, using nine coloured and shaped pieces of wood. Teaching the shape terms and the colour/shape marking took a total of seven sessions, at the end of which he could reliably produce and respond to five symbol strings of the form 'agent-action-colour-shape-object'.

In contrast, Catherine's performance was disappointing. She failed to master even the first two colour symbols over ten sessions, although, as we noted earlier, she alone of these three children could comprehend spoken colour terms. A possible explanation of her difficulty was the conflict between the colours of the symbols themselves, and the colours to which they referred (cf. Stroop 1935). To check this, we painted all the colour symbols black, retaining their shapes, and continued to use the same training method. She met criterion on all three colours within four sessions of the change. Thus, while we were unable to run the control procedures necessary to check the hypothesis rigorously, it did appear that the physical characteristics of the symbols had been interfering with the process of associating them with their colour referents.

We have described how Mick and Catherine were successfully taught to place symbols appropriately according to the object presented ('nouns') and to certain attributes of the presented object ('adjectives'). Such behaviour could reflect nothing more than a set of mechanical responses occasioned by, and constrained by, the regularities of the training situation. A question arises, therefore, as to what we have actually taught, and in particular as to whether the symbols in any sense represented their referents for the children. To investigate some aspects of this question we conducted a number of tests, some of which we shall now describe.

Assessing the use of 'noun' symbols

Throughout 'noun' training we used only one particular object as referent for each of the symbols (apple being an exception to this, for obvious reasons). Thus 'cup', for example, was always the same cracked, yellow stoneware mug. In asking what the symbol 'means' to the child, then, we need to ask whether the child classifies together objects corresponding to the concept we label 'cup', and, if so, whether he will spontaneously extend his symbol usage from the original exemplar used in training to *any* exemplar of that class.

To examine this, we collected together four further cups, four dishes, four dolls, four boxes and four balls. These were chosen to give a wide range of instances; the cups, for example, included a teacup, a paper cup, and a plastic beaker. In the first phase of testing the child was given the five noun symbols, and the novel objects were presented one at a time in random order. The child responded each time by placing a symbol on the board, and was reinforced socially regardless of his symbol choice. The sequence of 20 trials was repeated twice more for Mick, once more for Catherine. Both then entered a second phase of testing designed to establish whether they shared our conceptual grouping of the objects. Instead of five symbols, the children had before them the five original objects used in training. The novel objects were presented one at a time as before and the child's task was to match it by pointing to one of the five objects in front of him. The sequence of 20 trials was repeated twice for both children. Finally, we checked for any effect of the object matching on symbol selection by repeating the first phase of testing.

Catherine's performance was clearcut with three of the five nouns. All the novel cups were consistently responded to with the cup symbol in the first phase, all were matched with the cup used in training in the second phase, and again all were responded to with the cup symbol in the third phase. The same was true with the dolls and balls. Thus she could evidently classify these objects as we do, and despite being trained with a single object she was able to generalize what she had learned to novel exemplars without difficulty. However, results with the novel dishes and boxes were less clearcut. As can be seen from Table 9.1, in the first and third phases (object-symbol test and retest) Catherine labelled both novel boxes and novel dishes with the *box* symbol on almost all occasions. Interestingly, in the second phase (object-object test) she also matched both novel. boxes and novel dishes with the original exemplar of box. Thus, while we cannot pretend to understand her classification of these objects, her symbol usage was quite consistent with the way she appeared to group the objects.

Mick's data were similar to Catherine's in some respects. Like her, he responded to novel cups, dolls and balls with the appropriate symbols and also matched them appropriately with the training objects. However, a rather different picture emerged with boxes and dishes (Table 9.1). In the second phase (object-object test) he matched the novel objects appropriately (with the exception of box 3). As can be seen from the object-symbol test and retest, though, his symbol choices were far from consistent. Thus, for example while the novel dishes were virtually always matched to the original dish, they were never responded to with the dish symbol.

How can we account for Mick's performance? The possibility that he had come to associate the symbols only with the particular box and dish used in training and failed to generalize was unattractive for two reasons. Firstly, Mick showed a generalized usage of cup, ball and doll symbols, which were taught in exactly the same way, and secondly one of the novel boxes (box 1) was always responded to correctly. We decided to examine the issue further by attempting to teach Mick to use the *box* and *dish* symbols in response to two completely new exemplars. This was accomplished very quickly, with reliable performance after only five no-choice trials on each, so that there were then two dishes and two boxes which he would always respond to with the appropriate symbol. However, when we repeated the generalization test (Table 9.1, retest 2) there was no increase in 'correct' symbol choices in response to

Table 9.1 Some 'noun' generalization data for Catherine and Mick. Each appropriate matching response is marked with a tick: in the case of errors the matching response produced by the child is indicated.

CATHERINE		Object-symbol test	Object-object test	Object-symbol retest 1
BOX	1	Dish	✓	✓
	2	Dish	✓	✓
	3	✓	✓	✓
	4	✓	✓	✓
DISH	1	Box	✓	Box
	2	Box	Box	✓
	3	Box	Box	Box
	4	Box	Box	Box

MICK		Object-symbol test	Object-object test	Object-symbol retest 1	Object-symbol retest 2	Object-symbol retest 3	Object-symbol retest 4
BOX	1	✓	✓	✓	✓	✓	✓
	2	Dish	Ball	Ball	Ball	Ball	Cup
	3	Cup	Cup	Cup	Cup	Cup	Cup
	4	Ball	Ball	✓	Ball	Ball	Cup
DISH	1	Cup	Cup	Cup	Cup	Cup	Cup
	2	Cup	Cup	Box	Box	Cup	Cup
	3	Cup	Cup	Box	Cup	Cup	Cup
	4	Box	Cup	Box	Cup	Cup	Cup

the novel objects. We went further, teaching him to use the *dish* symbol for one of the dishes which had been used in the generalization test (dish 1) and to use the *box* symbol for a further completely new exemplar. His performance on the generalization test (Table 9.1, retest 3) remained the same, and indeed, apart from settling down to use the cup symbol for all novel boxes and dishes, his responses were the same when retested after a twelve-month break (Table 9.1, retest 4). His performance with the novel balls, dolls and cups remained faultless.

The contrast between Mick's object-object test performance and his symbol choices (object-symbol test and retest) for the novel boxes and dishes suggests that the attributes which governed the former were not the same as those which governed the latter. Thus, for example, the original dish used in training happened to be wooden, so that Mick could have learned to associate the *dish* symbol with 'wooden-ness' rather than 'dishness'. This would have no effect on his ability to group dishes together but would account for his reluctance to respond to them with the *dish* symbol. The failure of our subsequent procedures to alter his symbol choices may reflect the fact that the earlier learned meaning predominates and is insensitive to alteration through later training, or it may reflect a limitation of the test procedure. Repeated testing without contingent reinforcement may simply have led Mick to settle into a habitual response pattern.

Overall, these generalization tests showed that symbols learned in response to particular objects can be associated by the child with novel objects of the same class. Thus generalization will occur without specific training, though this procedure gives us little control of which attributes of the original objects the child will attend to.

Assessing the use of 'adjective' symbols

We were unable to do further work with Catherine, but we carried out a series of tests to evaluate Mick's understanding of colour and shape symbols. Our first concern was to establish whether these symbols had acquired meanings which were 'detachable' from the original training objects, i.e. whether they could be used productively.

Following the initial colour training sessions with Lego bricks, we taught Mick a new symbol for a different Lego component (an arch). We then performed a series of 26 trials, in which Mick had the three colour symbols available while arches of different colours were presented in a random sequence. He made only one error. However, in the second half of the sequence he was also required to place the appropriate noun, choosing between *brick* and *arch*. His performance on noun placement was at chance level. Although perfect performance was achieved over subsequent sessions, any claim for successful extension of colour naming to novel objects is weakened by the possibility that he was not in fact discriminating the new objects from the old. We therefore carried out a further test. Mick was taught a symbol for 'piece of cloth', and then the previous procedure was repeated using large coloured bundles of cloth as objects. On the first test session his performance was perfect in respect of colour symbol selection, and he was also correct in respect of noun choice on 85 per cent of the trials. A parallel test on shape adjectives using moulded pieces of plasticine as objects gave similar results.

These results convinced us that Mick was able to use single adjectival symbols productively. When he had been taught to mark both colour and shape attributes of the same object (see above) we were able to conduct a further test. This was done using nine small pieces of cloth which had both colour and shape attributes. As these were presented, one at a time in a random order, Mick had to choose appropriate colour and shape adjectives as well as having a choice of noun. He made no mistakes in 18 trials.

The 'transparent' nature of the symbols

The fact that the symbols for colours were themselves coloured pieces of perspex made it possible for us to assess the degree to which the 'meanings' of the symbols could transcend their physical characteristics. We attempted to put the two into conflict by designing a colour-sorting task in which a symbol could be sorted according to its meaning (red, yellow or blue) or according to its actual colour (white, green or orange). Mick was given a 'set' to sort for meaning by a brief exposure to a task on which he matched concrete noun symbols with photographs of their referents, arranged in a matrix on a board. A matrix of colour squares was then substituted for the photographs, including three which matched the colours marked by the symbols, three which matched the colours of the symbols themselves, and six 'filler' items. The three colour symbols were then presented one at a time, each being presented twice in an arbitrarily-ordered series of six trials without contingent reinforcement. Further trials using the photographs were followed by another sequence of six using the colours. There was no indication of any tendency to match the symbols with their actual colours. Mick always matched for meaning, his only error in the 12 trials being occasioned by there being two confusingly similar shades of blue.

Despite the artificiality of this testing procedure the results do seem to provide some evidence that the symbols had become 'transparent' for Mick — he was able to respond to them *as if* they were the things they represented, ignoring their characteristics as things in themselves. This transparency is a conspicuous feature of language use, and the results obtained with Mick are comforting in the light of our earlier failure to teach Catherine using symbols conflicting in colour with their referents.

Concluding discussion

In normal speech, most words correspond precisely enough with particular object, actions or ideas (or with classes of these things) for us to be able to enter their 'meanings' in a dictionary. These words can be said to have a labelling or naming function. But even when used without a verbal context, they can often function as more than labels (see Brinker, this volume). When a young child says to his mother 'drink', she may take him to mean 'I want a drink', 'You have a drink', or any one of a number of things, depending on the context. The child may use the word simply to point out the presence of a drink, but insofar as its object is to establish joint attention, the word is still clearly part of a social act. Words have been described (Koestler 1969) as 'levers for making things happen'.

A Skinner box also has a 'lever for making things happen', and a rat can be taught to use it. We would not, however, wish to interpret the lever press as a label for the resultant sugar pellet, nor would we regard the rat as demanding or requesting the pellet. We would simply say that it has learned an arbitrary association, established by us, between the lever press and the food.

In the earlier part of this chapter we reviewed a number of studies which demonstrated that nonspeaking children could be taught to associate manual signs or enduring symbols with particular objects, attributes or actions. Such demonstration has often been taken as equivalent to showing that the signs or symbols are functioning as words. We have raised a number of methodological criticisms in relation to these studies, but perhaps the more important issue concerns the inference from associations to words.

In our own training studies reported here we have tried to meet some of the methodological objections to earlier studies, by complete arbitrariness of symbol allocation, non-use of referential speech in training, and so on. Our teaching procedures have been essentially mechanical, geared to establishing appropriate associations, while our testing procedures have been used as probes to try to explore what the children have actually learned. We have described three testing procedures: noun generalization, adjectival productivity and transparency. The results presented have been complex, and illustrate some of the problems involved in this type of work. While they provide some indication of resemblances between symbol usage and the labelling function of words in natural language, many more questions remain than have been answered.

We have described a teaching procedure in which single 'functions' are taught in separate sessions, and all teaching is done by one person. We need to be sure that the children can use what they have learned flexibly, combining separately-learned items, and that they can perform as well with other people as with their teacher. The teaching procedures have emphasized the child's 'production' of symbols or symbol strings, and we have not here considered the issue of his 'comprehension' of symbols placed on the board by his teacher. We are devising and conducting tests of these questions as we proceed with the teaching of more complex aspects of symbol use.

Perhaps the most important point is that the teacher has always had control of the situation, and consequently the social transactions within which symbol usage has been situated have been limited and artificial. The objects used as referents are only means to an end within the teaching situation; they have no intrinsic importance for the child. By contrast with Brinker (this volume), we have adopted an approach which involves teaching language-related skills in relative isolation from the context of communication within which language has its function. Before we can confidently regard symbol use as an alternative to speech we shall need to see the child using the symbols referentially to pursue his own ends in a variety of social settings.

References

Archer, L. 1977: Blissymbolics: a nonverbal communication system. *J. Speech and Hearing Disorders* **42**, 568–79.

Baker, L., Cantwell, D., Rutter, M. and Bartak, L. 1976: Language and autism. In E. Ritvo (ed.), *Autism: diagnosis, current research and management*. New York: Spectrum.

Bartak, L., Rutter, M. and Cox, A. 1975: A comparative study of infantile autism and specific developmental receptive language disorder, I: The children. *Br. J. Psychiatry* **126**, 127–45.

Bellugi, U., Klima, E. and Siple, P. 1975: Remembering in signs. *Cognition* **3**, 93–125.

Bonvillian, J. and Nelson, K. 1978: Development of sign language in autistic children and other language handicapped individuals. In P. Siple (ed.), *Understanding language through sign language research*. New York: Academic.

Boucher, J. 1976: Is autism primarily a language disorder? *Br. J. Disorders of Communication* **11**, 135–43.

Bryson, Q. 1970: Systematic identification of perceptual disabilities in autistic children. *Perceptual and Motor Skills* **31**, 239–46.

Carrier, J. 1974: Application of functional analysis and a nonspeech response mode to teaching language. In L. McReynolds (ed.), *Developing systematic procedures for training children's language*. ASHA Monographs **18**.

Carrier, J. 1979: Perspectives on non-speech symbol systems. In R. Schiefulbusch and J. Hollis (eds.), *Language intervention from ape to child*. Baltimore: University Park Press.

Cobrinik, L. 1974: Unusual reading ability in severely disturbed children. *J. Autism and Childhood Schizophrenia* **4**, 163–75.

Condon, W. 1975: Multiple responses to sound in dysfunctional children. *J. Autism and Childhood Schizophrenia* 5, 37–56.

Condon, W. and Sander, L. 1974: Neonate movement is synchronized with adult speech: interactional participation and language acquisition. *Science* 183, 99–101.

Cromer, R. 1976: The cognitive hypothesis of language acquisition and its implications for child language deficiency. In D. Morehead and A. Morehead (eds.), *Normal and deficient child language*. Baltimore: University Park Press.

Davis, B. 1970: A clinical approach to the development of communication in young schizophrenic children. *J. Communication Disorders* 3, 211–222.

Deich, R. and Hodges, P. 1977: *Language without speech*. London: Souvenir Press.

De Villiers, J. and Naughton, J. 1974: Teaching a symbol language to autistic children. *J. Consulting and Clinical Psychology* 42, 111–17.

Eimas, P. 1974: Linguistic processing of speech by young infants. In R. Schiefelbusch and L. Lloyd (eds.), *Language perspectives: acquisition, retardation and intervention*. Baltimore: University Park Press.

Folstein, S. and Rutter, M. 1978: A twin study of individuals with infantile autism. In M. Rutter and E. Schopler (eds.), *Autism: a reappraisal of concepts and treatment*. New York: Plenum.

Gardner, A. and Gardner, B. 1969: Teaching sign language to a chimpanzee. *Science* 165, 644–72.

Gardener, H., Zurif, E., Berry, T. and Baker, E. 1976: Visual communication in aphasics. *Neuropsychologia* 14, 275–92.

Glass, A., Gazzaniga, M. and Premack, D. 1973: Artificial language training in global aphasics. *Neuropsychologia* 11, 95–103.

Goetz, L., Schuler, A. and Sailor, W. 1979: Teaching functional speech to the severely handicapped: current issues. *J. Autism and Developmental Disorders* 9, 325–43.

Guess, D., Sailor, W. and Baer, D. 1974: To teach language to retarded children. In R. Schiefelbusch and L. Lloyd (eds.), *Language perspectives: acquisition, retardation and intervention*. Baltimore: University Park Press.

Hermelin, B. 1976: Coding and the sense modalities. In L. Wing (ed.), *Early childhood autism: clinical, educational and social aspects*. Oxford: Pergamon.

—— 1978: Images and language. In M. Rutter and E. Schopler (eds.), *Autism: a reappraisal of concepts and methods*. New York: Plenum.

Hewett, F. 1964: Teaching reading to an autistic boy through operant conditioning. *The Reading Teacher* 17, 613–18.

Hodges, P. and Deich, R. 1978: Teaching an artificial language to nonverbal retardates. *Behavior Modification* 2, 489–509.

— 1979: Language intervention strategies with manipulable symbols. In R. Schiefulbusch and J. Hollis (eds.), *Language intervention from ape to child.* Baltimore: University Park Press.

Hughes, J. 1975: Acquisition of a nonvocal language by aphasic children. *Cognition* 3, 41–55.

Kiernan, C. 1977: Alternatives to speech: a review of research on manual and other forms of communication with the mentally handicapped and other non-communicating populations. *Br. J. Mental Subnormality* 23, 6–28.

Koegel, R. and Egel, A. 1979: Motivating autistic children. *J. Abnormal Psychology* 88, 418–26.

Koestler, A. 1969: *The act of creation.* London: Hutchinson.

Konstantareas, M., Oxman, J. and Webster, C. 1978: Iconicity: effects on the acquisition of sign language by autistic and other severely dysfunctional children. In P. Siple (ed.), *Understanding language through sign language research.* New York: Academic.

Kuntz, J., Carrier, J. and Hollis, J. 1978: A nonvocal system for teaching retarded children to read and write. In C. Meyers (ed.), *Quality of life in severely and profoundly retarded people: research foundations for improvement.* Washington: American Association on Mental Deficiency.

La Vigna, G. 1977: Communication training in mute autistic adolescents. *J. Autism and Childhood Schizophrenia* 7, 135–49.

Lotter, V. 1967: Epidemiology of autistic conditions in young children: II, Some characteristics of the parents and children. *Social Psychiatry* 1, 163–73.

Lovaas, O. 1967: *A behavior therapy approach to the treatment of childhood schizophrenia.* Minneapolis: University of Minnesota Press.

Lovaas, O., Berberick, J., Perloff, B. and Schaeffer, B. 1966: Acquisition of imitative speech by schizophrenic children. *Science* 151, 705–6.

Marshall, N. and Hargrenes, J. 1972: The use of written language as a communication system for an autistic child. *J. Speech and Hearing Disorders* 37, 258–61.

McLean, L. and McLean, J. 1974: A language training program for nonverbal autistic children. *J. Speech and Hearing Disorders* 39, 186–93.

Mittler, P. 1970: Language disorders. In P. Mittler (ed.), *The psychological assessment of mental and physical handicaps.* London: Methuen.

Morton-Evans, A. and Hensley, R. 1978: Paired associate learning in early infantile autism and receptive developmental aphasia. *J. Autism and Childhood Schizophrenia* 8, 61–9.

O'Connor, N. and Hermelin, B. 1973: The spatial and temporal organization of short-term memory. *Q. J. Experimental Psychology* 25,

335–43.

—— 1978: *Seeing and hearing in space and time*. London: Academic.

Olson, D. 1975: The language of experience: on natural language and formal education. *Bulletin of the British Psychological Society* **28**, 363–73.

Oxman, J., Webster, C. and Konstantareas, M. 1978: The perception and processing of information by severely dysfunctional nonverbal children. *Sign Language Studies* **21**, 289–316.

Premack, D. 1970: A functional analysis of language. *J. Experimental Analysis of Behavior* **14**, 107–25.

—— 1976: *Intelligence in ape and man*. New Jersey: Lawrence Erlbaum.

Premack, D. and Premack, A. 1974: Teaching visual language to apes and language deficient persons. In R. Schiefelbusch and L. Lloyd (eds.), *Language perspectives: acquisition, retardation and intervention*. Baltimore: University Park Press.

Ratusnik, C. and Ratusnik, D. 1974: A comprehensive communication approach for a ten year old nonverbal autistic child. *Am. J. Orthopsychiatry* **44**, 396–403.

Rutter, M. 1978: Diagnosis and definition. In M. Rutter and E. Schopler (eds.), *Autism: a reappraisal of concepts and treatment*. New York: Plenum.

Ryan, J. 1971: When is an apparent deficit a real defect? Language assessment in the subnormal. Paper presented at CIBA Conference on the Psychological Assessment of the Mentally Handicapped. London, December.

Seligman, M. 1975: *Helplessness*. San Francisco: Freeman.

Stroop, J. 1935: Studies of interference in serial verbal reactions. *J. Experimental Psychology* **18**, 643–62.

Tallal, P. and Piercey, M. 1973: Developmental aphasia: impaired rate of nonverbal processing as a function of sensory modality. *Neuropsychologia* **11**, 389–98.

Tubbs, V. 1966: Types of linguistic disability in psychotic children. *J. Mental Deficiency Research* **10**, 230–40.

Yule, W., Berger, M. and Howlin, P. 1975: Language deficit and behaviour modification. In N. O'Connor (ed.), *Language, cognitive deficits and retardation*. London: Butterworth.

10

Contextual contours and the development of language

Richard P. Brinker

Recently at a friend's house, we were preparing the grill for a barbecue and the three-year-old son, Danny, was busily assisting in the preparation. As the flames leaped about the coals, Danny, a few weeks short of his third birthday, pointed excitedly and said, 'Ribbons, there's the ribbons.' I immediately appreciated the metaphor of the situation and offered the interpretation that the flames looked like ribbons to the child; an overextension of a new lexical item, no doubt. The child's mother thought that a plausible explanation but as the child's intonation changed and as he persisted in saying 'Ribbons,' she finally asked what he was talking about. In reply, Danny whined, 'Where's the ribbons?' Since the flames were dying down, the mother said, 'Those aren't ribbons, they're flames. Now don't get too close.' Danny's 14-year-old sister resolutely asserted that he was just being silly and was making no sense. Then the child's father emerged with a plate full of spare ribs and the child triumphantly pointed to the spare ribs and said, 'There's the ribbons. Dad, put 'em on the gil.'

There are several interesting features of the discussion of 'spare ribbons' which illustrate aspects of communicative development.

First, there was the fact that for several minutes the conversation of an adolescent and two adults was completely dominated by a three-year-old who had said a few interesting words about a topic of his choosing. The topic was not clear; it was an intrusion upon the conversation the adults were having; but nevertheless they were quite willing to suspend their conversation to establish a new conversation around this unknown topic.

Second, the adults and the adolescent differed in their willingness to assume that the child had anything sensible to say. To his sister, Danny was being a nuisance, getting in the way of an 'adult' conversation in which she was participating. To both myself and the mother, it was clear that the child was trying to communicate something. The mother was the first to realize the inadequacy of our initial interpretation.

Third, the search for the meaning of Danny's 'ribbons' began with attention to the immediate perceptual situation. The assumption was that the child and the adults shared the situation and the meaning of the

239

child's utterance could be sorted out on this common ground. In this particular instance, this assumption of a shared understanding of the context was false. The 'ribbons' were not there.

Fourth, the child had to persist in maintaining the communication until his message was understood. He detected both the misunderstanding and finally the understanding of his message by the listeners. He negotiated this process by changing the words used ('There's the ribbons' became 'Where's the ribbons?'), by changing his intonation, and by changing his nonverbal behaviour.

It is clear from the above example that the message being communicated was not encoded completely in Danny's utterance. Nor was all of the message encoded by highlighting aspects of the context. Rather, the listeners gradually constructed the message by searching for information in the context and by searching for recasts of the utterance form.

The purpose of this chapter will be to explore the processes by which contexts are constructed in order to understand children's messages. The requirements for understanding children's messages involve the intersection of four kinds of information:

(1) the child's background of experience;
(2) the objects and events within the physical environment in which the communication occurs;
(3) the listener's experience as interpreter of that child; and
(4) the clarity of the message.

A second purpose will be to explore the implications of the constructivist view of contexts for language intervention. This author has been attempting for the last several years to apply the most recent advances in language research to the language and communication problems of moderately to profoundly-retarded children (Beveridge and Brinker 1980, Brinker 1978, Brinker and Bricker 1980, Brinker and Goldbart 1981). At the outset, it was hoped that the expansion of information about normal language development would provide the content for language intervention programs (Bricker and Bricker 1974, Bricker and Carlson 1980a). This content would be translated into educational practice through the use of behaviour-modification techniques (Jones and Robson 1979). This translation of content from theoretical language development research into language intervention practice has not been realized. However, the process of language development research does have some important implications for how we devise language intervention strategies. These issues will be discussed later in the chapter.

Initially there is no differentiation between the contexts of representational acts and the contexts of communicative acts. However, the actions which become the basis for representation and the actions which become the basis for communication can eventually be distinguished. It is important therefore, at the outset, to recall the distinction often made in the Russian developmental literature between the first and second signalling systems (Luria 1976, Vygotsky 1962). Language is a tool for exchanging messages between individuals. It is also a tool for representing and classifying experience.

The child's background of experience

Communication in social contexts

The 'cradle of meaning' is the mother's lap (Lewis and Freedle 1973, Newson and Newson 1979). As Beveridge and Lloyd (1977) described it, 'the child is developing an ever-increasing range of ways in which he participates closely with his mother in understanding the world. The mother and child respond to each other so sensitively as to make the child's world view an essentially joint construct. In other words, "he sees that she sees what he sees" ' (Beveridge and Brinker 1980, 53).

Even at the very early stages of infancy, there may be some differentiation between the functions which vocalizations serve. In one context vocalizations may simply be interesting things to do. Thus, infants simply play with sound outside of any interactive or object play context. However, early vocalizations provide an excellent medium around which to structure interaction. Lewis and Freedle (1973) found that, although more utterances occurred when the baby was in an infant seat, the greatest probability of an interactive exchange occurred when the infant was sitting on the mother's lap. Thus, the communicative nature of these early utterances (with the exception of cries) is defined by the social context. That is, someone must be exclusively focused on the child for these early utterances to take on a communicative character. This communicative character is provided by the mother breaking into the child's stream of behaviour and thereby imposing a structure on it (Bruner 1975, Stern 1974). Such 'structuring' is possible for the mother only if there are spaces in the infant's stream of behaviour (Jones 1977).

The introduction of referents

Paradoxically, the meanings in this cradle seem initially to be without content. That is, the exchanges which are the substrate of communicative dialogue generally have no referents or topic of conversation. Trevarthen and Hubley (1978) noted that when an object was introduced into a mother-child interaction when the child was 6 months old, the child became wholly focused on the object but seemed oblivious to the social nature of the context. That is, there was no exchange of utterances and no eye contact between mother and child. By 7 months, the child acted more directly upon objects introduced by the mother but again did not focus attention upon the mother. These situations were characterized by secondary circular reactions in which the infant used 'magical' means to repeat a spectacle (Piaget 1952). However, these means did not involve any activities or attention directed specifically to the mother.

When the child did focus attention on the mother, the object ceased to exist from the child's point of view. It was not until 8½ months that the child interspersed object actions and social actions; and there was still no coordination of social and object actions so that the mother could be included as a participant in the activity. Such social interactions in which both mother and child participated together with an object were not evidenced until 10 months (Trevarthen and Hubley 1978).

Coordinating people and objects

Communication about a shared topic does not seem to emerge until somewhat later, around 13 months. Sugarman-Bell (1978) studied the development of coordination between socially-directed and object-directed actions. She found a developmental sequence in which simple actions were directed exclusively either to persons or to objects. These simple actions included individual acts such as mouthing an object or smiling at an adult. Around 5 months, more complicated sequences of behaviour emerged, such as crawling to and picking up an object or reaching for and vocalizing to an adult. However, these complex actions were directed exclusively to objects or to people, with no switching between person-directed and object-directed actions. At about 13 months, the first examples of coordinated object and person interactions were noted. This sequence of development would be supported by Trevarthen and Hubley's (1978) data, although their child moved through this sequence more quickly than the children studied by Sugarman-Bell (1978).

Bricker and Carlson (1980b) extended Sugarman-Bell's findings to developmentally-delayed children. They found the same sequence of development from simple to complex to coordinated object and social schemes. However, the coordination of object and social schemes did not begin until approximately 18 months for the developmentally-delayed children. When mental ages were used instead of chronological age, there was an increase in the use of coordinated schemes at MA = 13 months, but simple schemes still predominated over complex and coordinated schemes. Unfortunately, data was not yet available to demonstrate the mental age at which the coordination of social and object schemes predominated over schemes employed exclusively towards either objects or people (Bricker and Carlson, 1980b). It would be premature to conclude that the developmentally-delayed children followed the same developmental path until the end point of this particular path (i.e. coordinated object and social schemes) was reached.

Thus it seems that what a child can do with objects and what a child can do with people are treated separately by the child until about 10 to 13 months of age. The ability to use objects in relation to people and vice versa is a sensorimotor development in the patterning of behaviour to achieve goals. Therefore, the introduction of referents into conversations will be part of a more general cognitive development and this general level of cognitive development will have an impact upon the patterns of interaction between mother and child. In terms of the mechanisms of development, the mother's or father's problem is to find the best match between the complexity of their own behaviour and that of the infant's. Presumably caregiver behaviour which structures situations slightly beyond the infant's abilities will result in developmental change (Hunt 1961, Robinson and Robinson 1978).

Dunst (1980) studied the relationships among sensorimotor levels, maternal behaviour, and the coordination of cues which young retarded and nonretarded children used in their communications. He videotaped mothers and their children in a play situation. Six dyads with a Down's syndrome child and six dyads with a normal child were studied. Children's gestures were coded in terms of their sensorimotor levels; for example: Stage 5 gestures included communicative pointing, giving or showing an object, requesting an object by reaching, and pulling an adult; Stage 4 gestures included nonintegrative pointing, extending arms, waving, hugging an adult, grabbing, taking, pushing an adult, and protesting. Stage 3 gestures included touching the mother, reaching for an object, and holding out an object.

Dunst (1980) found that the level of communication gesture in the play session was clearly related to the sensorimotor level of the child as independently assessed (Uzgiris and Hunt 1975). Thus the children assessed as being at Stage 5 sensorimotor development emitted predominantly Stage 5 gestures. These gestures involved the interpatterning of action, looking, and vocalization. The Stage 4 children emitted more Stage 3 gestures and these generally consisted of an action towards an object or a person. The Stage 3 gestures did not include the interpatterning of gesture, vocalization or looking. More of the Down's syndrome children's gestures were elicited by the children's mothers in comparison to the gestures of the nonretarded children, a greater proportion of which were spontaneously emitted.

Mothers differed in their responses to gestures combined with looking and vocalization when compared to mothers' responses to gestures alone. Mothers' responses were categorized as *complete*, *incomplete*, or *no response*. Complete responses by the mother referred back to the child's gesture and provided some consequence based upon the presumed meaning of the child's gesture. Incomplete responses included an acknowledgement of the child's gesture but no demonstration to the child that his behaviour was understood. For example, pointing to an object and vocalizing would be attended to and commented on by the mother but the child would not be given the object. Mothers responded more often to gestures combined with vocalizations and looking than to gestures alone. Incomplete responses and no response from the mother occurred more frequently when the child emitted a gesture with no interpatterning of vocalization and/or looking. Finally, the mothers of the Down's syndrome children emitted more incomplete responses to gestures, while mothers of nonretarded children emitted more complete responses.

The results of Dunst's (1980) study substantiates a generally-held view for which little data has been available (Bates 1976, Edwards 1974, Moerk 1976). That is, the complexity of communicative development is a function of the sensorimotor level of the child. The second implication of Dunst's study is that a style of maternal interaction is associated with the child's ability to combine gesture, vocalization and looking. Without such interpatterning on the child's part, the mother will acknowledge but not understand the child's behaviour. The construction of an understanding of the child's behaviour requires structuring the interactive context so the child's responses are elicited by the mother rather than being spontaneously emitted[1]. Mothers of developmentally-delayed children must depend upon this strategy for a longer time than mothers of nonretarded children (Buckhalt *et al.* 1978, Marshall *et al.* 1973). I will further explore the implications of this interactive strategy later in the chapter.

To summarize thus far, the caregiver must construct an interactive context within which communication takes place. She must build this context around the behaviour of the child (Lewis and Rosenblum 1974, Stern 1974) by selecting actions and vocalizations to imbue with meaning. Until the child has learned to switch attention from objects to mother and from mother to object, the messages exchanged are not referential. Thus the mother is free to make up any meaning, since the point is to maintain a dialogue rather than to exchange information. However, once the child reaches sensorimotor Stage 5 he can clearly take charge of the communicative situation and talk about things. Then the context for understanding become crucial if the child's caregivers are to extend and elaborate the messages generated by the child.

Somewhat before the child takes responsibility for the speaker's role, adults begin systematically to simplify their speech to the child. Sherrod

---

Editor's note:
[1] It should be pointed out that Trevarthen takes the view that from birth human infants are socially motivated and intentional in their interactive behaviour. This is in contrast to the position adopted by the author of this chapter. However, Trevarthen would not disagree that mothers do on many occasions *interpret* children's actions, and it is this point which is central to the argument presented here.

et al. (1978) have noted that this simplification of speech normally occurs when the child is about 8 months old. At this point, the child's development of schemes for acting on objects and people probably leads adults to conclude that there is something for the child to talk about. However, as we have seen (Bricker and Carlson 1980b, Dunst 1980, Sugarman-Bell 1978, Trevarthen and Hubley 1978), the child spends some time consolidating his knowledge about objects before actually referring to them in his communications.

Representing experience

The growth of concepts of action and concepts of objects

Several authors have noted the parallels between sensorimotor behaviour and the early acquisition of language (Bates 1976, Brown 1973, Leonard 1978, Moerk 1976). The substrates for concepts of nouns and verbs may be found in the social schemes and object schemes which eventually become coordinated as described in the preceding section.

Social schemes Social schemes result in a dynamic flow of events from some person in the environment. Social schemes seem to have a different physical and temporal pattern than object schemes. Object schemes incorporate objects into an activity. The activity and the object are cotemporaneous. The action of shaking a rattle doesn't result in feedback from the rattle except during the action.

Social schemes, on the other hand, activate consequences which occur *after* the actions themselves. Piaget (1952) has described such a dynamic flow of events as a 'spectacle'. Piaget's discussion of 'spectacles' emphasized objects (e.g., a hanging mobile) accidentally activated and then reactivated through circular reactions. The circular reactions become differentiated into procedures for making interesting sights last. However, the discussion of circular reactions and procedures for making interesting sights last is conceptually distinct from the discussion of object schemes.

We might speculate that most of the 'spectacles' which a child experiences during the first three or four stages of sensorimotor development are the result of social schemes rather than object schemes. The temporal parameters of crying and being attended to by an adult or smiling and eliciting an excited vocalization from an adult are certainly very different from the temporal parameters of sucking and receiving feedback from the object sucked or waving a rattle and hearing the sound of the rattle. The first two activities are better conceptualized as procedures and their consequent events, while the second two activities are more clearly activities for objects rather than for events. The complex patterning of mother and infant behaviour (Newson and Newson 1979) clearly has the temporal character of procedures and consequent spectacles. These social interactions may form the basis for a concept of event.

Object schemes While social schemes may provide the strongest basis for action concepts, object schemes have not been clearly implicated as the basis for lexical representation (Moerk 1976, Nelson 1974). The process would begin with simple reflexive acts which are elicited by certain classes of sufficient stimuli. Gradually, the reflexive action becomes less fixed in pattern and can be elicited by less than the sufficient stimuli. The actions can be classified as object schemes once the child is observed to actively seek to employ them. This would not generally be possible until visually-directed reaching had been established. Once the child is capable of being able to select objects to which to apply the schemes, object differentiation would begin.

Initially, each scheme would be applied to each object. Thus, a variety of objects would be grasped, mouthed, shaken, banged, crumpled and thrown. By applying these schemes to a wide variety of objects, the baby develops an understanding of different properties of objects. Some objects are more conducive to shaking and banging but cannot be easily crumpled. Other objects have properties which make them difficult to grasp and shake (e.g., balls) but which are more interesting to hit or throw.

The physical properties of objects, then, are gradually discovered by applying a small number of actions to a wide variety of objects. Ultimately, different schemes are applied to different classes of objects, presumably because the physical properties of the objects are differentially conducive to the action scheme. From the Piagetian perspective (Piaget 1952), concepts of objects are constructed on the basis of differentiated action schemes. Until such concepts are constructed, it is not possible to represent an object with a name.

Object Differentiation by the Retarded Child

Beveridge and Brinker (1980) reviewed several studies which indicated that retarded children did not differentiate objects by their actions as clearly as nonretarded children. Chatelanat, Hendersen and Robinson (cited in Bricker and Bricker 1974) found that developmentally-delayed toddlers, when compared to normal toddlers of the same age, emitted more actions with objects. However, the developmentally-delayed children tended to use the same somewhat simple set of actions indiscriminately. The normal children used fewer actions but the actions tended to be more clearly differentiated according to the properties of the objects. For example, the 2- to 3-year-old retarded children, when presented with a set of objects, applied simple schemes such as holding, shaking, banging, and throwing each object in sequence. The nonretarded children did different things with different objects. Brinker (1978) found that retarded children between 2 and 4 years of age used objects in socially appropriate ways in a teaparty or bedtime context; but that, in addition to actions such as using a spoon to put sugar in a cup of tea, they performed actions such as waving the spoon or hitting various objects with the spoon. Thus, complex socially appropriate play routines were embedded in the child's repertoire along with very simple object schemes. This would suggest that an incomplete differentiation of objects may be the basis for some of the representational problems of retarded children.

D. Bricker (1972) provided an interesting demonstration of the value of differentiating objects by actions prior to being able to represent objects. She demonstrated that acquisition of receptive vocabulary was facilitated by teaching children a 'motor mediator' prior to teaching the object labels. For example, one group of retarded children learned to perform a specific unique action when presented with a particular object (e.g. a strumming action when presented with a guitar). These children were superior to traditional intervention groups in subsequently learning to select these objects when named.

Action as a specific representational substrate

The work by Bricker (1972) suggests that actions may provide a direct representational linkage for the acquisition of specific lexical items. This position has been argued cogently by Nelson (1974) and is in contrast to Clark's (1973, 1974) position that lexical items are initially acquired by linking a word to a class of objects on the basis of the objects' perceptual attributes. Rather, Nelson (1974, 280) argues that:

> . . . when instances of these first concepts came to be named, it would be expected that they would be named only in the context of one of the definitionally specified actions and relationships. The word, the object, the action, and the relations to other objects would all be used in a totality that included the child as definer and integral member . . . The proposition here is that the word refers to the object in one of a set of relations that defines the concept. The concept contains all of the known relational information; the word that is attached to it then may refer to the whole concept while naming the concept in one of its defining relations as an instance of that concept.

Brinker (1978) attempted to apply this functional notion of early concepts and labelling within an intervention program. Two simple play contexts were used: a teatime and a bedtime context. Within these contexts intervention would follow the developmental progression (1) acquisition of functional differentiation of objects, (2) receptive acquisition of lexical items, (3) imitation of words, and using words in response to requests for object names.

The assessment of these various skills took place in a play situation and was led by the child's behaviour. For example, if a child was playing with the cup, after a certain amount of such play the experimenter would ask the child, 'What's that?' Sensorimotor actions were scored from videotapes and an interobserver agreement of .79 was obtained for classifications of actions as simple schemes versus functionally-differentiated actions appropriate to the objects. From each play context, data were obtained about the imitation, comprehension, and production of each lexical item for eight words (see Table 10.1).

An interesting difference emerged between the two contexts. The number of words understood initially in both contexts did not differ.

Table 10.1 Receptive syntax: objects available and requests made

Objects available	Request ('Make the . . . .')
Reversible subjects and objects	
boy, lady, soap, dog	boy wash the lady
horse, dog, lady, bed	horse jump the dog
boy, girl, wagon, door	boy kick the girl
boy, lady, soap, spoon	lady wash the boy
horse, cow, door, dog	horse ride the cow
dog, lady, car, horse	dog jump the horse
car, man, truck, pan	car push the truck
horse, cow, door, dog	cow ride the horse
boy, girl, wagon, door	girl kick the boy
car, man, truck, pan	truck push the car
Irreversible subjects and objects	
man, door, chair, horse	man shut the door
boy, car, horse, can	boy drive the car
window, hat, lady, hair	lady open the window
baby, milk, spoon, pan	baby drink the milk
lady, cookie, chair, boy	lady eat the cookie
Locatives	
dog, truck, boy, box	truck drive in the box
girl, bed, shoe, cup	girl sleep in the bed
dog, wagon, apple, sand	dog ride in the wagon
boy, chair, cup, cookie	boy sit in the chair
baby, sack, spoon, can	baby hide in the sack

Nor did the proportion of actions which were socially appropriate to the objects differ in the two contexts. However, the relationship between actions and objects and understanding of the object names was different in the two contexts during the pretest assessment. In the bed-time situation the correlation between socially appropriate actions with objects and word understanding was $r = .71$ ($p < .10$). In the tea party context the correlation between socially appropriate actions with objects and understanding of object names was $r = -.88$ ($p < .05$). One would expect from the Piagetian perspective as articulated by Nelson (1974) that there would be a positive relationship in any context between word comprehension and the degree of object differentiation.

Since this difference was found with a very small group of developmentally-delayed children, the results were interpreted with caution (Brinker 1978). However, there did appear to be differences in the way objects in the two contexts might be differentiated by a child's actions. Figure 10.1 is an attempt to conceptualize the relationships among the objects in these contexts in terms of the actions relating them.

This model suggests that the teaparty context would require the integration of five divergent sets of action-object relationships. Although the same number of actions can be used to characterize the bedtime situation, the entire situation is integrated by a single object, *the baby*. All of the action-object relationships could be viewed as a subset of a more general concept of *doll baby*, with each action-object relationship being an aspect of that concept. Four such aspects are evident from the model in Figure 10.1.

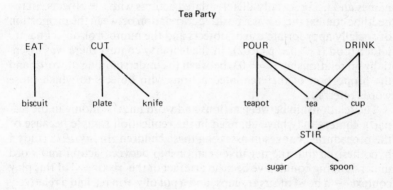

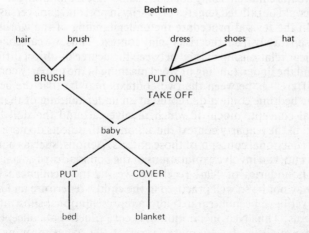

Figure 10.1 Target words and their relationship to socially appropriate actions.

Subsequent to my 1978 study, I assessed a second group of nine retarded children (CA = 33 to 47 months, MA = 12 to 33 months) and two nonretarded children (18 and 23 months). Several modifications of the procedure were made to ensure a more systematic sampling of imitation, comprehension and production skills than was possible when these skills were assessed within an ongoing play context in the classroom. Specifically, each child was assessed in two sessions. In one, the objects of the play context were all available and the child was encouraged to interact with the objects. In another session, the child was presented with pairs of objects from the context and asked, 'Give me the *(object name).*' Then each object was presented individually and the child was asked 'What's this?' Finally, the child was asked to imitate each object name.

Again, a difference was found between understanding objects' names and using socially-differentiated actions with the objects. In the bedtime context there was a positive correlation between the proportion of socially appropriate use of objects and the number of object names understood (r = .78, p < .02). In the teaparty context there was essentially no relationship (r = .03) between the understanding of words and the proportion of differentiated actions with objects to which those words referred.

The relationship between actions and word understanding in the teaparty context may have changed in the replication sample because of the procedural changes in assessing these children. In my 1978 study I hypothesized that the negative relationship between action and word understanding could have been an artefact of the 'riskiness' of this play context – a bowl of sugar, cups, and a pot of warm tea had a relatively high probability of being spilled. Thus, I was torn between allowing free rein to the children's play but at the same time maintaining the context so it could be utilized (e.g. tea primarily in pot, and cups versus elsewhere). In the revised procedure the understanding of the words was assessed separately from the 'risky' play context. Thus, we can conclude that no clear relationship existed between the degree of object differentiation and the understanding of word meaning in the teaparty context.

The differences between the two contexts may be that the actions within the bedtime context do represent an understanding of that core functional concept, much of which revolves around the doll baby. However, in the teaparty context the actions with objects do not represent core functional concepts of those objects. Actions, such as pouring tea into a cup, can involve explorations of the boundaries of social skills and the boundaries of 'care-receiving' versus independence. These actions may not be so well practised in the child's repertoire and hence may not yet have been integrated into a representational substrate for lexical items. Thus Nelson's notion of a core functional concept may have to be qualified by an appreciation of the social meaning of a context for the child.

Bowerman (1978) argues that the notion of a core functional concept based on object uses is not adequate for the explanation of her children's uses of first words. She argues that theories of lexical acquisition must account for classification of objects on the basis of many different kinds of similarities and not just on the basis of what the child typically does with objects. The data from the teaparty and bedtime contexts suggests that the quality of actions with objects may reflect different cognitive and representational skills in different contexts.

The confusion whether words need concepts or whether concepts need words leads us back to the two aspects of language: the first and second signalling systems. At this point it appears that some children use words to formulate and clarify concepts of a referent class, while others need a core functional concept to which words may be attached. Unfortunately, distinctions of words in terms of their communicative versus cognitive functions seems to be an idiosyncratic process based on a child's experience and personality.

Second signalling system

Thus far the discussion has focused on language as a communicative device. A second aspect of language is that of a primary tool for thought. The distinction has most clearly been drawn by the Russian researchers, who have referred to these two functions of language as the first and second signalling systems (Luria and Yudovich 1971, Vygotsky 1962). From this perspective, the second signalling system actually shapes perception and thought. As noted by Luria and Yudovich (1971, 25):

> The word connected with direct perception of the object isolates its essential features; to name the perceived object 'a glass' adding its functional role 'for drinking' isolates the essential and inhibits the less essential properties of the object. . . . In sum speech, the basic means of communication, becomes also a means of deeper analysis and synthesis of reality and, more fundamentally important, a higher regulator of behaviour.

The two signalling systems are clearly related, but the developmental progression is not so simple as, for example, mastering communicative aspects of the system and subsequently mastering the cognitive aspects.

Luria and Yudovich provide an interesting case study of a pair of twins who shared a communicative system which was quite primitive in comparison to that of normal four-year-olds. Interestingly, no generalized developmental delay was present. However, they noted that the context of their play was primitive, repetitive, and consisted primarily of manipulating objects according to their physical functions. Luria and Yudovich observed no games in which different roles were represented, no fantasy or representational play, no evidence of a more general semiotic functioning such as might be found in drawing, constructive play, or modelling with clay.

Most of the communication by these twins consisted of strings of sounds, only 40 per cent of which were words, which were incomprehensible outside of the specific situation in which the utterance occurred. Although this system clearly involved the communication of messages between the twins, Luria and Yudovich point out three drawbacks of this 'grammar of amorphous speech'. First, it could not carry out complex orienting functions, for example to objects outside the immediate contexts. Second, the variability in forms of a word could not reflect the external situation with objectivity or generalizability. Third, speech was so related to action that it could not fulfil the roles either of regulation or of planning future behaviour.

They conducted two kinds of intervention for the twins. The first was to place them in separate nursery classes so that they no longer had access to their primary interpreter. One of the twins was then given an intervention programme which emphasized the use of verbal forms, answering questions in grammatical sentences, and talking about events and objects which were not physically present but which were related to available objects. The separation alone led to a dramatic reduction for both twins in the percentage of utterances which were comprehensible only in context. After only three months, the twin who received no intervention was producing utterances only 19 per cent of which were incomprehensible outside of the context, compared to 78 per cent incomprehensible utterances prior to separation from his brother. The major impact of the intervention programme for the second twin was an increase after three months from 9 per cent to 63 per cent utterances which were grammatical sentences. The twin who did not receive the intervention programme increased the percentage of grammatical sentences from 10 per cent to 36 per cent in the same period. Thus the separation alone had some positive effects upon the twins; but the provision of intervention during the separation produced much more dramatic language development than the separation alone. Nevertheless, the study does suggest that intersubjectivity such as that between the twins sometimes can have detrimental effects upon communicative development.

Enacting simple grammatical sentences

When does language begin to function as the second signalling system, the regulator of behaviour and a primary classificatory tool? Brinker and Bricker (1980) conducted a study which provided data which can be used to address this question.

We presented children with sets of toys, two of which were involved in a requested action. The actions requested and the objects available are presented in Table 1. Brinker and Bricker (1980) found that the best predictor of the child's ability to enact the statements was the child's mean length of utterance. This confirms the findings by de Villiers and de Villiers (1973) with nonhandicapped children.

An analysis of the types of errors which children made in enacting these requested relationships provided some information on the acquisition of the second signalling system. Twelve retarded children and 22 nonretarded children participated in the study. Further information on the sample and design may be obtained from Brinker and Bricker (1980). The children's actions with objects were recorded. These actions were then classified as simple object schemes, functionally appropriate use of an object, and reversal errors. In addition, each of these types of action were further analyzed to determine the extent to which the objects acted upon were the objects named in the request. Definitions of each of the types of action are as follows:

Simple object schemes Simple actions with objects which can be applied to a variety of objects, for example: hitting, mouthing, throwing, crumpling, waving, examining.

Functionally appropriate use of objects Simple actions with objects which are congruent with the physical properties of the object, or which constitute the appropriate social use of the object, for example: drinking from a cup, feeding a baby with a spoon, putting objects in a box.

Reversal errors Reversal of the actor-object relationship requested. This kind of error requires selection of named objects from the available objects and use of the requested action, for example: making the car push the truck when requested 'make the truck push the car'.

Table 10.2 Proportion of error types for enacting simple requests as a function of Mean Length of Utterance

Mean Length of Utterance	Schemes	Functionally appropriate use	Reversals
1.0 – 1.9	.14	.77	.09
2.0 – 3.0	.00	.56	.44
3.0 – 4.5	.00	.27	.73
> 4.5	.00	.00	1.00

The types of actions with objects when the child did not perform the requested action are presented in Table 10.2. It is clear from the table that as MLU increases so does the probability that misunderstandings will not involve use of the lexical information but reversals of the actor-object relationship. This kind of error requires that the child has decoded the actor, action and object of an utterance but has reversed the actor and object roles. Thus, by the time a child is using three-word utterances, his behaviour can be clearly regulated by verbal input and his mistakes are based on verbal input. However, prior to an MLU of

3.0 the child may adopt a strategy of selecting the named objects within the array of objects and proceed to play with the objects with no further indication of linguistic regulation of behaviour. (See Bridges, this volume, for a detailed discussion of strategies adopted by children in comprehension tasks.)

The distinction between children who are using primarily one-word utterances and the children using primarily two-word utterances is the extent to which named referents are selected. The proportion of errors involving one or two of the named objects is present in Table 10.3. For the children between MLU of 2.0 and 3.0, .76 of the errors involved selection of the two named objects but use of these objects in a way which had not been requested. The errors of children at MLU 1.0 to 2.0 indicated that they generally did not decode both of the referent words. Instead, they would simply play with the objects available without attending to the verbal request. However, these children seemed to have differentiated these objects by their actions, since .86 of their actions were functionally or socially appropriate for the objects selected.

Table 10.3 Proportion of errors involving one or both named objects

Mean Length of Utterance	One named	Both named
1.0 – 1.9 (N = 17)	.28	.37
2.0 – 2.9 (N = 7)	.08	.76
3.0 – 4.5 (N = 5)	.09	.91
> 4.5 (N = 7)	.00	1.00

These data suggest that specifically linguistic errors are not encountered in decoding multiword utterances until the child is using simple syntactic constructions (i.e. MLU 3.0). However, prior to this regulation of an entire action by speech, the child attended to those words which she did know and selected their referents from those available. Since she didn't understand the proposition, she then played with the objects in a socially or functionally appropriate way. Even those children at the one-word stage of development had a strategy for dealing with these contexts. The strategy tended to be to select a favoured object and demonstrate its social function. Thus, the strategy which a child used was based upon her own skills in using language expressively. As these skills increased, so did the relationship between the child's strategy and the linguistic information in the context.

The problem of intersubjectivity for language research

To summarize, we have traced the course of language development from its roots in the social cradle of communication to its use as a tool for thought. The data suggests that language becomes a tool for thought only after it is being used as a communicative device (Smith 1975; Zachry, 1972). Language for communication depends upon a listener who *shares* a context with the speaker[2]. The intersubjectivity required for communication, especially at the early stages of development, presents some problems for an objective science of language development. It presents perhaps greater problems for language interventionists.

The problem of intersubjectivity in descriptions of language development

There has been a methodological shift over the last 20 years in the study of language. This shift is most evident in the study of child language. Chomsky's (1965) rational method for formally describing the structure of a language was largely intrasubjective. This rational intuitive method relied upon the linguist's competence as a native speaker to generate sentences and induce the rules which bring these sentences from deep to surface structure. The linguist's description of a formal rule depends upon his ability to construct meaningful exemplars of the rule and his inability to generate exceptions. Thus the explication of a grammatical rule by a linguist and the data to support the rule interact at all levels of theory development.

As Bloom (1970, 32) pointed out, 'The intuition of the native speaker is inaccessible in an investigation of children's language and the problem of testing the adequacy of a theory of children's language is difficult, if indeed such a test of adequacy is possible at all.' Child language researchers were well aware of the problem of intrasubjectivity in Chomsky's rational method and responded to this problem by adopting a more objective approach (Braine 1963, Brown and Fraser 1964, Miller and Ervin 1964). They decided to treat child language as a foreign language, the structure of which was to be discovered by a distributional analysis of corpuses of speech.

Bloom (1970) pointed out that a distributional analysis was inadequate for detecting structural differences in the use of the same words. Thus she argued that the utterance 'Mommy sock' could be classified as two different grammatical structures on the basis of the two different contexts in which the child said it. *Mommy* was a possessive adjective modifying *sock* in the context in which the child was referring to her

---

[2] *Editor's note:* Urwin, this volume, argues that this language/context distinction is based on the visual/auditory sensory distinction. She goes on to argue that the evidence from the study of blind children suggests that the language/context distinction is a false dichotomy which presents unnecessary and irrelevant problems. Walkerdine, this volume, presents a similar argument and presents a view of language as a semiotic system which drives certain events or objects into significance. The reader might reflect on whether the two signalling systems referred to by Brinker in this chapter sit better with his view or with that of Urwin and Walkerdine.

mother's sock hanging on a chair, whereas *Mommy* was the subject and *sock* the object of a sentence in the context in which the mother was putting on the child's sock. These grammatical differences would have been lost if one had simply done a distributional analysis to determine with what other words these words occurred and in what position. However, by introducing the shared understanding of the context and the utterance by speaker and listener, one runs the risk of imposing a structure on children's language rather than discovering a structure in their language (Greenfield and Smith 1976).

The notion of a shared context and the intersubjectivity required to define context is a significant methodological problem for an objective science of language development (Brinker and Goldbart 1980). However, for the purposes of an individual child's language development, this intersubjectivity seems to be a necessary aspect for the process to occur (Bruner 1975, Snow and Ferguson 1974). That is, there must be someone who segments a child's behaviour into units, someone who interprets as meaningful the unintentional movements and sounds which the infant makes. The accuracy or objectivity of individual interpretations is not so important so long as the child discovers the foundations for later language such as dialogue, joint reference and representation.

Thus our theories of language development emphasize the intersubjectivity between mother and child as an essential component in the developmental process. However, criteria of scientific rigour would require an objective and replicable evidence for stages within that developmental process. To train observers to agree in their description of communication, it would help if we understood how contexts are constructed by mothers and other members of the language community.

Contextual relativity

Different people will construe situations different ways. These different constructions will depend upon the novelty or familiarity of a person with the context and the relationships among people within a context as well as upon the physical structure of the context. The contention is that messages cannot be understood in the absence of an understanding of these contextual dimensions. Communicative development will be difficult to study if the carriers of message units are not understood.

The messages of very young children lead adult listeners to several strategies for understanding. The first is to attempt to discover the referent which the child is talking about. (See Freeman, Sinha and Stedmon, this volume). Clues to the referent are to be found in what the child is holding or what the child is looking at (Bruner 1975, Collis and Schaffer 1975). These clues were not sufficient for understanding Danny's 'There's the ribbons' when he was pointing at the flames. The second clue would be found in the relationship between the speaker and listener. Who is listening and what does the speaker expect them to understand? Both of these considerations apply to messages in general – not just vocalizations. The third clue applies primarily to vocalizations. What sounds like what the speaker just said?

Describing communicative acts

In 1977 it became apparent to me that there were no adequate observational systems for describing communicative acts across a developmental period ranging from preverbal nonvocal messages to simple sentences. Rather, the literature provided increasingly complex descriptions of children within a sharply-circumscribed developmental range. Obviously some focus is necessary; but we are often faced with clear descriptions of the trees and little description of the forest in our studies of language and communicative development.

The concepts and categories for describing preverbal communicative attempts and their social contexts were readily available (Bates 1976, Greenfield and Smith 1976, Smith and Connolly 1972). However, these concepts had not been integrated into a system which would enable one to discover the level of communicative development that a particular child had achieved. Rather, the concepts emerged through the study of children who were within the same developmental level.

The pragmatic and semantic concepts adopted were clear enough and could be instantiated by the behaviour of children in our sample (Brinker and Goldbart 1980). For example, Bates *et al.* (1975) define 'proto-declaratives' as the use of an object as a means of gaining or holding an adult's attention. For example, a child points to an object, says 'dah' and looks at an adult who replies 'Yes, that's a car.' 'Proto-imperatives' are defined as the use of an adult as a means of obtaining an object. For example, a child looks at a jack-in-the-box which is on a shelf and out of reach. While pointing toward the object and looking at an adult, the child says emphatically 'uh'.

Unfortunately we had serious difficulties in obtaining reliable use of these concepts in describing the children's communicative repertoires. The problem was not so much that the observers disagreed in their coding of a specific communicative act; rather, they extracted different communicative acts from the stream of behaviour and its context. The correlations were adequate (average; $r = .84$) between observers for frequencies of different types of communicative acts summed across a 15-minute observation. However, comparisons of observers' transcripts on each event yielded proportion agreements (Cohen's Kappa) ranging from .13 to .25 among the four observers. Comparing the total number of proto-declaratives for two observers across a 15-minute observation yielded a Pearson correlation of .76. The Pearson correlation between two observers for proto-imperatives was .69. Furthermore, the stability of proto-declaratives and proto-imperatives across four 15-minute samples of children's behaviour was .61 and .83 respectively.

Thus our data (Brinker and Goldbart 1980) both provide evidence for the existence of constructs such as 'proto-imperative' and 'proto-declarative' and point the fuzziness of such concepts. Perhaps the source of this fuzziness is to be found in the observer's task. The observer must believe in the possibility of messages embedded in ambiguous forms. Thus, he is continually trying to construct meanings from the ambiguous forms and their contexts.

The difficulties in establishing inter-observer agreement in the above study were disappointing since considerable effort had been expended in training the observers. The problem was that it was very difficult to topographically define the boundaries of communicative and social acts. The concept of a communicative act seemed to imply some listener/interpreter who had decoded some message. The decoding depended upon how the listener/interpreter defined the context. Unfortunately, the understanding of contexts and how to characterize them is not sufficient to have helped our observers (Beveridge and Brinker 1980, Lewis 1967, 1978). The problems will be illustrated with an example which occurred in the course of our observations.

Mathew fell down and said 'ee' as he was falling. All four observers initially coded this as a *'perlocution* – a nonverbal vocal utterance from which no clear meaning can be inferred from gesture or context or for which no meaning seemed intended by the child' (Brinker and Goldbart 1980). This particular segment of behaviour had been video-taped, and upon reviewing the tape, one of the observers changed his coding of Mathew's utterance from a perlocution to an action word – in this case, 'eat'. His rationale was based upon an increased reliance upon the context of the utterance and a broader time frame for defining that context. For 2 or 3 minutes prior to the utterance, Mathew was engaged in an elaborate play routine in the house area. He went to the cooker, stirred in the pan with a spoon, went to the table, made motions with the spoon from the pan to a plate as if dishing up the imaginary food, sat down and pretended to eat with the spoon, and fed the teddy bear sitting at the table. Then he spotted one of the teachers across the room. He toddled over to her with cup and spoon in hand, stopping twice to stir in the cup with the spoon. Mathew then took the spoon from the cup and offered it to the teacher who leaned forward and pretended to eat from it, saying, 'Yum, yum, that's good.' Mathew stumbled backward and said 'ee' as he was falling.

Given this information, one might suspect that the four observers had been lulled into a comatose state by the videotape and had incorrectly coded an obvious example of a poorly articulated 'eat'. Add the information that Mathew was a three-year-old Down's syndrome child who did not use many (if any) words at the time and you are left with ambiguity.

The problem of intersubjectivity for language intervention

An interesting question about the above example is whether Mathew 'really' could use words if no one believed him capabable of it. In this case 'belief' would constitute a very active process of constructing contexts and potential messages within them. However, too much intersubjectivity for too long a time can prevent communicative development. It can lead to the kind of closed, private communication system shared by the twins in Luria and Yudovich's 1971 study.

The key questions for interventionists revolve around:

(1) the extent to which we actively interpret children's messages so they continue to attempt to communicate; and

(2) the extent to which we demand messages in forms that approximate those used by the language community.

The emphasis, especially within American education for the handicapped, has been to specify clearly the form of behaviour which is expected of the child. The danger of rigorously specifying the form of behaviour is that we may inadvertently extinguish behaviours which serve the same function. The danger of failing to specify educational objectives is that:

(a) the teacher may not generate a consistent educational plan since educational goals are vague and/or constantly changing;

(b) the child will remain at a low level of functioning; and

(c) social stereotypes of a low ultimate functioning for handicapped people will be confirmed.

Two examples illustrate each of these dangers. The first occurred when a team of professionals were appointed to help the courts determine if a large urban American school system was fulfilling the mandate of 'free appropriate public education in the least restrictive setting'. One teacher was observed teaching a multiply-handicapped child to use the manual sign for 'eat' in order to receive a bite of food. Instead of using the correct hand posture, the child was putting his hand on the side of his face and saying 'ee'. He was not receiving food since the form of his behaviour was not judged to be sufficiently close to the target behaviour.

The second example occurred when a group of mothers from the Anson House Preschool in the Hester Adrian Research Centre visited their local education authority ESN(S) school. They were in a state of considerable agitation because the classes which they observed had exactly the same puzzles and some of the same equipment which their children had mastered two years previously. Moreover, some of these materials were being used with Down's syndrome children as old as eight. In response to their concern, they were told that materials were selected for each child's level of functioning. Nevertheless, all of the available materials seemed to the mothers to be suited for preschool rather than for primary school children.

The intersubjectivity of the teacher

It is easy to be critical of educational environments and teachers' behaviour within those environments. However, a major problem is achieving an appreciation of the teacher's intersubjectivity with the children. In order legitimately to criticise educational practice it is necessary to understand the teacher's intentions. Within those intentions the teacher constructs the meaning of the child's behaviour. I have argued elsewhere that educational objectives for preschool retarded children should be based upon a broader observational framework than would be found in most available developmental curricula (Brinker and Bricker 1980).

A broad observational framework leads to a characterization of the child's behavioural repertoire without specific reference to curriculum objectives. The task of the creative educator is to determine which developmental processes are instantiated both by the predominant behaviours and by the most sophisticated behaviours within a child's repertoire.

When the process begins with a developmental curricula, that is, when our view of a child consists of those developmental pinpoints (Cohen *et al*. 1976) which a child has or doesn't have, we run the risk of removing intersubjectivity from the educational process. For many years this was viewed as a desirable goal – a truly objective education (Skinner 1968). However, the process of language development seems to require some element of intersubjectivity. Miller and Yoder (1974) have emphasized the need for characterizing the linguistic functions which a child is already using as well as the specific forms which the child uses. They recommend that effective language intervention consist of extending functions with known forms and introducing new forms in the context of known linguistic functions. This recommendation should serve as a guiding light which teachers might use to organize the bases of their educational intentions.

In conclusion, it appears that the study of language development will be inextricably bound to the study of contexts or situations in which language is used. Some have argued that it is impossible to separate linguistic from extralinguistic information in the study of communication (Cook-Gumperz and Gumperz 1978). However, we may begin to study the basis of intersubjectivity and the process by which contexts come to be shared. To retreat into a rigorous objectivity, especially in language intervention, will lead to a few fixed forms with inconsistent linkage to communicative functions. On the other hand, the construction of a maternal intersubjectivity may lead to a communicative system which never gains the child entry into the language community of the society. Mischel (1979, 747) stated:

Structure, I believe, exists neither all in the head of the perceiver nor all in the person perceived; it is instead a function of an interaction between the beliefs of the observers and the characteristics of the observed, in the person domain as well as in the common object domain.

Our task is to learn how to characterize these beliefs and the aspects of contexts which are incorporated into them. In doing so we may discover the developmentally-changing mix of speaker and listener responsibility in constructing messages.

References

Bates, E. 1976: *Language and context: The acquisition of pragmatics*. New York: Academic.

Bates, E., Camaioni, L. and Volterra, V. 1975: The acquisition of performatives prior to speech. *Merrill-Palmer Quarterly* **21**, 205–26.

Beveridge, M. and Brinker, R.P. 1980: An ecological-developmental approach to communication in retarded children. In M. Jones (ed.), *Language disability in children*. Lancaster: MTP Press, 45–67.

Beveridge, M. and Lloyd, P. 1977: The developing person as a communicator. Paper presented at the Annual Conference of the Developmental Section of the British Psychological Society, Cambridge, England, September.

Bloom, L. 1970: *Language development: Form and function in emerging grammars*. Cambridge, Mass: MIT Press.

Bowerman, M. 1978: The acquisition of word meaning: an investigation into some current conflicts. In N. Waterson and C. Snow (eds.), *The development of communication*. Chichester: Wiley, 263–87.

Braine, M.D.R. 1963: The ontogeny of English phrase structure: The first phase. *Language* **39**, 1–13.

Bricker, D.D. 1972: Imitative sign training as a facilitator of word-object association with low-functioning children. *Am. J. Mental Deficiency* **76**, 509–16.

Bricker, W.A. and Bricker, D.D. 1974: An early language training strategy. In R.L. Schiefelbusch and L.L. Lloyd (eds.), *Language perspectives: acquisition, retardation and intervention*. Baltimore: University Park Press, 429–68.

Bricker, D.D. and Carlson, L. 1980a: Issues in early language intervention. In D. Bricker and R.L. Schiefelbusch (eds.), *Early language intervention: theory and practice*. Baltimore: University Park Press.

— 1980b: The relationship of object and prelinguistic social-communicative schemes to the acquisition of early linguistic skills in developmentally delayed infants. Paper presented at the Conference on Handicapped and At-Risk Infants: Research and Application, Asilimar, California, April.

Brinker, R.P. 1978: Teaching language in context: a feasibility study. *Revue de Phonetique Appliquée* **46**–7, 195–203.

Brinker, R.P. and Bricker, D.D. 1980: Teaching a first language: building complex structures from simpler components. In J. Hogg and P. Mittler (eds.), *Advances in mental handicap research*. Chichester: Wiley, 197–223.

Brinker, R.P. and Goldbart, J.G. 1981: The problem of reliability in the study of early communication skills. *Br. J. Psychology* **72**, 27–41.

Brown, R. 1973: *A first language*. Cambridge, Mass: Harvard University Press.

Brown, R.W. and Fraser, C. 1964: The acquisition of syntax. In U. Bellugi and R.W. Brown (eds.), *The acquisition of language*. Monographs of the Society for Research in Child Development **29(1)**, 43–79.

Bruner, J.S. 1975: The ontogenesis of speech acts. *J. Child Language* **2**, 1–19.

Buckhalt, J., Rutherford, R. and Goldberg, K. 1978: Verbal and nonverbal interaction of mothers with their Down's syndrome and nonretarded infants. *Am. J. Mental Deficiency* **82**, 337–43.

Chomsky, N. 1965: *Aspects of a theory of syntax*. Cambridge, Mass: MIT Press.

Clark, E.V. 1973: What's in a word? On the child's acquisition of semantics in his first language. In T.E. Moore (ed.), *Cognitive development and the acquisition of language*. New York: Academic, 65–110.

— 1974: Some aspects of the conceptual basis for first language acquisition. In R.L. Schiefelbusch and L.L. Lloyd (eds.), *Language perspectives: acquisition, retardation and intervention*. Baltimore: University Park Press, 105–128.

Cohen, M., Gross, P. and Haring, N. 1976: Developmental pinpoints. In N. Haring and L. Brown (eds.), *Teaching the severely handicapped*, vol. 1. New York: Grune and Stratton.

Collis, G.M. and Schaffer, H.R. 1975: Synchronization of visual attention in mother-infant pairs. *J. Child Psychology and Psychiatry* **16**, 315–24.

Cook-Gumperz, J. and Gumperz, J.J. 1978: Context in children's speech. In N. Waterson and C. Snow (eds.), *The development of communication*. Chichester: Wiley, 3–23.

de Villiers, J.G. and de Villiers, P.A. 1973: Development of the use of word order in comprehension. *J. Psycholinguistic Research* **2**, 331–41.

Dunst, C.J. 1980: Developmental characteristics of communicative acts among Down's syndrome infants and nonretarded infants. Paper presented at the Biennial meeting of the Southeastern Conference on Human Development, Alexandria, Virginia, April.

Edwards, D. 1974: Sensory-motor intelligence and semantic relations in early child grammar. *Cognition* 2, 395–434.

Greenfield, P.M. and Smith, J.H. 1976: *The structure of communication in early language development*. New York: Academic.

Hunt, J. McV. 1961: *Intelligence and experience*. New York: Ronald Press.

Jones, O.H.M. 1977: Mother-child communication with prelinguistic Down's syndrome and normal infants. In H.R. Schaffer (ed.), *Studies in mother-infant interaction*. London: Academic, 319–401.

Jones, A. and Robson, C. 1979: Language training the severely mentally handicapped. In N. Ellis (ed.), *Handbook of mental deficiency, psychological theory and research*, 2nd edn. Hillsdale, NJ: Erlbaum, 367–400.

Leonard, L.B. 1978: Cognitive factors in early linguistic development. In R.L. Schiefelbusch (ed.), *Bases of language intervention*. Baltimore: University Park Press, 67–96.

Lewis, M. 1967: The meaning of a response or why researchers in infant behavior should be oriental metaphysicians. *Merrill-Palmer Quarterly* 13, 7–18.

— 1978: Situational analysis and the study of behavioral development. In L. Pervin and M. Lewis (eds.), *Perspectives in interactional psychology*. New York: Plenum, 49–66.

Lewis, M. and Freedle, R. 1973: Mother-infant dyad: the cradle of meaning. In P. Pliner, L. Krames and T. Alloway (eds.), *Communication and affect: language and thought*. New York: Academic, 127–55.

Lewis, M. and Rosenblum, L. (eds.) 1974: *The effect of the infant on its caregiver: the origins of behavior*, vol. 1. New York: Wiley.

Luria, A.R. 1976: *Basic problems of neurolinguistics*. The Hague: Mouton.

Luria, A.R. and Yudovich, F.A. 1971: *Speech and the development of mental processes in the child*. London: Penguin.

Marshall, N., Henegrenes, J. and Goldstein, S. 1973: Verbal interactions: mothers and their retarded children versus mothers and their nonretarded children. *Am. J. Mental Deficiency* 77, 415–19.

Miller, W. and Ervin, S.M. 1964: The development of grammar in child language. In U. Bellugi and R. Brown (eds.), *The acquisition of language*. Monographs of the Society for Research in Child Development 29 (Serial No. 92), 9–34.

Miller, J.F. and Yoder, D.E. 1974: An ontogenetic language teaching strategy for retarded children. In R.L. Schiefelbusch and L.L. Lloyd (eds.), *Language perspectives: acquisition, retardation and intervention*. Baltimore: University Park Press, 505–28.

Mischel, W. 1979: On the interface of cognition and personality: beyond the person-situation debate. *Am. Psychologist* 34, 740–54.

Moerk, E. 1976: Processes of language teaching and training in the interactions of mother-child dyads. *Child Development* **47**, 1064–78.

Nelson, K. 1974: Concept, word, and sentence: interrelations in acquisition and development. *Psychological Review* **81**, 267–85.

Newson, J. and Newson, E. 1979: *Toys and playthings*. London: Penguin.

Piaget, J. 1952: *The origins of intelligence in children*. London: International Universities Press.

Robinson, C. and Robinson, J. 1978: Sensorimotor functions and cognitive development. In M. Snell (ed.), *Systematic instruction of the moderately and severely handicapped*. Columbus: Merrill.

Sherrod, K., Crawley, S., Peterson, G. and Bennett, P. 1978: Maternal language to prelinguistic infants: semantic aspects. *Infant Behavior and Development* **1**, 335–45.

Skinner, B.F. 1968: *The technology of teaching*. New York: Meredith.

Smith, R.A. 1975: *Effects of mother-to-sample training with class stimuli on subsequent name acquisition and generalization in developmentally-delayed and nondelayed preschool age children*. Unpublished doctoral dissertation, George Peabody College for Teachers, Nashville, Tennessee.

Smith, P.K. and Connolly, K. 1972: Patterns of play and social interaction in preschool children. In N. Blurton-Jones (ed.), Ethological studies of child behavior. Cambridge: CUP, 65–95.

Snow, C.E. and Ferguson, C.A. (eds.) 1977: Talking to children: language input and acquisition. Cambridge: CUP.

Stern, D.N. 1974: Mother and infant at play: the dyadic interaction involving facial, vocal, and gaze behaviors. In M. Lewis and L.A. Rosenblum (eds.), *The effect of the infant on its caregiver*. New York: Wiley, 187–213.

Sugarman-Bell, S. 1978: Some organizational aspects of preverbal communication. In I. Markova (ed.), *The social context of language*. New York: Wiley.

Trevarthen, C. and Hubley, P. 1978: Secondary intersubjectivity: confidence, confiding and acts of meaning in the first year. In A. Lock (ed.), *Action, gesture and symbol: the emergence of language*. London: Academic.

Uzgiris, I.C. and Hunt, J. McV. 1975: *Assessment in infancy: ordinal scales of psychological development*. Urbana, Illinois: University of Illinois Press.

Vygotsky, L.S. 1962: *Thought and language*. Cambridge, Mass: MIT Press.

Zachry, W. 1972: *The relation of language development to sensorimotor level in second-year infants*. Unpublished doctoral dissertation, Memphis State University, Memphis, Tennessee.

Index